Traeger Grill & Smoker Cookbook

1000 Days of Mouth-Wateringly Easy Recipes That Will Drive Your Taste Buds Crazy.

Melissa Miranda

All Rights Reserved.

The content contained within this book may not be reproduced, duplicated, or transmitted without direct written permission from the author or the publisher. Under no circumstances will any blame or legal responsibility be held against the publisher, or author, for any damages, reparation, or monetary loss due to the information contained within this book, either directly or indirectly.

Legal Notice: This book is copyright protected. It is only for personal use. You cannot amend, distribute, sell, use, quote or paraphrase any part, or the content within this book, without the consent of the author or publisher.

Disclaimer Notice:

Please note the information contained within this document is for educational and entertainment purposes only. All effort has been executed to present accurate, up to date, reliable, complete information. No warranties of any kind are declared or implied. Readers acknowledge that the author is not engaged in the rendering of legal, financial, medical, or professional advice. The content within this book has been derived from various sources. Please consult a licensed professional before attempting any techniques outlined in this book. By reading this document, the reader agrees that under no circumstances is the author responsible for any losses, direct or indirect, that are incurred as a result of the use of the information contained within this document, including, but not limited to, errors, omissions, or inaccuracies.

CONTENTS

What is a Wood Pellet Grill? 11
Benefits - Versatility 11
What are the advantages of wood pellet grills? 11

Beef, pork & Lamb Recipes 12

Wood Pellet Grilled Aussie Leg Of Lamb Roast 12
Bbq Party Pork Ribs 12
Cheesy Lamb Burgers 12
Thai Beef Skewers 13
Spicy Pork Chops 13
Versatile Beef Tenderloin 13
Braised Lamb Shank 14
Smoked Ham 14
Simple Traeger Grilled Lamb Chops 14
Traeger Beef Short Rib Lollipop 14
Simply Delicious Tri Tip Roast 15
Bbq Sweet Pepper Meatloaf 15
Bacon-swiss Cheesesteak Meatloaf 15
Deliciously Spicy Rack Of Lamb 16
Wine Braised Lamb Shank 16
Midweek Dinner Pork Tenderloin 16
Traeger Beef Jerky 17
Apple-smoked Bacon 17
Smoked Spicy Candied Bacon 17
Chinese Bbq Pork 17
Thai Beef Salad 18
Grilled Butter Basted Rib-eye 18
Leg Of A Lamb 19
Wood Pellet Grilled Lamb With Brown Sugar Glaze 19
Texas Shoulder Clod 19
Barbecued Tenderloin 20
Traeger Stuffed Peppers 20
French Onion Burgers 20
Cajun Double-smoked Ham 21
Smoked Lamb Chops 21
Simple Wood Pellet Smoked Pork Ribs 21
Traeger Bacon 21
Grilled Lamb Chops With Rosemary 22
Smoked Midnight Brisket 22

Beef Shoulder Clod 22
Grilled Filet Mignon 23
Flavorsome Pork Loin 23
Rub-injected Pork Shoulder 23
Kalbi Beef Ribs 24
Naked St. Louis Ribs 24
Teriyaki Pineapple Pork Tenderloin Sliders 24
Baby Back Ribs 25
Chili Rib Eye Steaks 25
Traeger Kalbi Beef Short Ribs 25
Perfect Roast Prime Rib 26
Buttermilk Pork Loin Roast 26
Korean Style Bbq Prime Ribs 26
St. Patrick Day's Corned Beef 26
Smoked New York Steaks 27
Blackened Steak 27
St. Louis Bbq Ribs 27
Grilled Butter Basted Porterhouse Steak 28
Smoked Roast Beef 28
Cheeseburger Hand Pies 28
Traditional Tomahawk Steak 29
Roasted Pork With Blackberry Sauce 29
Grilled Hanger Steak 30
Santa Maria Tri-tip 30
Aromatic Herbed Rack Of Lamb 30
Grilled Venison Kabob 31

Poultry Recipes 31

Rustic Maple Smoked Chicken Wings 31
Hot And Sweet Spatchcocked Chicken 31
South-east-asian Chicken Drumsticks 32
Jamaican Jerk Chicken Quarters 32
Wild Turkey Egg Rolls 32
Smoked Whole Chicken 33
Wood Pellet Smoked Spatchcock Turkey 33
Applewood-smoked Whole Turkey 33
Bacon-wrapped Chicken Tenders 33
Honey Garlic Chicken Wings 34
Chicken Wings 34
Smo-fried Chicken 34
Trager Smoked Spatchcock Turkey 35

Savory-sweet Turkey Legs 35
Whole Smoked Chicken 35
Turkey Meatballs 36
Lemon Chicken Breast 36
Chicken Cordon Bleu 36
Perfectly Smoked Turkey Legs 37
Wood Pellet Smoked Spatchcock Turkey 37
Serrano Chicken Wings 38
Game Day Chicken Drumsticks 38
Beer Can Chicken 38
Buffalo Chicken Flatbread 39
Special Occasion's Dinner Cornish Hen 39
Hellfire Chicken Wings 39
Roasted Chicken With Pimenton Potatoes 40
Cajun Chicken 40
Maple And Bacon Chicken 40
Christmas Dinner Goose 40
Traeger Smoked Cornish Hens 41
Smoked Airline Chicken 41
Roasted Whole Chicken 42
Rosemary Orange Chicken 42
Glazed Chicken Thighs 42
Herb Roasted Turkey 42
Wood Pellet Grilled Chicken Kabobs 43
Chinese Inspired Duck Legs 43
Wood Pellet Smoked Cornish Hens 44
Turkey Legs 44
Sweet Sriracha Bbq Chicken 44
Buttered Thanksgiving Turkey 45
Authentic Holiday Turkey Breast 45
Smoked Fried Chicken 45
Smoked Turkey Breast 46
Bbq Sauce Smothered Chicken Breasts 46
Skinny Smoked Chicken Breasts 46
Wood Pellet Sheet Pan Chicken Fajitas 46
Paprika Chicken 47
Smoked Chicken Drumsticks 47
Smoked And Fried Chicken Wings 47
Wood-fired Chicken Breasts 48
Thanksgiving Dinner Turkey 48
Wood Pellet Grilled Buffalo Chicken 48

Hickory Smoked Chicken ... 48
Traeger Grilled Buffalo Chicken Legs ... 49
Traeger Asian Miso Chicken Wings ... 49
Traeger Chicken Breast ... 49
Smoked Chicken With Apricot Bbq Glaze ... 49
Barbecue Chicken Wings ... 50

Fish And Seafood Recipes ... 50

Dijon-smoked Halibut ... 50
Cajun-blackened Shrimp ... 50
Spicy Shrimps Skewers ... 51
Traeger Grilled Lingcod ... 51
Oysters In The Shell ... 51
Grilled Shrimp Scampi ... 51
Jerk Shrimp ... 52
Wood Pellet Rockfish ... 52
Super-tasty Trout ... 52
Grilled Blackened Salmon ... 53
Cod With Lemon Herb Butter ... 53
Citrus Salmon ... 53
Hot-smoked Salmon ... 53
Octopus With Lemon And Oregano ... 53
Citrus-smoked Trout ... 54
Cajun Seasoned Shrimp ... 54
Halibut In Parchment ... 54
Traeger Rockfish ... 55
Bbq Oysters ... 55
Grilled Tilapia ... 55
Grilled Lingcod ... 56
Grilled Rainbow Trout ... 56
Smoked Shrimp ... 56
Barbeque Shrimp ... 57
Blackened Salmon ... 57
Grilled Salmon ... 57
Cajun Catfish ... 57
Wood Pellet Teriyaki Smoked Shrimp ... 58
Barbecued Shrimp ... 58
Wood Pellet Smoked Buffalo Shrimp ... 58
Halibut With Garlic Pesto ... 58
Peppercorn Tuna Steaks ... 59
Cider Salmon ... 59

Grilled Herbed Tuna ... 59
Sriracha Salmon ... 59
Wood-fired Halibut ... 60
Traeger Lobster Tail ... 60
Wine Infused Salmon ... 60
Charleston Crab Cakes With Remoulade ... 61
Wood Pellet Grilled Scallops ... 61
Teriyaki Smoked Shrimp ... 61
Juicy Smoked Salmon ... 62
Cajun Smoked Catfish ... 62
Lively Flavored Shrimp ... 62
Buttered Crab Legs ... 63
Grilled King Crab Legs ... 63
Smoked Scallops ... 63
Chilean Sea Bass ... 63
Halibut ... 64
Spicy Shrimp ... 64
Seared Tuna Steaks ... 64
Lobster Tails ... 65
Traeger Smoked Shrimp ... 65
Grilled Shrimp Kabobs ... 65
Grilled Lobster Tail ... 66
Traeger Salmon With Togarashi ... 66
No-fuss Tuna Burgers ... 66
Grilled Teriyaki Salmon ... 67
Enticing Mahi-mahi ... 67
Grilled Shrimp ... 67

Vegetable & Vegetarian Recipes ... 68

Smoked Pumpkin Soup ... 68
Baked Cheesy Corn Pudding ... 68
Wood Pellet Cold Smoked Cheese ... 68
Grilled Corn With Honey & Butter ... 69
Caldereta Stew ... 69
Roasted Root Vegetables ... 69
Grilled Artichokes ... 70
Smoked Tomato And Mozzarella Dip ... 70
Smoked Pickles ... 70
Wood Pellet Grilled Zucchini Squash Spears ... 71
Grilled Zucchini ... 71
Potluck Salad With Smoked Cornbread ... 71

Twice-smoked Potatoes 72

Vegan Smoked Carrot Dogs 72

Roasted Peach Salsa 72

Roasted Sheet Pan Vegetables 73

Smoked Baked Beans 73

Smoked Hummus 73

Traeger Smoked Mushrooms 73

Bunny Dogs With Sweet And Spicy Jalapeño Relish 74

Smoked Healthy Cabbage 74

Blt Pasta Salad 74

Smoked Mushrooms 75

Smoked Deviled Eggs 75

Roasted Vegetable Medley 75

Grilled Sugar Snap Peas 76

Mexican Street Corn With Chipotle Butter 76

Split Pea Soup With Mushrooms 76

Ramen Soup 77

Chicken Tortilla Soup 77

Smoked Balsamic Potatoes And Carrots 77

Grilled Zucchini Squash 78

Whole Roasted Cauliflower With Garlic Parmesan Butter 78

Wood Pellet Grilled Mexican Street Corn 78

Wood Pellet Grilled Vegetables 78

Grilled Sweet Potato Planks 79

Smoked Mashed Red Potatoes 79

Salt-crusted Baked Potatoes 79

Smoked Eggs 79

Easy Smoked Vegetables 79

Roasted Okra 80

Coconut Bacon 80

Garlic And Herb Smoke Potato 80

Corn Chowder 81

Grilled Asparagus With Wild Mushrooms 81

Smokey Roasted Cauliflower 81

Smoked Stuffed Mushrooms 82

Crispy Maple Bacon Brussels Sprouts 82

Roasted Hasselback Potatoes 82

Broccoli-cauliflower Salad 83

Garlic And Rosemary Potato Wedges 83

Traeger Fries With Chipotle Ketchup 83

Grilled Corn On The Cob With Parmesan And Garlic 83

Scampi Spaghetti Squash 84
Sweet Jalapeño Cornbread 84
Wood Pellet Smoked Asparagus 85
Vegetable Skewers 85
Roasted Parmesan Cheese Broccoli 85
Southern Slaw 86
Feisty Roasted Cauliflower 86

Other Favorite Recipes 86

Braised Pork Carnitas 86
White Bbq Sauce 87
Grilled Tuna Burger With Ginger Mayonnaise 87
Smoked Soy Sauce 87
Grilled Pineapple With Chocolate Sauce 87
Sweet And Spicy Cinnamon Rub 88
Grilled Clam With Lemon-cayenne Butter 88
Smoked Tuna 88
Rosemary Chicken Glazed With Balsamic With Bacon Pearl Onions 88
Succulent Lamb Chops 89
Smoking Burgers 89
Ginger And Chili Grilled Shrimp 89
Twice Grilled Potatoes 90
Cornish Game Hens 90
Smoked Pork Ribs With Fresh Herbs 90
Cajun Rub 91
Smoked Cheese Dip 91
Pizza Bianca 91
Traeger Smoked Italian Meatballs 92
Hickory Smoked Green Beans 92
Crusty Artisan Dough Bread 92
Smoked Pork Tenderloin With Mexican Pineapple Sauce 93
Grilled Fruit And Cream 93
Smoked Ribs 93
Grilled Peaches And Cream 94
Smoked Brats 94
Roasted Ham 94
Savory Applesauce On The Grill 95
Thanksgiving Turkey Brine 95
Smoked Sriracha Sauce 95
Simple Roasted Butternut Squash 95
Red Wine Beef Stew 96

Vegan Pesto	96
Cherry Smoked Strip Steak	96
Smoked Brisket Pie	96
Fall Season Apple Pie	97
All-purpose Dry Rub	97
Coffee-chile Rub	97
Pellet Grill Funeral Potatoes	97
Bruschetta	98
Banana Walnut Bread	98
Grilled Bacon Dog	98
Fennel And Almonds Sauce	98
Grilled Pizza	99
Smoked Teriyaki Tuna	99
Classic Apple Pie	99
Bradley Maple Cure Smoked Salmon	99
Baked Breakfast Casserole	100
Dill Seafood Rub	100
Smoked Up Salmon And Dungeness Crab Chowder	100
Grilled Lime Chicken	101
Rosemary-smoked Lamb Chops	101
Bourbon Braised Beef Short Ribs	101
Potluck Favorite Baked Beans	102
Smoked Sausage & Potatoes	102
Butter-braised Springs Onions With Lots Of Chives	102
Barbecue Pork Belly	102
Lemon And Thyme Roasted With Bistro Chicken	103
Roasted Almonds	103
Grapefruit Juice Marinade	103

RECIPES INDEX 104

What is a Wood Pellet Grill?

Do you love food grilled on the fire but hate having to manage barbecues that are too complex to clean? Quiet, the Traeger Grill is just for you!

This type of grill is also very convenient for combining several cooking options at once. It does not reach the same temperature as the classic charcoal, but it manages to heat the plate or the grill in no time, and above all, you will not waste time preparing your barbecue!

Benefits - Versatility

The great thing about this incredible grill is that you can really prepare everything: from beef to chicken or whatever you like, you will no longer have to limit your barbecues with family or friends due to the too much maintenance that this type of grill usually requires!

What are the advantages of wood pellet grills?

- Saves you a lot of time

Designed to allow anyone to prepare everything in a range of 10 to 15 minutes maximum.

- Easy

Getting the best result from cooking on a grill is complicated even for the most experienced, as the food must be cooked evenly for it to be really at its best. Wood Pellet Grills are designed to facilitate cooking evenly, thus giving you the ability to To get the best cooking flavor and taste, your food needs to be cooked evenly.

- Great results

Wood Pellet Traeger Grills are well known for imparting a distinctive flavor. Seeing is believing!

- Temperature regulation

It is much easier to monitor the heat and temperature it has generated with this type of grill.

So, these, and many more, are the countless benefits that wood pellet grill smokers have to offer. Without a doubt, they enjoy a jaw-dropping level of popularity and before moving on with some of the most jaw-dropping recipes in the book,

we want you to find yourself one of the perfect wood pellet grills. Trust me; the barbecue would be much more

fun than you would like to host a BBQ party every weekend and call your friends!

The smoky effect and extra flavor infusion will help you earn more of the coveted chef title.

Beef, pork & Lamb Recipes

Wood Pellet Grilled Aussie Leg Of Lamb Roast

Servings: 8
Cooking Time: 2 Hours
Ingredients:
- 5 lb Aussie leg of lamb, boneless
- Smoked Paprika Rub
- 1 tbsp raw sugar
- 1 tbsp kosher salt
- 1 tbsp black pepper
- 1 tbsp smoked paprika
- 1 tbsp garlic powder
- 1 tbsp rosemary, dried
- 1 tbsp onion powder
- 1 tbsp cumin
- 1/2 tbsp cayenne pepper
- Roasted Carrots
- 1 bunch rainbow carrots
- Olive oil
- Salt
- pepper

Directions:
1. Heat the wood pellet grill to 3750 F.
2. Trim any excess fat from the lamb.
3. Combine all the rub ingredients and rub all over the lamb. Place the lamb on the grill and smoke for 2 hours.
4. Toss the carrots in oil, salt, and pepper then add to the grill after the lamb has cooked for 1-1/2 hour.
5. Cook until the roast internal temperature reaches 1350 F. Remove the lamb from the grill and cover with foil. Let rest for 30 minutes.
6. Remove the carrots from the grill once soft and serve with the lamb. Enjoy.

Nutrition Info:
- InfoCalories 257, Total fat 8g, Saturated fat 2g, Total Carbs 6g, Net Carbs 5g, Protein 37g, Sugar 3g, Fiber 1g, Sodium: 431mg, Potassium 666mg

Bbq Party Pork Ribs

Servings: 6
Cooking Time: 1 Hour 55 Minutes
Ingredients:
- 2 bone-in racks of pork ribs, silver skin removed
- 6 oz. BBQ rub
- 8 oz. apple juice
- ½ C. BBQ sauce

Directions:
1. Coat each rack of ribs with BBQ rub generously.
2. Arrange the racks onto a platter and set aside for about 30 minutes.
3. Set the temperature of Traeger Grill to 225 degrees F and preheat with closed lid for 15 minutes.
4. Arrange the racks onto the grill, bone side down and cook for about 1 hour.
5. In a food-safe spray bottle, place apple juice.
6. Spray the racks with vinegar mixture evenly.
7. Cook for about 3½ hours, spraying with vinegar mixture after every 45 minutes.
8. Now, coat the racks with a thin layer of BBQ sauce evenly and cook for about 10 minutes more.
9. Remove the racks from grill and place onto a cutting board for about 10-15 minutes before slicing.
10. With a sharp knife, cut each rack into individual ribs and serve.

Nutrition Info:
- Calories per serving: 801; Carbohydrates: 44.9g; Protein: 60.4g; Fat: 406g; Sugar: 37.4g; Sodium: 558mg; Fiber: 0.8g

Cheesy Lamb Burgers

Servings: 4
Cooking Time: 20 Minutes
Ingredients:
- 2 lb. ground lamb
- 1 C. Parmigiano-Reggiano cheese, grated
- Salt and freshly ground black pepper, to taste

Directions:
1. Set the temperature of Traeger Grill to 425 degrees F and preheat with closed lid for 15 minutes.
2. In a bowl, add all ingredients and mix well.
3. Make 4 (¾-inch thick) patties from mixture.
4. With your thumbs, make a shallow but wide depression in each patty.
5. Arrange the patties onto the grill, depression-side down and cook for about 8 minutes.
6. Flip and cook for about 8-10 minutes.
7. Serve immediately.

Nutrition Info:
- Calories per serving: 502; Carbohydrates: 0g; Protein: 71.7g; Fat: 22.6g; Sugar: 0g; Sodium: 331mg; Fiber: 0g

Thai Beef Skewers

Servings: 6
Cooking Time: 8 Minutes
Ingredients:
- ½ of medium red bell pepper, destemmed, cored, cut into a ¼-inch piece
- ½ of beef sirloin, fat trimmed
- ½ cup salted peanuts, roasted, chopped
- For the Marinade:
- 1 teaspoon minced garlic
- 1 tablespoon grated ginger
- 1 lime, juiced
- 1 teaspoon ground black pepper
- 1 tablespoon sugar
- 1/4 cup soy sauce
- 1/4 cup olive oil

Directions:
1. Prepare the marinade and for this, take a small bowl, place all of its ingredients in it, whisk until combined, and then pour it into a large plastic bag.
2. Cut into beef sirloin 1-1/4-inch dice, add to the plastic bag containing marinade, seal the bag, turn it upside down to coat beef pieces with the marinade and let it marinate for a minimum of 2 hours in the refrigerator.
3. When ready to cook, switch on the Traeger grill, fill the grill hopper with cherry flavored wood pellets, power the grill on by using the control panel, select 'smoke' on the temperature dial, or set the temperature to 425 degrees F and let it preheat for a minimum of 5 minutes.
4. Meanwhile, remove beef pieces from the marinade and then thread onto skewers.
5. When the grill has preheated, open the lid, place prepared skewers on the grill grate, shut the grill, and smoke for 4 minutes per side until done.
6. When done, transfer skewers to a dish, sprinkle with peanuts and red pepper, and then serve.

Nutrition Info:
- InfoCalories: 124 Cal ;Fat: 5.5 g ;Carbs: 1.7 g ;Protein: 15.6 g ;Fiber: 0 g

Spicy Pork Chops

Servings: 4
Cooking Time: 10-15 Minutes
Ingredients:
- 1 tbsp. olive oil
- 2 cloves garlic, crushed and minced
- 1 tbsp. cayenne pepper
- ½ tsp. hot sauce
- ¼ cup lime juice
- 2 tsp. ground cumin
- 1 tsp. ground cinnamon
- 4 pork chops
- Lettuce

Directions:
1. Mix the olive oil, garlic, cayenne pepper, hot sauce, lime juice, cumin and cinnamon.
2. Pour the mixture into a re-sealable plastic bag. Place the pork chops inside. Seal and turn to coat evenly. Chill in the refrigerator for 4 hours. Grill for 10 to 15 minutes, flipping occasionally.

Nutrition Info:
- Calories: 196 Cal Fat: 9 g Carbohydrates: 3 g   Protein: 25 g Fiber: 1 g

Versatile Beef Tenderloin

Servings: 6
Cooking Time: 2 Hours 5 Minutes
Ingredients:
- For Brandy Butter:
- ½ C. butter
- 1 oz. brandy
- For Brandy Sauce:
- 2 oz. brandy
- 8 garlic cloves, minced
- ¼ C. mixed fresh herbs (parsley, rosemary and thyme), chopped
- 2 tsp. honey
- 2 tsp. hot English mustard
- For Tenderloin:
- 1 (2-lb.) center-cut beef tenderloin
- Salt and cracked black peppercorns, to taste

Directions:
1. Set the temperature of Traeger Grill to 230 degrees F and preheat with closed lid for 15 minutes.
2. For brandy butter: in a pan, melt butter over medium-low heat.
3. Stir in brandy and remove from heat.
4. Set aside, covered to keep warm.
5. For brandy sauce: in a bowl, add all ingredients and mix until well combined.
6. Season the tenderloin with salt and black peppercorns generously.
7. Coat tenderloin with brandy sauce evenly.
8. With a baster-injector, inject tenderloin with brandy butter.
9. Place the tenderloin onto the grill and cook for about 1½-2 hours, injecting with brandy butter occasionally.

10. Remove the tenderloin from grill and place onto a cutting board for about 10-15 minutes before serving.
11. With a sharp knife, cut the tenderloin into desired-sized slices and serve.
Nutrition Info:
- Calories per serving: 496; Carbohydrates: 4.4g; Protein: 44.4g; Fat: 29.3g; Sugar: 2g; Sodium: 240mg; Fiber: 0.7g

Braised Lamb Shank

Servings: 6
Cooking Time: 4 Hours
Ingredients:
- 6 whole lamb shanks
- Traeger Prime Rib Rub
- 1 cup beef broth
- 1 cup red wine
- 4 sprig rosemary and thyme

Directions:
1. Season the lamb shanks with Traeger Prime Rib Rub.
2. When ready to cook, fire the Traeger Grill to 5000F. Use desired wood pellets when cooking. Close the lid and preheat for 15 minutes.
3. Place the lamb shanks directly on the grill grate and cook for 20 minutes or until the surface browns.
4. Transfer the shanks to a Dutch oven and pour in beef broth.
5. Place the Dutch oven back on the grill grate and reduce the temperature to 3250F. Cook for another 3 to 4 hours.
Nutrition Info:
- InfoCalories per serving: 532 ; Protein: 55.2g; Carbs: 10.2g; Fat: 21.4g Sugar: 2.3g

Smoked Ham

Servings: 12 To 15
Cooking Time: 5 Or 6 Hours
Ingredients:
- 1 (10-pound) fresh ham, skin removed
- 2 tablespoons olive oil
- 1 batch Rosemary-Garlic Lamb Seasoning

Directions:
1. Supply your smoker with wood pellets and follow the manufacturer's specific start-up procedure. Preheat the grill, with the lid closed, to 180°F.
2. Rub the ham all over with olive oil and sprinkle it with the seasoning.
3. Place the ham directly on the grill grate and smoke for 3 hours.
4. Increase the grill's temperature to 375°F and continue to smoke the ham until its internal temperature reaches 170°F.
5. Remove the ham from the grill and let it rest for 10 minutes, before carving and serving.

Simple Traeger Grilled Lamb Chops

Servings: 6
Cooking Time: 20 Minutes
Ingredients:
- 1/4 cup white vinegar, distilled
- 2 tbsp olive oil
- 2 tbsp salt
- 1/2 tbsp black pepper
- 1 tbsp minced garlic
- 1 onion, thinly sliced
- 2 lb lamb chops

Directions:
1. In a resealable bag, mix vinegar, oil, salt, black pepper, garlic, and sliced onions until all salt has dissolved.
2. Add the lamb and toss until evenly coated. Place in a fridge to marinate for 2 hours.
3. Preheat your Traeger.
4. Remove the lamb from the resealable bag and leave any onion that is stuck on the meat. Use an aluminum foil to cover any exposed bone ends.
5. Grill until the desired doneness is achieved. Serve and enjoy when hot.
Nutrition Info:
- InfoCalories 519, Total fat 44.8g, Saturated fat 18.4g, Total carbs 2.3g, Net carbs 1.9g Protein 25g, Sugars 0.8g, Fiber 0.4g, Sodium 861mg, Potassium 358.6mg

Traeger Beef Short Rib Lollipop

Servings: 4
Cooking Time: 3 Hours
Ingredients:
- 4 beef short rib lollipops
- BBQ Rub
- BBQ Sauce

Directions:
1. Preheat your Traeger to 2750F.
2. Season the short ribs with BBQ rub and place them on the grill.
3. Cook for 4 hours while turning occasionally until the meat is tender.
4. Apply the sauce on the meat in the last 30 minutes of cooking.
5. Serve and enjoy.
Nutrition Info:
- Calories: 265 Cal Fat: 19 g Carbohydrates: 1 g Protein: 22 g Fiber: 0 g

Simply Delicious Tri Tip Roast

Servings: 8
Cooking Time: 35 Minutes
Ingredients:
- 1 tbsp. granulated onion
- 1 tbsp. granulated garlic
- Salt and freshly ground black pepper, to taste
- 1 (3-lb.) tri tip roast, trimmed

Directions:
1. In a bowl, add all ingredients except for roast and mix well.
2. Coat the roast with spice mixture generously.
3. Set aside at room temperature until grill heats.
4. Set the temperature of Traeger Grill to 250 degrees F and preheat with closed lid for 15 minutes.
5. Place the roast onto the grill and cook for about 25 minutes.
6. Now, set the grill to 350-400 degrees F and preheat with closed lid for 15 minutes. and sear roast for about 3-5 minutes per side.
7. Remove the roast from grill and place onto a cutting board for about 15-20 minutes before slicing.
8. With a sharp knife, cut the roast into slices across the grain and serve.

Nutrition Info:
- Calories per serving: 313; Carbohydrates: 0.8g; Protein: 45.7g; Fat: 14.2g; Sugar: 0.3g; Sodium: 115mg; Fiber: 0.1g

Bbq Sweet Pepper Meatloaf

Servings: 8
Cooking Time: 3 Hours And 15 Minutes
Ingredients:
- 1 cup chopped red sweet peppers
- 5 pounds ground beef
- 1 cup chopped green onion
- 1 tablespoon salt
- 1 tablespoon ground black pepper
- 1 cup panko bread crumbs
- 2 tablespoon BBQ rub and more as needed
- 1 cup ketchup
- 2 eggs

Directions:
1. Switch on the Traeger grill, fill the grill hopper with Texas beef blend flavored wood pellets, power the grill on by using the control panel, select 'smoke' on the temperature dial, or set the temperature to 225 degrees F and let it preheat for a minimum of 5 minutes.
2. Meanwhile, take a large bowl, place all the ingredients in it except for ketchup and then stir until well combined.
3. Shape the mixture into meatloaf and then sprinkle with some BBQ rub.
4. When the grill has preheated, open the lid, place meatloaf on the grill grate, shut the grill, and smoke for 2 hours and 15 minutes.
5. Then change the smoking temperature to 375 degrees F, insert a food thermometer into the meatloaf and cook for 45 minutes or more until the internal temperature of meatloaf reaches 155 degrees F.
6. Brush the top of meatloaf with ketchup and then continue cooking for 15 minutes until glazed. When done, transfer food to a dish, let it rest for 10 minutes, then cut it into slices and serve.

Nutrition Info:
- InfoCalories: 160.5 Cal ;Fat: 2.8 g ;Carbs: 13.2 g ;Protein: 17.2 g ;Fiber: 1 g

Bacon-swiss Cheesesteak Meatloaf

Servings: 4
Cooking Time: 2 Hours
Ingredients:
- 1 tablespoon canola oil
- 2 garlic cloves, finely chopped
- 1 medium onion, finely chopped
- 1 poblano chile, stemmed, seeded, and finely chopped
- 2 pounds extra-lean ground beef
- 2 tablespoons Montreal steak seasoning
- 1 tablespoon A.Steak Sauce
- ½ pound bacon, cooked and crumbled
- 2 cups shredded Swiss cheese
- 1 egg, beaten
- 2 cups breadcrumbs
- ½ cup Tiger Sauce

Directions:
1. On your stove top, heat the canola oil in a medium sauté pan over medium-high heat. Add the garlic, onion, and poblano, and sauté for 3 to 5 minutes, or until the onion is just barely translucent
2. Supply your smoker with wood pellets and follow the manufacturer's specific start-up procedure. Preheat, with the lid closed, to 225°F.
3. In a large bowl, combine the sautéed vegetables, ground beef, steak seasoning, steak sauce, bacon, Swiss cheese, egg, and breadcrumbs. Mix with your hands until well incorporated, then shape into a loaf.
4. Put the meatloaf in a cast iron skillet and place it on the grill. Close the lid and smoke for 2 hours, or until a meat thermometer inserted in the loaf reads 165°F.

5. Top with the meatloaf with the Tiger Sauce, remove from the grill, and let rest for about 10 minutes before serving.

Deliciously Spicy Rack Of Lamb

Servings: 6
Cooking Time: 3 Hours
Ingredients:
- 2 tbsp. paprika
- ½ tbsp. coriander seeds
- 1 tsp. cumin seeds
- 1 tsp. ground allspice
- 1 tsp. lemon peel powder
- Salt and freshly ground black pepper, to taste
- 2 (1½-lb.) rack of lamb ribs, trimmed

Directions:
1. Set the temperature of Traeger Grill to 225 degrees F and preheat with closed lid for 15 minutes.
2. In a coffee grinder, add all ingredients except rib racks and grind into a powder.
3. Coat the rib racks with spice mixture generously.
4. Arrange the rib racks onto the grill and cook for about 3 hours.
5. Remove the rib racks from grill and place onto a cutting board for about 10-15 minutes before slicing.
6. With a sharp knife, cut the rib racks into equal-sized individual ribs and serve.

Nutrition Info:
- Calories per serving: 545; Carbohydrates: 1.7g; Protein: 64.4g; Fat: 29.7g; Sugar: 0.3g; Sodium: 221mg; Fiber: 1g

Wine Braised Lamb Shank

Servings: 2
Cooking Time: 10 Hours
Ingredients:
- 2 (1¼-lb.) lamb shanks
- 1-2 C. water
- ¼ C. brown sugar
- 1/3 C. rice wine
- 1/3 C. soy sauce
- 1 tbsp. dark sesame oil
- 4 (1½x½-inch) orange zest strips
- 2 (3-inch long) cinnamon sticks
- 1½ tsp. Chinese five-spice powder

Directions:
1. Set the temperature of Traeger Grill to 225-250 degrees F and preheat with closed lid for 15 minutes. , using charcoal and soaked apple wood chips.
2. With a sharp knife, pierce each lamb shank at many places.
3. In a bowl, add remaining all ingredients and mix until sugar is dissolved.
4. In a large foil pan, place the lamb shanks and top with sugar mixture evenly.
5. Place the foil pan onto the grill and cook for about 8-10 hours, flipping after every 30 minutes. (If required, add enough water to keep the liquid ½-inch over).
6. Remove from the grill and serve hot.

Nutrition Info:
- Calories per serving: 1200; Carbohydrates: 39.7g; Protein: 161.9g; Fat: 48.4; Sugar: 29g; Sodium: 2000mg; Fiber: 0.3g

Midweek Dinner Pork Tenderloin

Servings: 6
Cooking Time: 3 Hours
Ingredients:
- ½ C. apple cider
- 3 tbsp. honey
- 2 (1¼-1½-lb.) pork tenderloins, silver skin removed
- 3 tbsp. sweet rub

Directions:
1. In a small bowl, mix together apple cider and honey.
2. Coat the outside of tenderloins with honey mixture and season with the rub generously.
3. With a plastic wrap, cover each tenderloin and refrigerate for about 2-3 hours.
4. Set the temperature of Traeger Grill to 225 degrees F and preheat with closed lid for 15 minutes.
5. Arrange the tenderloins onto the grill and cook for about 2½-3 hours.
6. Remove the pork tenderloins from grill and place onto a cutting board for about 10 minutes before slicing.
7. With a sharp knife, cut each pork tenderloin into desired-sized slices and serve.

Nutrition Info:
- Calories per serving: 498; Carbohydrates: 11.1g; Protein: 67.8g; Fat: 18.4g; Sugar: 10.9g; Sodium: 146mg; Fiber: 0g

Traeger Beef Jerky

Servings: 10
Cooking Time: 5 Hours
Ingredients:
- 3 pounds sirloin steaks
- 2 cups soy sauce
- 1 cup pineapple juice
- 1/2 cup brown sugar
- 2 tbsp sriracha
- 2 tbsp hoisin
- 2 tbsp red pepper flake
- 2 tbsp rice wine vinegar
- 2 tbsp onion powder

Directions:
1. Mix the marinade in a zip lock bag and add the beef. Mix until well coated and remove as much air as possible.
2. Place the bag in a fridge and let marinate overnight or for 6 hours. Remove the bag from the fridge an hour prior to cooking
3. Startup the Traeger and set it on the smoking settings or at 1900F.
4. Lay the meat on the grill leaving a half-inch space between the pieces. Let cool for 5 hours and turn after 2 hours.
5. Remove from the grill and let cool. Serve or refrigerate

Nutrition Info:
- Calories: 309 Cal Fat: 7 g Carbohydrates: 20 g   Protein: 34 g Fiber: 1 g

Apple-smoked Bacon

Servings: 4 To 6
Cooking Time: 20 To 30 Minutes
Ingredients:
- 1 (1-pound) package thick-sliced bacon

Directions:
1. Supply your smoker with wood pellets and follow the manufacturer's specific start-up procedure. Preheat the grill, with the lid closed, to 275°F.
2. Supply your smoker with wood pellets and follow the manufacturer's specific start-up procedure. Preheat the grill, with the lid closed, to 275°F.

Smoked Spicy Candied Bacon

Servings: 6
Cooking Time: 35 Minutes
Ingredients:
- 1 lb. center cut bacon
- 1/2 cup dark brown sugar
- 1/2 cup real maple syrup
- 1 tbsp sriracha hot sauce
- 1/2 tbsp. cayenne pepper

Directions:
1. In a small mixing bowl, whisk together sugar, maple syrup, hot sauce, and cayenne until well combined.
2. Preheat your Traeger to 3000F and line a baking sheet with parchment paper.
3. Lay the bacon on a single layer and brush with the sugar mixture on both sides.
4. Place the baking sheet in the Traeger and cook for 20 minutes. Flip the bacon and cook for 15 more minutes.
5. Remove the baking sheet from the Traeger and let cool for 15 minutes before serving.

Nutrition Info:
- InfoCalories 458, Total fat 15g, Saturated fat 10g, Total carbs 37g, Net carbs 15g Protein 9g, Sugars 33g, Fiber 0g, Sodium 565mg

Chinese Bbq Pork

Servings: 8
Cooking Time: 2 Hours
Ingredients:
- 2 pork tenderloins, silver skin removed
- For the Marinade:
- ½ teaspoon minced garlic
- 1 1/2 tablespoon brown sugar
- 1 teaspoon Chinese five-spice
- 1/4 cup honey
- 1 tablespoon Asian sesame oil
- 1/4 cup hoisin sauce
- 2 teaspoons red food coloring
- 1 tablespoon oyster sauce, optional
- 3 tablespoons soy sauce
- For the Five-Spice Sauce:
- 1/4 teaspoon Chinese five-spice
- 3 tablespoons brown sugar
- 1 teaspoon yellow mustard
- 1/4 cup ketchup

Directions:
1. Prepare the marinade and for this, take a small bowl, place all of its ingredients in it and whisk until combined.
2. Take a large plastic bag, pour marinade in it, add pork tenderloin, seal the bag, turn it upside down to coat the pork and let it marinate for a minimum of 8 hours in the refrigerator.
3. Switch on the Traeger grill, fill the grill hopper with maple-flavored wood pellets, power the grill on by using the control panel, select 'smoke' on the temperature dial, or set

the temperature to 225 degrees F and let it preheat for a minimum of 5 minutes.

4. Meanwhile, remove pork from the marinade, transfer marinade into a small saucepan, place it over medium-high heat and cook for 3 minutes, and then set aside until cooled.

5. When the grill has preheated, open the lid, place pork on the grill grate, shut the grill and smoke for 2 hours, basting with the marinade halfway.

6. Meanwhile, prepare the five-spice sauce and for this, take a small saucepan, place it over low heat, add all of its ingredients, stir until well combined and sugar has dissolved and cooked for 5 minutes until hot and thickened, set aside until required.

7. When done, transfer pork to a dish, let rest for 15 minutes, and meanwhile, change the smoking temperature of the grill to 450 degrees F and let it preheat for a minimum of 10 minutes.

8. Then return pork to the grill grate and cook for 3 minutes per side until slightly charred.

9. Transfer pork to a dish, let rest for 5 minutes, and then serve with prepared five-spice sauce.

Nutrition Info:
- InfoCalories: 280 Cal ;Fat: 8 g ;Carbs: 12 g ;Protein: 40 g ;Fiber: 0 g

Thai Beef Salad

Servings: 4
Cooking Time: 10 Minutes
Ingredients:
- 1 ½ pound skirt steak
- 1 ½ teaspoon salt
- 1 teaspoon ground white pepper
- For the Dressing:
- 4 jalapeño peppers, minced
- ½ teaspoon minced garlic
- 4 tablespoons Thai fish sauce
- 4 tablespoons lime juice
- 1 tablespoon brown sugar
- For the Salad:
- 1 small red onion, peeled, thinly sliced
- 6 cherry tomatoes, halved
- 2 green onions, ¼-inch diced
- 1 cucumber, deseeded, thinly sliced
- 1 heart of romaine lettuce, chopped
- ½ cup chopped mint
- 2 tablespoons cilantro
- ½ teaspoon red pepper flakes
- 1 tablespoon lime juice
- 2 tablespoons fish sauce

Directions:
1. Switch on the Traeger grill, fill the grill hopper with cherry flavored wood pellets, power the grill on by using the control panel, select 'smoke' on the temperature dial, or set the temperature to 450 degrees F and let it preheat for a minimum of 15 minutes.

2. Meanwhile, prepare the steak, and for this, season it with salt and black pepper until well coated.

3. When the grill has preheated, open the lid, place steak on the grill grate, shut the grill and smoke for 10 minutes until internal temperature reaches 130 degrees F.

4. Meanwhile, prepare the dressing and for this, take a medium bowl, place all of its ingredients in it and then stir until combined.

5. Take a large salad, place all the ingredients for the salad in it, drizzle with dressing and toss until well coated and mixed.

6. When done, transfer steak to a cutting board, let it rest for 10 minutes and then cut it into slices.

7. Add steak slices into the salad, toss until mixed, and then serve.

Nutrition Info:
- InfoCalories: 128 Cal ;Fat: 6 g ;Carbs: 6 g ;Protein: 12 g ;Fiber: 1 g

Grilled Butter Basted Rib-eye

Servings: 4
Cooking Time: 20 Minutes
Ingredients:
- 2 rib-eye steaks, bone-in
- Slat to taste
- Pepper to taste
- 4 tbsp butter, unsalted

Directions:
1. Mix steak, salt, and pepper in a ziplock bag. Seal the bag and mix until the beef is well coated. Ensure you get as much air as possible from the ziplock bag.

2. Set the wood pellet grill temperature to high with closed lid for 15 minutes. Place a cast-iron into the grill.

3. Place the steaks on the hottest spot of the grill and cook for 5 minutes with the lid closed.

4. Open the lid and add butter to the skillet. When it's almost melted place the steak on the skillet with the grilled side up.

5. Cook for 5 minutes while busting the meat with butter. Close the lid and cook until the internal temperature is 130°F.

6. Remove the steak from skillet and let rest for 10 minutes before enjoying with the reserved butter.

Nutrition Info:

- InfoCalories 745, Total fat 65g, Saturated fat 32g, Total Carbs 5g, Net Carbs 5g, Protein 35g, Sugar 0g, Fiber 0g

Leg Of A Lamb

Servings: 10
Cooking Time: 2 Hours And 30 Minutes
Ingredients:
- 1 (8-ounce) package softened cream cheese
- ¼ cup cooked and crumbled bacon
- 1 seeded and chopped jalapeño pepper
- 1 tablespoon crushed dried rosemary
- 2 teaspoons garlic powder
- 1 teaspoon onion powder
- 1 teaspoon paprika
- 1 teaspoon cayenne pepper
- Salt, to taste
- 1 (4-5-pound) butterflied leg of lamb
- 2-3 tablespoons olive oil

Directions:
1. For filling in a bowl, add all ingredients and mix till well combined.
2. For spice mixture in another small bowl, mix together all ingredients.
3. Place the leg of lamb onto a smooth surface. Sprinkle the inside of leg with some spice mixture.
4. Place filling mixture over the inside surface evenly. Roll the leg of lamb tightly and with a butcher's twine, tie the roll to secure the filling
5. Coat the outer side of roll with olive oil evenly and then sprinkle with spice mixture.
6. Preheat the pallet grill to 225-240 degrees F.
7. Arrange the leg of lamb in pallet grill and cook for about 2-2½ hours. Remove the leg of lamb from pallet grill and transfer onto a cutting board.
8. With a piece of foil, cover leg loosely and transfer onto a cutting board for about 20-25 minutes before slicing.
9. With a sharp knife, cut the leg of lamb in desired sized slices and serve.

Nutrition Info:
- Calories: 715 Cal Fat: 38.9 g   Carbohydrates: 2.2 g Protein: 84.6 g Fiber: 0.1 g

Wood Pellet Grilled Lamb With Brown Sugar Glaze

Servings: 4
Cooking Time: 10 Minutes
Ingredients:
- 1/4 cup brown sugar
- 2 tbsp ginger, ground
- 2 tbsp tarragon, dried
- 1 tbs cinnamon, ground
- 1 tbsp black pepper, ground
- 1 tbsp garlic powder
- 1/2 tbsp salt
- 4 lamb chops

Directions:
1. In a mixing bowl, mix sugar, ginger, dried tarragon, cinnamon, black pepper, garlic, and salt.
2. Rub the lamb chops with the seasoning and place it on a plate.refrigerate for an hour to marinate.
3. Preheat the grill to high heat then brush the grill grate with oil.
4. Arrange the lamb chops on the grill grate in a single layer and cook for 5 minutes on each side.
5. Serve and enjoy.

Nutrition Info:
- InfoCalories 241, Total fat 13.1g, Saturated fat 6g, Total Carbs 15.8g, Net Carbs 15.1g, Protein 14.6g, Sugar 14g, Fiber 0.7g, Sodium: 339mg,

Texas Shoulder Clod

Servings: 16 To 20
Cooking Time: 12 To 16 Hours
Ingredients:
- ½ cup sea salt
- ½ cup freshly ground black pepper
- 1 tablespoon red pepper flakes
- 1 tablespoon minced garlic
- 1 tablespoon cayenne pepper
- 1 tablespoon smoked paprika
- 1 (13- to 15-pound) beef shoulder clod

Directions:
1. In a small bowl, combine the salt, pepper, red pepper flakes, minced garlic, cayenne pepper, and smoked paprika to create a rub. Generously apply it to the beef shoulder.
2. Supply your smoker with wood pellets and follow the manufacturer's specific start-up procedure. Preheat, with the lid closed, to 250°F.
3. Put the meat on the grill grate, close the lid, and smoke for 12 to 16 hours, or until a meat thermometer inserted deeply into the beef reads 195°F. You may need to cover the clod with aluminum foil toward the end of smoking to prevent overbrowning.
4. Let the meat rest for about 15 minutes before slicing against the grain and serving.

Barbecued Tenderloin

Servings: 4 To 6
Cooking Time: 30 Minutes
Ingredients:
- 2 (1-pound) pork tenderloins
- 1 batch Sweet and Spicy Cinnamon Rub

Directions:
1. Supply your smoker with wood pellets and follow the manufacturer's specific start-up procedure. Preheat the grill, with the lid closed, to 350°F.
2. Generously season the tenderloins with the rub. Using your hands, work the rub into the meat.
3. Place the tenderloins directly on the grill grate and smoke until their internal temperature reaches 145°F.
4. Remove the tenderloins from the grill and let them rest for 5 to 10 minutes, before thinly slicing and serving.

Traeger Stuffed Peppers

Servings: 6
Cooking Time: 5 Minutes
Ingredients:
- 3 bell peppers, sliced in halves
- 1 pound ground beef, lean
- 1 onion, chopped
- 1/2 tbsp red pepper flakes
- 1/2 tbsp salt
- 1/4 tbsp pepper
- 1/2 tbsp garlic powder
- 1/2 tbsp onion powder
- 1/2 cup white rice
- 15 oz stewed tomatoes
- 8 oz tomato sauce
- 6 cups cabbage, shredded
- 1-1/2 cup water
- 2 cups cheddar cheese

Directions:
1. Arrange the pepper halves on a baking tray and set aside.
2. Preheat your grill to 3250F.
3. Brown the meat in a large skillet. Add onions, pepper flakes, salt, pepper garlic, and onion and cook until the meat is well cooked.
4. Add rice, stewed tomatoes, tomato sauce, cabbage, and water. Cover and simmer until the rice is well cooked, the cabbage is tender and there is no water in the rice.
5. Place the cooked beef mixture in the pepper halves and top with cheese.
6. Place in the grill and cook for 30 minutes.
7. Serve immediately and enjoy it.

Nutrition Info:
- Calories: 422 Cal Fat: 22 g Carbohydrates: 24 g Protein: 34 g Fiber: 5 g

French Onion Burgers

Servings: 4
Cooking Time: 20-25 Minutes
Ingredients:
- 1-pound lean ground beef
- 1 tablespoon minced garlic
- 1 teaspoon Better Than Bouillon Beef Base
- 1 teaspoon dried chives
- 1 teaspoon freshly ground black pepper
- 8 slices Gruyère cheese, divided
- ½ cup soy sauce
- 1 tablespoon extra-virgin olive oil
- 1 teaspoon liquid smoke
- 3 medium onions, cut into thick slices (do not separate the rings)
- 1 loaf French bread, cut into 8 slices
- 4 slices provolone cheese

Directions:
1. In a large bowl, mix together the ground beef, minced garlic, beef base, chives, and pepper until well blended.
2. Divide the meat mixture and shape into 8 thin burger patties.
3. Top each of 4 patties with one slice of Gruyère, then top with the remaining 4 patties to create 4 stuffed burgers.
4. Supply your smoker with wood pellets and follow the manufacturer's specific start-up procedure. Preheat, with the lid closed, to 425°F.
5. Arrange the burgers directly on one side of the grill, close the lid, and smoke for 10 minutes. Flip and smoke with the lid closed for 10 to 15 minutes more, or until a meat thermometer inserted in the burgers reads 160°F. Add another Gruyère slice to the burgers during the last 5 minutes of smoking to melt.
6. Meanwhile, in a small bowl, combine the soy sauce, olive oil, and liquid smoke.
7. Arrange the onion slices on the grill and baste on both sides with the soy sauce mixture. Smoke with the lid closed for 20 minutes, flipping halfway through.
8. Lightly toast the French bread slices on the grill. Layer each of 4 slices with a burger patty, a slice of provolone cheese, and some of the smoked onions. Top each with another slice of toasted French bread. Serve immediately.

Nutrition Info:
- Calories: 704 Cal Fat: 43 g Carbohydrates: 28 g Protein: 49 g Fiber: 2 g

Cajun Double-smoked Ham

Servings: 12 To 15
Cooking Time: 4 Or 5 Hours
Ingredients:
- 1 (5- or 6-pound) bone-in smoked ham
- 1 batch Cajun Rub
- 3 tablespoons honey

Directions:
1. Supply your smoker with wood pellets and follow the manufacturer's specific start-up procedure. Preheat the grill, with the lid closed, to 225°F.
2. Generously season the ham with the rub and place it either in a pan or directly on the grill grate. Smoke it for 1 hour.
3. Drizzle the honey over the ham and continue to smoke it until the ham's internal temperature reaches 145°F.
4. Remove the ham from the grill and let it rest for 5 to 10 minutes, before thinly slicing and serving.

Smoked Lamb Chops

Servings: 4
Cooking Time: 50 Minutes
Ingredients:
- 1 rack of lamb, fat trimmed
- 2 tbsp rosemary, fresh
- 2 tbsp sage, fresh
- 1 tbsp garlic cloves, roughly chopped
- 1/2 tbsp salt
- 1/2 tbsp pepper, coarsely ground
- 1/4 cup olive oil
- 1 tbsp honey

Directions:
1. Preheat your wood pellet smoker to 225°F using a fruitwood.
2. Combine all the ingredients except the lamb in a food processor. Liberally apply the mixture on the lamb.
3. Place the lamb on the smoker for 45 minutes or until the internal temperature reaches 120°F.
4. Sear the lamb on the grill for 2 minutes per side. let rest for 5 minutes before serving.
5. Slice and enjoy.

Nutrition Info:
- InfoCalories 704, Total fat 56g, Saturated fat 14g, Total Carbs 24g, Net Carbs 23g, Protein 27g, Sugar 6g, Fiber 1g, Sodium: 124mg

Simple Wood Pellet Smoked Pork Ribs

Servings: 7
Cooking Time: 5 Hours
Ingredients:
- 3 rack baby back ribs
- 3/4 cup pork and poultry rub
- 3/4 cup Que BBQ Sauce

Directions:
1. Peel the membrane from the backside of the ribs and trim any fat.
2. Season the pork generously with the rub.
3. Set the wood pellet grill to 180°F and preheat for 15 minutes with the lid closed.
4. Place the pork ribs on the grill and smoke them for 5 hours.
5. Remove the pork from the grill and wrap them in a foil with the BBQ sauce.
6. Place back the pork and increase the temperature to 350°F. Cook for 45 more minutes.
7. Remove the pork from the grill and let it rest for 20 minutes before serving. Enjoy.

Nutrition Info:
- InfoCalories 762, Total fat 57g, Saturated fat 17g, Total Carbs 23g, Net Carbs 22.7g, Protein 39g, Sugar 18g, Fiber 0.5g, Sodium: 737mg, Potassium 618mg

Traeger Bacon

Servings: 6
Cooking Time: 25 Minutes
Ingredients:
- 1lb bacon

Directions:
1. Preheat your Traeger to 3750F.
2. Line a baking sheet with parchment paper then arrange the thick-cut bacon on it in a single layer.
3. Bake the bacon in the Traeger for 20 minutes. Flip the bacon pieces and cook for 20 more minutes or until the bacon is no longer floppy.
4. Serve and enjoy.

Nutrition Info:
- InfoCalories 315, Total fat 10g, Saturated fat 0g, Total carbs 0g, Net carbs 0g Protein 9g, Sugars 0g, Fiber 0g, Sodium 500mg

Grilled Lamb Chops With Rosemary

Servings: 4
Cooking Time: 12 Minutes
Ingredients:
- ½ cup extra virgin olive oil
- ¼ cup coarsely chopped onion
- 2 cloves of garlic, minced
- 2 tablespoons soy sauce
- 2 tablespoons balsamic vinegar
- 1 tablespoon fresh rosemary
- 2 teaspoons Dijon mustard
- 1 teaspoon Worcestershire sauce
- Salt and pepper to taste
- 4 lamb chops (8 ounce each)

Directions:
1. Heat oil in a saucepan over medium flame and sauté the onion and garlic until fragrant. Place in food processor together with the soy sauce, vinegar, rosemary, mustard, Worcestershire sauce, salt, and pepper. Pulse until smooth. Set aside.
2. Fire the Traeger Grill to 5000F. Use desired wood pellets when cooking. Close the lid and preheat for 15 minutes.
3. Brush the lamb chops on both sides with the paste.
4. Place on the grill grates and cook for 6 minutes per side or until the internal temperature reaches 1350F for medium rare.
5. Serve with the paste if you have leftover.

Nutrition Info:
- InfoCalories per serving: 442; Protein: 16.7g; Carbs: 6.1g; Fat:38.5 g Sugar: 3.7g

Smoked Midnight Brisket

Servings: 6
Cooking Time: 12 Hours
Ingredients:
- 1 tbsp Worcestershire sauce
- 1 tbsp Traeger beef Rub
- 1 tbsp Traeger Chicken rub
- 1 tbsp Traeger Blackened Saskatchewan rub
- 5 lb flat cut brisket
- 1 cup beef broth

Directions:
1. Rub the sauce and rubs in a mixing bowl then rub the mixture on the meat.
2. Preheat your grill to 180°F with the lid closed for 15 minutes. You can use super smoke if you desire.
3. Place the meat on the grill and grill for 6 hours or until the internal temperature reaches 160°F.
4. Remove the meat from the grili and double wrap it with foil.
5. Add beef broth and return to grill with the temperature increased to 225°F. Cook for 4 hours or until the internal temperature reaches 204°F.
6. Remove from grill and let rest for 30 minutes. Serve and enjoy with your favorite BBQ sauce.

Nutrition Info:
- InfoCalories 200, Total fat 14g, Saturated fat 6g, Total carbs 3g, Net carbs 3g, Protein 14g, Sugar 0g, Fiber 0g, Sodium: 680mg

Beef Shoulder Clod

Servings: 16-20
Cooking Time: 12-16 Hours
Ingredients:
- ½ cup sea salt
- ½ cup freshly ground black pepper
- 1 tablespoon red pepper flakes
- 1 tablespoon minced garlic
- 1 tablespoon cayenne pepper
- 1 tablespoon smoked paprika
- 1 (13- to 15-pound) beef shoulder clod

Directions:
1. Combine spices
2. Generously apply it to the beef shoulder.
3. Supply your smoker with wood pellets and follow the manufacturer's specific start-up procedure. Preheat, with the lid closed, to 250°F.
4. Put the meat on the grill grate, close the lid, and smoke for 12 to 16 hours, or until a meat thermometer inserted deeply into the beef reads 195°F. You may need to cover the clod with aluminum foil toward the end of smoking to prevent overbrowning.
5. Let the meat rest and serve

Nutrition Info:
- Calories: 290 Cal Fat: 22 g Carbohydrates: 0 g Protein: 20 g Fiber: 0 g

Grilled Filet Mignon

Servings: 3
Cooking Time: 20 Minutes
Ingredients:
- Salt
- Pepper
- Filet mignon - 3

Directions:
1. Preheat your grill to 450 degrees.
2. Season the steak with a good amount of salt and pepper to enhance its flavor.
3. Place on the grill and flip after 5 minutes.
4. Grill both sides for 5 minutes each.
5. Take it out when it looks cooked and serve with your favorite side dish.

Nutrition Info:
- Carbohydrates: 0 g Protein: 23 g Fat: 15 g Sodium: 240 mg Cholesterol: 82 mg

Flavorsome Pork Loin

Servings: 8
Cooking Time: 1 Hour 40 Minutes
Ingredients:
- 1 (12-oz.) bottle German lager
- 1/3 C. honey
- 2 tbsp. Dijon mustard
- 1 tsp. dried thyme
- 1 tsp. caraway seeds
- 1 (3-lb.) pork loin, silver skin removed
- 1 large Vidalia onion, chopped
- 3 garlic cloves, minced
- 3 tbsp. dry seasoned pork rub

Directions:
1. In a bowl, add German lager, honey, Dijon mustard, thyme and caraway seeds and mix well.
2. In a large sealable Ziploc bag, place pork loin, onion, garlic and honey mixture.
3. Seal the bag and shake to coat well.
4. Refrigerate to marinate overnight.
5. Set the temperature of Traeger Grill to 350 degrees F and preheat with closed lid for 15 minutes.
6. Remove the pork loin, onions and garlic from bag and place onto a plate.
7. Rub the pork loin with pork rub evenly.
8. Place the seasoned pork, onions, and garlic into a large roasting pan.
9. Arrange the pork tenderloin, fat side pointed up.
10. Place the marinade into a pan over medium heat and to a boil.
11. Cook for about 3-5 minutes or until the liquid reduces by half.
12. Remove from the heat and set aside.
13. Place the roasting pan onto the grill and cook for about 1 hour.
14. Carefully pour the reduced marinade on top of the pork loin evenly.
15. Cook for another 30-60 minutes, basting the meat with marinade occasionally.
16. Remove from the grill and place the pork loin onto a cutting board for about 10 minutes before slicing.
17. With a sharp knife, cut each pork tenderloin into desired-sized slices and serve with the topping of pan juices.

Nutrition Info:
- Calories per serving: 492; Carbohydrates: 16.3g; Protein: 47.2g; Fat: 23.9g; Sugar: 12.8g; Sodium: 277mg; Fiber: 0.6g

Rub-injected Pork Shoulder

Servings: 8 To 12
Cooking Time: 16 To 20 Hours
Ingredients:
- 1 (6- to 8-pound) bone-in pork shoulder
- 2 cups Tea Injectable made with Pork Rub
- 2 tablespoons yellow mustard
- 1 batch Pork Rub

Directions:
1. Supply your smoker with wood pellets and follow the manufacturer's specific start-up procedure. Preheat the grill, with the lid closed, to 225°F.
2. Inject the pork shoulder throughout with the tea injectable.
3. Coat the pork shoulder all over with mustard and season it with the rub. Using your hands, work the rub into the meat.
4. Place the shoulder directly on the grill grate and smoke until its internal temperature reaches 160°F and a dark bark has formed on the exterior.
5. Pull the shoulder from the grill and wrap it completely in aluminum foil or butcher paper.
6. Increase the grill's temperature to 350°F.
7. Return the pork shoulder to the grill and cook until its internal temperature reaches 195°F.
8. Pull the shoulder from the grill and place it in a cooler. Cover the cooler and let the pork rest for 1 or 2 hours.
9. Remove the pork shoulder from the cooler and unwrap it. Remove the shoulder bone and pull the pork apart using just your fingers. Serve immediately.

Kalbi Beef Ribs

Servings: 6
Cooking Time: 23 Minutes
Ingredients:
- Thinly sliced beef ribs - 2 ½ lbs
- Soy sauce - ½ cup
- Brown sugar - ½ cup
- Rice wine or mirin - ⅛ cup
- Minced garlic - 2 tbsp
- Sesame oil - 1 tbsp
- Grated onion - ⅛ cup

Directions:
1. In a medium-sized bowl, mix the mirin, soy sauce, sesame oil, brown sugar, garlic, and grated onion.
2. Add the ribs to the bowl to marinate and cover it properly with cling wrap. Put it in the refrigerator for up to 6 hours.
3. Once you remove the marinated ribs from the refrigerator, immediately put them on the grill. Close the grill quickly, so no heat is lost. Also, make sure the grill is preheated well before you place the ribs on it.
4. Cook on one side for 4 minutes and then flip it. Cook the other side for 4 minutes.
5. Pull it out once it looks fully cooked. Serve it with rice or any other side dish

Nutrition Info:
- Carbohydrates: 22 g Protein: 28 g Fat: 6 g Sodium: 1213 mg Cholesterol: 81 mg

Naked St. Louis Ribs

Servings: 6-8
Cooking Time: 5-6 Hours
Ingredients:
- 3 St. Louis-style pork blacks
- 1 cup and 1 tablespoon of Yang's original dry lab or your favorite pork club

Directions:
1. Insert the spoon handle between the membrane and the rib bone and remove the membrane under the rib bone rack. Grasp the membrane with a paper towel and pull it down slowly from the rack to remove it.
2. Rub both sides of the rib with a sufficient amount of friction.
3. Use of wood pellet smokers and grills
4. Configure a wood pellet smoker grill for indirect cooking and preheat to 225 ° F using hickory or apple pellets.
5. If using Reblack, place the ribs on the grill grid rack. Otherwise, you can use a Teflon-coated fiberglass mat or place the ribs directly on the grill.
6. Slice rib bone at 225 ° F for 5-6 hours with hickory pellets until the internal temperature of the thickest part of the ick bone reaches 185 ° F to 190 ° F.
7. Place ribs under loose foil tent for 10 minutes before carving and serving.

Nutrition Info:
- Calories: 320 Cal Fat: 26 g Carbohydrates: 0 g Protein: 19 g Fiber: 0 g

Teriyaki Pineapple Pork Tenderloin Sliders

Servings: 6
Cooking Time: 20 Minutes
Ingredients:
- 1-1/2 lb pork tenderloin
- 1 can pineapple rings
- 1 package king's Hawaiian rolls
- 8 oz teriyaki sauce
- 1-1/2 tbsp salt
- 1 tbsp onion powder
- 1 tbsp paprika
- 1/2 tbsp garlic powder
- 1/2 tbsp cayenne pepper

Directions:
1. Add all the ingredients for the rub in a mixing bowl and mix until well mixed. Generously rub the pork loin with the mixture.
2. Heat the pellet to 325°F. Place the meat on a grill and cook while you turn it every 4 minutes.
3. Cook until the internal temperature reaches 145°F.remove from the grill and let it rest for 5 minutes.
4. Meanwhile, open the pineapple can and place the pineapple rings on the grill. Flip the rings when they have a dark brown color.
5. At the same time, half the rolls and place them on the grill and grill them until toasty browned.
6. Assemble the slider by putting the bottom roll first, followed by the pork tenderloin, pineapple ring, a drizzle of sauce, and top with the other roll half.
7. Serve and enjoy.

Nutrition Info:
- InfoCalories 243, Total fat 5g, Saturated fat 2g, Total Carbs 4g, Net Carbs 15g, Protein 33g, Sugar 10g, Fiber 1g, Sodium: 2447mg

Baby Back Ribs

Servings: 12 To 15
Cooking Time: 5 To 6 Hours
Ingredients:

- 2 full slabs baby back ribs, back membranes removed
- 1 cup prepared table mustard
- 1 cup Pork Rub
- 1 cup apple juice, divided
- 1 cup packed light brown sugar, divided
- 1 cup of The Ultimate BBQ Sauce, divided

Directions:
1. Supply your Traeger with wood pellets and follow the manufacturer's specific start-up procedure. Preheat, with the lid closed, to 150° to 180°F, or to the "Smoke" setting.
2. Coat the ribs with the mustard to help the rub stick and lock in moisture.
3. Generously apply the rub
4. Place the ribs directly on the grill, close the lid, and smoke for 3 hoursIncrease the temperature to 225°F.
5. Remove the ribs from the grill and wrap each rack individually with aluminum foil, but before sealing tightly, add ½ cup apple juice and ½ cup brown sugar to each package
6. Return the foil-wrapped ribs to the grill, close the lid, and smoke for 2 more hours.
7. Carefully unwrap the ribs and remove the foil completely. Coat each slab with ½ cup of barbecue sauce and continue smoking with the lid closed for 30 minutes to 1 hour, or until the meat tightens and has a reddish bark. For the perfect rack, the internal temperature should be 190°F.

Chili Rib Eye Steaks

Servings: 4
Cooking Time: 1 Hour
Ingredients:

- 4 rib-eye steaks, each about 12 ounces
- For the Rub:
- 1 tablespoon minced garlic
- 1 teaspoon salt
- 1 teaspoon brown sugar
- 2 tablespoons red chili powder
- 1 teaspoon ground cumin
- 2 tablespoons Worcestershire sauce
- 2 tablespoons olive oil

Directions:
1. Prepare the rub and for this, take a small bowl, place all of its ingredients in it and then stir until mixed.
2. Brush the paste on all sides of the steak, rub well, then place steaks into a plastic bag and let it marinate for a minimum of 4 hours.
3. When ready to cook, switch on the Traeger grill, fill the grill hopper with mesquite flavored wood pellets, power the grill on by using the control panel, select 'smoke' on the temperature dial, or set the temperature to 225 degrees F and let it preheat for a minimum of 15 minutes.
4. When the grill has preheated, open the lid, place steaks on the grill grate, shut the grill, and smoke for 45 minutes until internal temperature reaches 120 degrees F.
5. When done, transfer steaks to a dish, let rest for 15 minutes, and meanwhile, change the smoking temperature of the grill to 450 degrees F and let it preheat for a minimum of 10 minutes.
6. Then return steaks to the grill grate and cook for 3 minutes per side until the internal temperature reaches 140 degrees F.
7. Transfer steaks to a dish, let rest for 5 minutes and then serve.

Nutrition Info:

- InfoCalories: 293 Cal ;Fat: 0 g ;Carbs: 0 g ;Protein: 32 g ;Fiber: 0 g

Traeger Kalbi Beef Short Ribs

Servings: 6
Cooking Time: 6 Hours
Ingredients:

- 1/2 cup soy sauce
- 1/2 cup brown sugar
- 1/8 cup rice wine
- 2 tbsp minced garlic
- 1 tbsp sesame oil
- 1/8 cup onion, finely grated
- 2-1/2 pound beef short ribs, thinly sliced

Directions:
1. Mix soy sauce, sugar, rice wine, garlic, sesame oil and onion in a medium mixing bowl.
2. Add the beef in the bowl and cover it in the marinade. Cover the bowl with a plastic wrap and refrigerate for 6 hours.
3. Heat your Traeger to high and ensure the grill is well heated.
4. Place on grill and close the lid ensuring you don't lose any heat.
5. Cook for 4 minutes, flip, and cook for 4 more minutes on the other side.
6. Remove the meat and serve with rice and veggies of choice. Enjoy.

Nutrition Info:

- Calories: 355 Cal Fat: 10 g Carbohydrates: 22 g Protein: 28 g Fiber: 0 g

Perfect Roast Prime Rib

Servings: 8 To 12
Cooking Time: 4 Or 5 Hours
Ingredients:
- 1 (3-bone) rib roast
- Salt
- Freshly ground black pepper
- 1 garlic clove, minced

Directions:
1. Supply your Traeger with wood pellets and follow the start-up procedure. Preheat the grill, with the lid closed, to 360°F.
2. Season the roast all over with salt and pepper and, using your hands, rub it all over with the minced garlic.
3. Place the roast directly on the grill grate and smoke for 4 or 5 hours, until its internal temperature reaches 145°F for medium-rare.
4. Remove the roast from the grill and let it rest for 15 minutes, before slicing and serving.

Buttermilk Pork Loin Roast

Servings: 4-6
Cooking Time: 3-3.5 Hours
Ingredients:
- 1 (3-3½lb) pork loin roast
- 1-quart buttermilk brine

Directions:
1. Cut out all fat and silver skin of pork roast.
2. Place the roast and buttermilk brine in a 1-gallon sealable plastic bag or brine container.
3. Refrigerate overnight, rotating roast every few hours if possible.
4. Use of wood pellet smokers and grills
5. Remove the salted pork roast from the salt water and dry it lightly with a paper towel.
6. In the part where the roast is thickest, incorporate the meat probe
7. Set the wood pellet smoker grill for indirect cooking and preheat to 225 ° F using apple or cherry pellets.
8. Suck roast for 3 to 3 1/2 hours until internal temperature reaches 145 ° F.
9. Place the roast under a loose foil tent for 15 minutes and carve it towards the grain.

Nutrition Info:
- Calories: 126 Cal Fat: 3 g Carbohydrates: 2 g Protein: 21 g Fiber: 0 g

Korean Style Bbq Prime Ribs

Servings: 5
Cooking Time: 8 Hours
Ingredients:
- 3 lbs beef short ribs
- 2 tbsp sugar
- 3/4 cup water
- 1 tbsp ground black pepper
- 3 tbsp white vinegar
- 2 tbsp sesame oil
- 3 tbsp soy sauce
- 6 cloves garlic, minced
- 1/3 cup light brown sugar
- 1/2 yellow onion, finely chopped

Directions:
1. Combine soy sauce, water, and vinegar in a bowl. Mix and whisk in brown sugar, white sugar, pepper, sesame oil, garlic, and onion. Whisk until the sugars have completely dissolved
2. Pour marinade into large bowl or baking pan with high sides. Dunk the short ribs in the marinade, coating completely. Cover marinaded short ribs with plastic wrap and refrigerate for 6 to 12 hours3. Preheat pellet grill to 225°F.
3. Remove plastic wrap from ribs and pull ribs out of marinade. Shake off any excess marinade and dispose of the contents left in the bowl.
4. Place ribs on grill and cook for about 6-8 hours, until ribs reach an internal temperature of 203°F. Measure using a probe meat thermometer
5. Once ribs reach temperature, remove from grill and allow to rest for about 20 minutes. Slice, serve, and enjoy!

St. Patrick Day's Corned Beef

Servings: 14
Cooking Time: 7 Hours
Ingredients:
- 6 lb. corned beef brisket, drained, rinsed and pat dried
- Freshly ground black pepper, to taste
- 8 oz. light beer

Directions:
1. Set the temperature of Traeger Grill to 275 degrees F and preheat with closed lid for 15 minutes.
2. Sprinkle the beef brisket with spice packet evenly.
3. Now, sprinkle the brisket with black pepper lightly.
4. Place the brisket onto the grill and cook for about 3-4 hours.
5. Remove from grill and transfer briskets into an aluminum pan.

6. Add enough beer just to cover the bottom of pan.
7. With a piece of foil, cover the pan, leaving one corner open to let out steam.
8. Cook for about 2-3 hours.
9. Remove the brisket from grill and place onto a cutting board for about 10-15 minutes before slicing.
10. With a sharp knife, cut the brisket in desired sized slices and serve.
11. Remove the brisket from grill and place onto a cutting board for about 25-30 minutes before slicing.
12. With a sharp knife, cut the brisket in desired sized slices and serve.

Nutrition Info:
- Calories per serving: 337; Carbohydrates: 0.6g; Protein: 26.1g; Fat: 24.3g; Sugar: 0g; Sodium: 1719mg; Fiber: 0g

Smoked New York Steaks

Servings: 4
Cooking Time: 1 To 2 Hours
Ingredients:
- 4 (1-inch-thick) New York steaks
- 2 tablespoons olive oil
- Salt
- Freshly ground black pepper

Directions:
1. Supply your Traeger with wood pellets and follow the start-up procedure. Preheat the grill, with the lid closed, to 180°F.
2. Rub the steaks all over with olive oil and season both sides with salt and pepper.
3. Place the steaks directly on the grill grate and smoke for 1 hour.
4. Increase the grill's temperature to 375°F and continue to cook until the steaks' internal temperature reaches 145°F for medium-rare.
5. Remove the steaks and let them rest 5 minutes, before slicing and serving.

Blackened Steak

Servings: 4
Cooking Time: 60 Minutes
Ingredients:
- 2 steaks, each about 40 ounces
- 4 tablespoons blackened rub
- 4 tablespoons butter, unsalted

Directions:
1. Switch on the Traeger grill, fill the grill hopper with hickory flavored wood pellets, power the grill on by using the control panel, select 'smoke' on the temperature dial, or set the temperature to 225 degrees F and let it preheat for a minimum of 15 minutes.
2. Meanwhile, prepare the steaks and for this, sprinkle rub on all sides of each steak and let marinate for 10 minutes.
3. When the grill has preheated, open the lid, place steaks on the grill grate, shut the grill and smoke for 40 minutes until internal temperature reaches 119 degrees F.
4. When done, remove steaks from the grill and wrap each in a piece of foil.
5. Change the smoking temperature to 400 degrees F, place a griddle pan on the grill grate, and when hot, add 2 tablespoons butter and when it begins to melts, add steak and sear it for 4 minutes per side until internal temperature reaches 125 degrees F.
6. Transfer steaks to a dish and then repeat with the remaining steak.
7. Let seared steaks rest for 10 minutes, then slice each steak across the grain and serve.

Nutrition Info:
- InfoCalories: 184.4 Cal ;Fat: 8.8 g ;Carbs: 0 g ;Protein: 23.5 g ;Fiber: 0 g

St. Louis Bbq Ribs

Servings: 4-6
Cooking Time: 4 Hours 20 Minutes
Ingredients:
- Traeger pork as well as a poultry rub - 6 oz
- St. Louis bone in the form of pork ribs - 2 racks
- Traeger Heat and Sweet BBQ sauce - 1 bottle
- Apple juice - 8 oz

Directions:
1. Trim the ribs and peel off their membranes from the back.
2. Apply an even coat of the poultry rub on the front and back of the ribs. Let the coat sit for at least 20 minutes. If you wish to refrigerate it, you can do so for up to 4 hours.
3. Once you are ready to cook it, preheat the pellet grill for around 15 minutes. Place the ribs on the grill grate, bone side down. Put the apple juice in an easy spray bottle and then spray it evenly on the ribs.
4. Smoke the meat for 1 hour.
5. Remove the ribs from the pellet grill and wrap them securely in aluminum foil. Ensure that there is an opening in the wrapping at one end. Pour the remaining 6 oz of apple juice into the foil. Wrap it tightly.
6. Place the ribs on the grill again, meat side down. Smoke the meat for another 3 hours.
7. Once the ribs are done and cooked evenly, get rid of the foil. Gently brush a layer of the sauce on both sides of the

ribs. Put them back on the grill to cook for another 10 minutes to ensure that the sauce is set correctly.
8. Once the sauce sets, take the ribs off the pellet grill and rest for at least 10 minutes to soak in all the juices.
9. Slice the ribs to serve and enjoy!

Nutrition Info:
- Carbohydrates: 13 g Protein: 67 g Fat: 70 g Sodium: 410 mg Cholesterol: 180 mg

Grilled Butter Basted Porterhouse Steak

Servings: 4
Cooking Time: 8 Minutes

Ingredients:
- 4 tablespoons melted butter
- 2 tablespoons Worcestershire sauce
- 2 tablespoons Dijon mustard
- Traeger Prime Rib Rub, as needed
- 2 porterhouse steaks, 1 ½ inch thick

Directions:
1. Fire the Traeger Grill to 2550F. Use desired wood pellets when cooking. Close the lid and preheat for 15 minutes.
2. In a bowl, mix the butter, Worcestershire sauce, mustard, and Prime Rib Rub.
3. Massage all over the steak on all sides. Allow steak to rest for an hour before cooking.
4. When ready to cook, fire the Traeger Grill to 5000F. Use desired wood pellets when cooking. Close the lid and preheat for 15 minutes.
5. Place the steaks on the grill grates and cook for 4 minutes on each side or until the internal temperature reads at 1300F for medium rare steaks.
6. Remove from the grill and allow to rest for 10 minutes before slicing.

Nutrition Info:
- InfoCalories per serving: 515 ; Protein: 65.3g; Carbs: 2.1g; Fat: 27.7g Sugar: 0.9g

Smoked Roast Beef

Servings: 5 To 8
Cooking Time: 12 To 14 Hours

Ingredients:
- 1 (4-pound) top round roast
- 1 batch Espresso Brisket Rub
- 1 tablespoon butter

Directions:
1. Supply your Traeger with wood pellets and follow the start-up procedure. Preheat the grill, with the lid closed, to 180°F.
2. Season the top round roast with the rub. Using your hands, work the rub into the meat.
3. Place the roast directly on the grill grate and smoke until its internal temperature reaches 140°F. Remove the roast from the grill.
4. Place a cast-iron skillet on the grill grate and increase the grill's temperature to 450°F. Place the roast in the skillet, add the butter, and cook until its internal temperature reaches 145°F, flipping once after about 3 minutes.
5. Remove the roast from the grill and let it rest for 10 to 15 minutes, before slicing and serving.

Cheeseburger Hand Pies

Servings: 4
Cooking Time: 10 Minutes

Ingredients:
- ½ pound lean ground beef
- 1 tablespoon minced onion
- 1 tablespoon steak seasoning
- 1 cup shredded Monterey Jack and Colby cheese blend
- 8 slices white American cheese, divided
- 2 (14-ounce) refrigerated prepared pizza dough sheets, divided
- 2 eggs, beaten with 2 tablespoons water (egg wash), divided
- 24 hamburger dill pickle chips
- 2 tablespoons sesame seeds
- 6 slices tomato, for garnish
- Ketchup and mustard, for serving

Directions:
1. Supply your smoker with wood pellets and follow the manufacturer's specific start-up procedure. Preheat, with the lid closed, to 325°F.
2. On your stove top, in a medium sauté pan over medium-high heat, brown the ground beef for 4 to 5 minutes, or until cooked through. Add the minced onion and steak seasoning.
3. Toss in the shredded cheese blend and 2 slices of American cheese, and stir until melted and fully incorporated.
4. Remove the cheeseburger mixture from the heat and set aside.
5. Make sure the dough is well chilled for easier handling. Working quickly, roll out one prepared pizza crust on parchment paper and brush with half of the egg wash.
6. Arrange the remaining 6 slices of American cheese on the dough to outline 6 hand pies.

7. Top each cheese slice with ¼ cup of the cheeseburger mixture, spreading slightly inside the imaginary lines of the hand pies.
8. Place 4 pickle slices on top of the filling for each pie.
9. Top the whole thing with the other prepared pizza crust and cut between the cheese slices to create 6 hand pies.
10. Using kitchen scissors, cut the parchment to further separate the pies, but leave them on the paper.
11. 1Using a fork dipped in egg wash, seal the edges of the pies on all sides. Baste the tops of the pies with the remaining egg wash and sprinkle with the sesame seeds.
12. 1Remove the pies from the parchment paper and gently place on the grill grate. Close the lid and smoke for 5 minutes, then carefully flip and smoke with the lid closed for 5 more minutes, or until browned.
13. 1Top with the sliced tomato and serve with ketchup and mustard.

Traditional Tomahawk Steak

Servings: 4 To 6
Cooking Time: 1 Or 2 Hours
Ingredients:
- 1 tomahawk ribeye steak (2 1/2 to 3 1/2 lbs)
- 5 garlic cloves, minced
- 2 tbsp kosher salt
- 1 bundle fresh thyme
- 2 tbsp ground black pepper
- 8 oz butter stick
- 1 tbsp garlic powder
- 1/8 cup olive oil

Directions:
1. Mix rub ingredients (salt, black pepper, and garlic powder) in a small bowl. Use this mixture to season all sides of the ribeye steak generously. You can also substitute your favorite steak seasoning. After applying seasoning, let the steak rest at room temperature for at least 30 minutes.
2. While the steak rests, preheat your pellet grill to 450°F - 550°F for searing
3. Sear the steak for 5 minutes on each side. Halfway through each side (so after 2 1/2 minutes), rotate the steak 90° to form grill marks on the tomahawk
4. After the tomahawk steak has seared for 5 minutes on each side (10 minutes total), move the steak to a raised rack
5. Adjust your pellet grill's temperature to 250°F and turn up smoke setting if applicable. Leave the lid open for a moment to help allow some heat to escape
6. Stick your probe meat thermometer into the very center of the cut to measure internal temperature.
7. Place butter stick, garlic cloves, olive oil, and thyme in the aluminum pan. Then place the aluminum pan under the steak to catch drippings. After a few minutes, the steak drippings and ingredients will mix together
8. Baste the steak with the aluminum pan mixture every 10 minutes until the tomahawk steak reaches your desired doneness
9. Once the steak reaches its desired doneness, remove from the grill and place on a cutting board or serving dish. The steak should rest for 10-15 minutes before cutting/serving.

Roasted Pork With Blackberry Sauce

Servings: 4
Cooking Time: 50 Minutes
Ingredients:
- 2 lb. pork tenderloin
- 2 tablespoons dried rosemary
- Salt and pepper to taste
- 2 tablespoons olive oil
- 12 blackberries, sliced
- 1 cup balsamic vinegar
- 4 tablespoons sugar

Directions:
1. Preheat the Traeger wood pellet grill to 350 degrees F for 15 minutes while the lid is closed.
2. Season the pork with the rosemary, salt and pepper.
3. In a pan over high heat, pour in the oil and sear pork for 2 minutes per side.
4. Transfer to the grill and cook for 20 minutes.
5. Take the pan off the grill.
6. Let rest for 10 minutes.
7. In a pan over medium heat, simmer the blackberries in vinegar and sugar for 30 minutes.
8. Pour sauce over the pork and serve.
9. Tips: You can also simmer the pork in the blackberry sauce for 10 minutes.

Grilled Hanger Steak

Servings: 6
Cooking Time: 50 Minutes
Ingredients:
- Hanger Steak - 1
- Salt
- Pepper
- For Bourbon Sauce
- Bourbon whiskey - ⅛ cup
- Honey - ⅛ cup
- Sriracha - 1 tbsp
- Garlic - ½ tbsp
- Salt - ¼ tbsp

Directions:
1. Preheat the grill to 225 degrees.
2. Use pepper and salt to season the steak liberally.
3. Place the steak on the grill and close the lid.
4. Let it cook until the temperature goes down to the finish.
5. Take an iron skillet and place it on the stove.
6. Add some butter to the pan and place the steak on it.
7. Cook on both sides for 2 minutes each.
8. Remove the steak from the stove.
9. Add the bourbon sauce ingredients to the pan.
10. Cook and whisk for 3-4 minutes. Pour it over your steak.
11. Serve with your favorite side dish or simply have it with the bourbon sauce.

Nutrition Info:
- Carbohydrates: 6 g Protein: 10 g Fat: 7 g Sodium: 180 mg Cholesterol: 36 mg

Santa Maria Tri-tip

Servings: 4
Cooking Time: 45 Minutes To 1 Hour
Ingredients:
- 2 teaspoons sea salt
- 2 teaspoons freshly ground black pepper
- 2 teaspoons onion powder
- 2 teaspoons garlic powder
- 2 teaspoons dried oregano
- 1 teaspoon cayenne pepper
- 1 teaspoon ground sage
- 1 teaspoon finely chopped fresh rosemary
- 1 (1½ – to 2-pound) tri-tip bottom sirloin

Directions:
1. Supply your Traeger with wood pellets and follow the start-up procedure. Preheat the grill, with the lid closed, to 425°F.
2. In a small bowl, combine the salt, pepper, onion powder, garlic powder, oregano, cayenne pepper, sage, and rosemary to create a rub.
3. Season the meat all over with the rub and lay it directly on the grill.
4. Close the lid and smoke for 45 minutes to 1 hour, or until a meat thermometer inserted in the thickest part of the meat reads 120°F for rare, 130°F for medium-rare, or 140°F for medium, keeping in mind that the meat will come up in temperature by about another 5°F during the rest period.
5. Remove the tri-tip from the heat, tent with aluminum foil, and let rest for 15 minutes before slicing against the grain.

Aromatic Herbed Rack Of Lamb

Servings: 3
Cooking Time: 2 Hours
Ingredients:
- 2 tbsp. fresh sage
- 2 tbsp. fresh rosemary
- 2 tbsp. fresh thyme
- 2 garlic cloves, peeled
- 1 tbsp. honey
- Salt and freshly ground black pepper, to taste
- ¼ C. olive oil
- 1 (1½-lb.) rack of lamb, trimmed

Directions:
1. In a food processor, add all ingredients except for oil and rack of lamb rack and pulse until well combined.
2. While motor is running, slowly add oil and pulse until a smooth paste is formed.
3. Coat the rib rack with paste generously and refrigerate for about 2 hours.
4. Set the temperature of Traeger Grill to 225 degrees F and preheat with closed lid for 15 minutes.
5. Arrange the rack of lamb onto the grill and cook for about 2 hours.
6. Remove the rack of lamb from grill and place onto a cutting board for about 10-15 minutes before slicing.
7. With a sharp knife, cut the rack into individual ribs and serve.

Nutrition Info:
- Calories per serving: 566; Carbohydrates: 9.8g; Protein: 46.7g; Fat: 33.5g; Sugar: 5.8g; Sodium: 214mg; Fiber: 2.2g

Grilled Venison Kabob

Servings: 6
Cooking Time: 15 Minutes
Ingredients:
- 1 venison, black strap steaks cut into large cubes
- 2 whole red onion, quartered
- 2 whole green bell pepper, sliced into big squares
- Oil as needs
- Salt and pepper to taste

Directions:
1. Place all ingredients in a mixing bowl. Toss to coat the meat and vegetables with the oil and seasoning.
2. Thread the meat and vegetables into metal skewers in an alternating manner.
3. Fire the Traeger Grill to 5000F. Use desired wood pellets when cooking. Close the lid and preheat for 15 minutes.
4. Place the kabobs on the grill grate and cook for 15 minutes. Make sure to turn once halfway through the cooking time.
5. Remove from the grill and serve with yogurt if desired.

Nutrition Info:
- InfoCalories per serving: 267; Protein: 32.4g; Carbs: 10.1g; Fat: 10.4g Sugar:4.8 g

Poultry Recipes

Rustic Maple Smoked Chicken Wings

Servings:16
Cooking Time: 35 Minutes
Ingredients:
- 16 chicken wings
- 1 tablespoon olive oil
- 1 tablespoon Traeger Chicken Rub
- 1 cup Traeger 'Que BBQ Sauce or other commercial BBQ sauce of choice

Directions:
1. Place all ingredients in a bowl except for the BBQ sauce. Massage the chicken breasts so that it is coated with the marinade.
2. Place in the fridge to marinate for at least 4 hours.
3. Fire the Traeger Grill to 3500F. Use maple wood pellets. Close the grill lid and preheat for 15 minutes.
4. Place the wings on the grill grate and cook for 12 minutes on each side with the lid closed.
5. Once the chicken wings are done, place in a clean bowl.
6. Pour over the BBQ sauce and toss to coat with the sauce.

Nutrition Info:
- InfoCalories per serving: 230 ; Protein: 37.5g; Carbs: 2.2g; Fat: 7g Sugar: 1.3g

Hot And Sweet Spatchcocked Chicken

Servings:8
Cooking Time:55 Minutes
Ingredients:
- 1 whole chicken, spatchcocked
- ¼ cup Traeger Chicken Rub
- 2 tablespoons olive oil
- ½ cup Traeger Sweet and Heat BBQ Sauce

Directions:
1. Place the chicken breastbone-side down on a flat surface and press the breastbone to break it and flatten the chicken. Sprinkle the Traeger Chicken Rub all over the chicken and massage until the bird is seasoned well. Allow the chicken to rest in the fridge for at least 12 hours.
2. When ready to cook, fire the Traeger Grill to 3500F. Use preferred wood pellets. Close the grill lid and preheat for 15 minutes.
3. Before cooking the chicken, baste with oil. Place on the grill grate and cook on both sides for 55 minutes.
4. 20 minutes before the cooking time, baste the chicken with Traeger Sweet and Heat BBQ Sauce.
5. Continue cooking until a meat thermometer inserted in the thickest part of the chicken reads at 1650F.
6. Allow to rest before carving the chicken.

Nutrition Info:

- InfoCalories per serving: 200; Protein: 30.6g; Carbs: 1.1g; Fat: 7.4g Sugar: 0.6g

South-east-asian Chicken Drumsticks

Servings: 6
Cooking Time: 2 Hours
Ingredients:
- 1 C. fresh orange juice
- ¼ C. honey
- 2 tbsp. sweet chili sauce
- 2 tbsp. hoisin sauce
- 2 tbsp. fresh ginger, grated finely
- 2 tbsp. garlic, minced
- 1 tsp. Sriracha
- ½ tsp. sesame oil
- 6 chicken drumsticks

Directions:
1. Set the temperature of Traeger Grill to 225 degrees F and preheat with closed lid for 15 minutes, using charcoal.
2. In a bowl, place all ingredients except for chicken drumsticks and mix until well combined.
3. Reserve half of honey mixture in a small bowl.
4. In the bowl of remaining sauce, add drumsticks and mix well.
5. Arrange the chicken drumsticks onto the grill and cook for about 2 hours, basting with remaining sauce occasionally.
6. Serve hot.

Nutrition Info:
- Calories per serving: 385; Carbohydrates: 22.7g; Protein: 47.6g; Fat: 10.5g; Sugar: 18.6g; Sodium: 270mg; Fiber: 0.6g

Jamaican Jerk Chicken Quarters

Servings: 4
Cooking Time: 1 To 2 Hours
Ingredients:
- 4 chicken leg quarters, scored
- ¼ cup canola oil
- ½ cup Jamaican Jerk Paste
- 1 tablespoon whole allspice (pimento) berries

Directions:
1. Supply your smoker with wood pellets and follow the manufacturer's specific start-up procedure. Preheat, with the lid closed, to 275°F.
2. Brush the chicken with canola oil, then brush 6 tablespoons of the Jerk paste on and under the skin. Reserve the remaining 2 tablespoons of paste for basting.
3. Throw the whole allspice berries in with the wood pellets for added smoke flavor.
4. Arrange the chicken on the grill, close the lid, and smoke for 1 hour to 1 hour 30 minutes, or until a meat thermometer inserted in the thickest part of the thigh reads 165°F.
5. Let the meat rest for 5 minutes and baste with the reserved jerk paste prior to serving.

Wild Turkey Egg Rolls

Servings: 4-6
Cooking Time: 40 Minutes
Ingredients:
- Corn - ½ cup
- Leftover wild turkey meat - 2 cups
- Black beans - ½ cup
- Taco seasoning - 3 tbsp
- Water ½ cup
- Rotel chilies and tomatoes - 1 can
- Egg roll wrappers- 12
- Cloves of minced garlic- 4
- 1 chopped Poblano pepper or 2 jalapeno peppers
- Chopped white onion - ½ cup

Directions:
1. Add some olive oil to a fairly large skillet. Heat it over medium heat on a stove.
2. Add peppers and onions. Sauté the mixture for 2-3 minutes until it turns soft.
3. Add some garlic and sauté for another 30 seconds. Add the Rotel chilies and beans to the mixture. Keeping mixing the content gently. Reduce the heat and then simmer.
4. After about 4-5 minutes, pour in the taco seasoning and ⅓ cup of water over the meat. Mix everything and coat the meat thoroughly. If you feel that it is a bit dry, you can add 2 tbsp of water. Keep cooking until everything is heated all the way through.
5. Remove the content from the heat and box it to store in a refrigerator. Before you stuff the mixture into the egg wrappers, it should be completely cool to avoid breaking the rolls.
6. Place a spoonful of the cooked mixture in each wrapper and then wrap it securely and tightly. Do the same with all the wrappers.
7. Preheat the pellet grill and brush it with some oil. Cook the egg rolls for 15 minutes on both sides until the exterior is nice and crispy.
8. Remove them from the grill and enjoy with your favorite salsa!

Nutrition Info:

- Info Carbohydrates: 26.1 g Protein: 9.2 g Fat: 4.2 g Sodium: 373.4 mg Cholesterol: 19.8 mg

Smoked Whole Chicken

Servings: 6 To 8
Cooking Time: 4 Hours
Ingredients:
- 1 whole chicken
- 2 cups Tea Injectable (using Not-Just-for-Pork Rub)
- 2 tablespoons olive oil
- 1 batch Chicken Rub
- 2 tablespoons butter, melted

Directions:
1. Supply your smoker with wood pellets and follow the manufacturer's specific start-up procedure. Preheat the grill, with the lid closed, to 180°F.
2. Inject the chicken throughout with the tea injectable.
3. Coat the chicken all over with olive oil and season it with the rub. Using your hands, work the rub into the meat.
4. Place the chicken directly on the grill grate and smoke for 3 hours.
5. Baste the chicken with the butter and increase the grill's temperature to 375°F. Continue to cook the chicken until its internal temperature reaches 170°F.
6. Remove the chicken from the grill and let it rest for 10 minutes, before carving and serving.

Wood Pellet Smoked Spatchcock Turkey

Servings: 6
Cooking Time: 1 Hour 45 Minutes
Ingredients:
- 1 whole turkey
- 1/2 cup oil
- 1/4 cup chicken rub
- 1 tbsp onion powder
- 1 tbsp garlic powder
- 1 tbsp rubbed sage

Directions:
1. Preheat your wood pellet grill to high.
2. Meanwhile, place the turkey on a platter with the breast side down then cut on either side of the backbone to remove the spine.
3. Flip the turkey and season on both sides then place it on the preheated grill or on a pan if you want to catch the drippings.
4. Grill on high for 30 minutes, reduce the temperature to 325°F, and grill for 45 more minutes or until the internal temperature reaches 165°F

5. Remove from the grill and let rest for 20 minutes before slicing and serving. Enjoy.

Nutrition Info:
- InfoCalories 156, Total fat 16g, Saturated fat 2g, Total Carbs 1g, Net Carbs 1g, Protein 2g, Sugar 0g, Fiber 0g, Sodium: 19mg

Applewood-smoked Whole Turkey

Servings: 6 To 8
Cooking Time: 5 To 6 Hours
Ingredients:
- 1 (10- to 12-pound) turkey, giblets removed
- Extra-virgin olive oil, for rubbing
- ¼ cup poultry seasoning
- 8 tablespoons (1 stick) unsalted butter, melted
- ½ cup apple juice
- 2 teaspoons dried sage
- 2 teaspoons dried thyme

Directions:
1. Supply your smoker with wood pellets and follow the manufacturer's specific start-up procedure. Preheat, with the lid closed, to 250°F.
2. Rub the turkey with oil and season with the poultry seasoning inside and out, getting under the skin.
3. In a bowl, combine the melted butter, apple juice, sage, and thyme to use for basting.
4. Put the turkey in a roasting pan, place on the grill, close the lid, and grill for 5 to 6 hours, basting every hour, until the skin is brown and crispy, or until a meat thermometer inserted in the thickest part of the thigh reads 165°F.
5. Let the bird rest for 15 to 20 minutes before carving.

Bacon-wrapped Chicken Tenders

Servings: 6
Cooking Time: 30 Minutes
Ingredients:
- 1-pound chicken tenders
- 10 strips bacon
- 1/2 tbsp Italian seasoning
- 1/2 tbsp black pepper
- 1/2 tbsp salt
- 1 tbsp paprika
- 1 tbsp onion powder
- 1 tbsp garlic powder
- 1/3 cup light brown sugar
- 1 tbsp chili powder

Directions:
1. Preheat your wood pellet smoker to 350°F.
2. Mix seasonings

3. Sprinkle the mixture on all sides of chicken tenders
4. Wrap each chicken tender with a strip of bacon
5. Mix sugar and chili then sprinkle the mixture on the bacon-wrapped chicken.
6. Place them on the smoker and smoker for 30 minutes with the lid closed or until the chicken is cooked.
7. Serve and enjoy.

Nutrition Info:
- Calories: 206 Cal Fat: 7.9 g Carbohydrates: 1.5 g Protein: 30.3 g Fiber: 0 g

Honey Garlic Chicken Wings

Servings: 4
Cooking Time: 1 Hour And 15 Minutes
Ingredients:
- 2 1/2 lb. chicken wings
- Poultry dry rub
- 4 tablespoons butter
- 3 cloves garlic, minced
- 1/2 cup hot sauce
- 1/4 cup honey

Directions:
1. Sprinkle chicken wings with dry rub.
2. Place on a baking pan.
3. Set the Traeger wood pellet grill to 350 degrees F.
4. Preheat for 15 minutes while the lid is closed.
5. Place the baking pan on the grill.
6. Cook for 50 minutes.
7. Add butter to a pan over medium heat.
8. Sauté garlic for 3 minutes.
9. Stir in hot sauce and honey.
10. Cook for 5 minutes while stirring.
11. Coat the chicken wings with the mixture.
12. Grill for 10 more minutes.
13. Tips: You can make the sauce in advance to reduce preparation time.

Chicken Wings

Servings: 4
Cooking Time: 15 Minutes
Ingredients:
- Fresh chicken wings
- Salt to taste
- Pepper to taste
- Garlic powder
- Onion powder
- Cayenne
- Paprika
- Seasoning salt
- Barbeque sauce to taste

Directions:
1. Preheat the wood pellet grill to low. Mix seasoning and coat on chicken. Put the wings on the grill and cook. Place the wings on the grill and cook for 20 minutes or until the wings are fully cooked. Let rest to cool for 5 minutes then toss with barbeque sauce. Serve with orzo and salad. Enjoy.

Nutrition Info:
- Calories: 311 Cal Fat: 22 g Carbohydrates: 22 g Protein: 22 g Fiber: 3 g

Smo-fried Chicken

Servings: 4 To 6
Cooking Time: 55 Minutes
Ingredients:
- 1 egg, beaten
- ½ cup milk
- 1 cup all-purpose flour
- 2 tablespoons salt
- 1 tablespoon freshly ground black pepper
- 2 teaspoons freshly ground white pepper
- 2 teaspoons cayenne pepper
- 2 teaspoons garlic powder
- 2 teaspoons onion powder
- 1 teaspoon smoked paprika
- 8 tablespoons (1 stick) unsalted butter, melted
- 1 whole chicken, cut up into pieces

Directions:
1. Supply your smoker with wood pellets and follow the manufacturer's specific start-up procedure. Preheat, with the lid closed, to 375°F.
2. In a medium bowl, combine the beaten egg with the milk and set aside.
3. In a separate medium bowl, stir together the flour, salt, black pepper, white pepper, cayenne, garlic powder, onion powder, and smoked paprika.
4. Line the bottom and sides of a high-sided metal baking pan with aluminum foil to ease cleanup.
5. Pour the melted butter into the prepared pan.
6. Dip the chicken pieces one at a time in the egg mixture, and then coat well with the seasoned flour. Transfer to the baking pan.
7. Smoke the chicken in the pan of butter ("smo-fry") on the grill, with the lid closed, for 25 minutes, then reduce the heat to 325°F and turn the chicken pieces over.
8. Continue smoking with the lid closed for about 30 minutes, or until a meat thermometer inserted in the thickest part of each chicken piece reads 165°F.
9. Serve immediately.

Trager Smoked Spatchcock Turkey

Servings: 8
Cooking Time: 1 Hour 15 Minutes;
Ingredients:
- 1 turkey
- 1/2 cup melted butter
- 1/4 cup Traeger chicken rub
- 1 tbsp onion powder
- 1 tbsp garlic powder
- 1 tbsp rubbed sage

Directions:
1. Preheat your Traeger to high temperature.
2. Place the turkey on a chopping board with the breast side down and the legs pointing towards you.
3. Cut either side of the turkey backbone, to remove the spine. Flip the turkey and place it on a pan
4. Season both sides with the seasonings and place it on the grill skin side up on the grill.
5. Cook for 30 minutes, reduce temperature, and cook for 45 more minutes or until the internal temperature reaches 1650F.
6. Remove from the Traeger and let rest for 15 minutes before slicing and serving.

Nutrition Info:
- InfoCalories 156, Total fat 16g, Saturated fat 2g, Total carbs 1g, Net carbs 1g Protein 2g, Sugars 0g, Fiber 0g, Sodium 19mg

Savory-sweet Turkey Legs

Servings: 4
Cooking Time: 4 To 5 Hours
Ingredients:
- 1 gallon hot water
- 1 cup curing salt (such as Morton Tender Quick)
- ¼ cup packed light brown sugar
- 1 teaspoon freshly ground black pepper
- 1 teaspoon ground cloves
- 1 bay leaf
- 2 teaspoons liquid smoke
- 4 turkey legs
- Mandarin Glaze, for serving

Directions:
1. In a large container with a lid, stir together the water, curing salt, brown sugar, pepper, cloves, bay leaf, and liquid smoke until the salt and sugar are dissolved; let come to room temperature.
2. Submerge the turkey legs in the seasoned brine, cover, and refrigerate overnight.
3. When ready to smoke, remove the turkey legs from the brine and rinse them; discard the brine.
4. Supply your smoker with wood pellets and follow the manufacturer's specific start-up procedure. Preheat, with the lid closed, to 225°F.
5. Arrange the turkey legs on the grill, close the lid, and smoke for 4 to 5 hours, or until dark brown and a meat thermometer inserted in the thickest part of the meat reads 165°F.
6. Serve with Mandarin Glaze on the side or drizzled over the turkey legs.

Whole Smoked Chicken

Servings: 6
Cooking Time: 3 Hours
Ingredients:
- ½ cup salt
- 1 cup brown sugar
- 1 whole chicken (3 ½ pounds)
- 1 teaspoon minced garlic
- 1 lemon, halved
- 1 medium onion, quartered
- 3 whole cloves
- 5 sprigs of thyme

Directions:
1. Dissolve the salt and sugar in 4 liters of water. Once dissolved, place the chicken in the brine and allow to marinate for 24 hours.
2. When ready to cook, fire the Traeger Grill up to 2500F and allow to preheat for 15 minutes with the lid closed. Use any wood pellet desired but we recommend using the maple wood pellet.
3. While the grill is preheating, remove the chicken from the brine and pat dry using paper towel. Rub the minced garlic all over the chicken. Stuff the cavity of the chicken with the remaining ingredients.
4. Tie the legs together with a natural string.
5. Place the stuffed chicken directly on the grill grate and smoke for 3 hours until the internal temperature of the chicken is 1600F particularly in the breast part.
6. Take the chicken out and grill.

Nutrition Info:
- InfoCalories per serving: 251; Protein: 32.6g; Carbs: 19g; Fat: 4.3g Sugar: 17.3g

Turkey Meatballs

Servings: 8
Cooking Time: 40 Minutes
Ingredients:
- 1 1/4 lb. ground turkey
- 1/2 cup breadcrumbs
- 1 egg, beaten
- 1/4 cup milk
- 1 teaspoon onion powder
- 1/4 cup Worcestershire sauce
- Pinch garlic salt
- Salt and pepper to taste
- 1 cup cranberry jam
- 1/2 cup orange marmalade
- 1/2 cup chicken broth

Directions:
1. In a large bowl, mix the ground turkey, breadcrumbs, egg, milk, onion powder, Worcestershire sauce, garlic salt, salt and pepper.
2. Form meatballs from the mixture.
3. Preheat the Traeger wood pellet grill to 350 degrees F for 15 minutes while the lid is closed.
4. Add the turkey meatballs to a baking pan.
5. Place the baking pan on the grill.
6. Cook for 20 minutes.
7. In a pan over medium heat, simmer the rest of the ingredients for 10 minutes.
8. Add the grilled meatballs to the pan.
9. Coat with the mixture.
10. Cook for 10 minutes.
11. Tips: You can add chili powder to the meatball mixture if you want spicy flavor.

Lemon Chicken Breast

Servings: 4
Cooking Time: 30 Minutes
Ingredients:
- 6 chicken breasts, skinless and boneless
- ½ cup oil
- 1-3 fresh thyme sprigs
- 1 teaspoon ground black pepper
- 2 teaspoon salt
- 2 teaspoons honey
- 1 garlic clove, chopped
- 1 lemon, juiced and zested
- Lemon wedges

Directions:
1. Take a bowl and prepare the marinade by mixing thyme, pepper, salt, honey, garlic, lemon zest, and juice. Mix well until dissolved
2. Add oil and whisk
3. Clean breasts and pat them dry, place in a bag alongside marinade and let them sit in the fridge for 4 hours
4. Preheat your smoker to 400 degrees F
5. Drain chicken and smoke until the internal temperature reaches 165 degrees, for about 15 minutes
6. Serve and enjoy!

Nutrition Info:
- Calories: 230 Fats: 7g Carbs: 1g Fiber: 2g

Chicken Cordon Bleu

Servings: 6
Cooking Time: 40 Minutes
Ingredients:
- 6 boneless skinless chicken breasts
- 6 slices of ham
- 12 slices swiss cheese
- 1 cup panko breadcrumbs
- ½ cup all-purpose flour
- 1 tsp ground black pepper or to taste
- 1 tsp salt or to taste
- 4 tbsp grated parmesan cheese
- 2 tbsp melted butter
- ½ tsp garlic powder
- ½ tsp thyme
- ¼ tsp parsley

Directions:
1. Butterfly the chicken breast with a pairing knife. Place the chicken breast in between 2 plastic wraps and pound with a mallet until the chicken breasts are ¼ inch thick.
2. Place a plastic wrap on a flat surface. Place one fat chicken breast on it.
3. Place one slice of swiss cheese on the chicken. Place one slice of ham over the cheese and place another cheese slice over the ham.
4. Roll the chicken breast tightly. Fold both ends of the roll tightly. Pin both ends of the rolled chicken breast with a toothpick.
5. Repeat step 3 and 4 for the remaining chicken breasts
6. In a mixing bowl, combine the all-purpose flour, ½ tsp salt, and ½ tsp pepper. Set aside.
7. In another mixing bowl, combine breadcrumbs, parmesan, butter, garlic, thyme, parsley, ½ tsp salt, and ½ tsp pepper. Set aside.
8. Break the eggs into another mixing bowl and whisk. Set aside.

9. Grease a baking sheet.
10. Bake one chicken breast roll. Dip into the flour mixture, brush with eggs and dip into breadcrumb mixture. The chicken breast should be coated.
11. Place it on the baking sheet.
12. Repeat steps 9 and 10 for the remaining breast rolls.
13. Preheat your grill to 375°F with the lid closed for 15 minutes.
14. Place the baking sheet on the grill and cook for about 40 minutes, or until the chicken is golden brown.
15. Remove the baking sheet from the grill and let the chicken rest for a few minutes.
16. Slice cordon bleu and serve.

Nutrition Info:
- Calories: 560 Total Fat: 27.4 g Saturated Fat: 15.9 g Cholesterol: 156mg Sodium: 1158 mg Total Carbohydrate: 23.2 g Dietary Fiber: 1.1 g Total Sugars: 1.2 g Protein: 54.3 g

Perfectly Smoked Turkey Legs

Servings: 6
Cooking Time: 4 Hours

Ingredients:
- For Turkey:
- 3 tbsp. Worcestershire sauce
- 1 tbsp. canola oil
- 6 turkey legs
- For Rub:
- ¼ C. chipotle seasoning
- 1 tbsp. brown sugar
- 1 tbsp. paprika
- For Sauce:
- 1 C. white vinegar
- 1 tbsp. canola oil
- 1 tbsp. chipotle BBQ sauce

Directions:
1. For turkey in a bowl, add the Worcestershire sauce and canola oil and mix well.
2. With your fingers, loosen the skin of legs.
3. With your fingers coat the legs under the skin with oil mixture.
4. In another bowl, mix together rub ingredients.
5. Rub the spice mixture under and outer surface of turkey legs generously.
6. Transfer the legs into a large sealable bag and refrigerate for about 2-4 hours.
7. Remove the turkey legs from refrigerator and set aside at room temperature for at least 30 minutes before cooking.
8. Set the temperature of Traeger Grill to 200-220 degrees F and preheat with closed lid for 15 minutes.
9. In a small pan, mix together all sauce ingredients on low heat and cook until warmed completely, stirring continuously.
10. Place the turkey legs onto the grill cook for about 3½-4 hours, coating with sauce after every 45 minutes.
11. Serve hot.

Nutrition Info:
- Calories per serving: 430; Carbohydrates: 4.9g; Protein: 51.2g; Fat: 19.5g; Sugar: 3.9g; Sodium: 1474mg; Fiber: 0.5g

Wood Pellet Smoked Spatchcock Turkey

Servings: 6
Cooking Time: 1 Hour And 45 Minutes

Ingredients:
- 1 whole turkey
- 1/2 cup oil
- 1/4 cup chicken rub
- 1 tbsp onion powder
- 1 tbsp garlic powder
- 1 tbsp rubbed sage

Directions:
1. Preheat your wood pellet grill to high.
2. Meanwhile, place the turkey on a platter with the breast side down then cut on either side of the backbone to remove the spine.
3. Flip the turkey and season on both sides then place it on the preheated grill or on a pan if you want to catch the drippings. Grill on high for 30 minutes, reduce the temperature to 325°F, and grill for 45 more minutes or until the internal temperature reaches 165°F Remove from the grill and let rest for 20 minutes before slicing and serving. Enjoy.

Nutrition Info:
- Calories: 156 Cal Fat: 16 g Carbohydrates: 1 g Protein: 2 g Fiber: 0 g

Serrano Chicken Wings

Servings: 4
Cooking Time: 40 Minutes
Ingredients:
- 4 lb. chicken wings
- 2 cups beer
- 2 teaspoons crushed red pepper
- Cajun seasoning powder
- 1 lb. Serrano chili peppers
- 1 teaspoon fresh basil
- 1 teaspoon dried oregano
- 4 cloves garlic
- 1 cup vinegar
- Salt and pepper to taste

Directions:
1. Soak the chicken wings in beer.
2. Sprinkle with crushed red pepper.
3. Cover and refrigerate for 12 hours.
4. Remove chicken from brine.
5. Season with Cajun seasoning.
6. Preheat your Traeger wood pellet grill to 325 degrees F for 15 minutes while the lid is closed.
7. Add the chicken wings and Serrano chili peppers on the grill.
8. Grill for 5 minutes per side.
9. Remove chili peppers and place in a food processor.
10. Grill the chicken for another 20 minutes.
11. Add the rest of the ingredients to the food processor.
12. Pulse until smooth.
13. Dip the chicken wings in the sauce.
14. Grill for 5 minutes and serve.
15. Tips: You can also use prepared pepper sauce to save time.

Game Day Chicken Drumsticks

Servings: 8
Cooking Time: 1 Hour
Ingredients:
- For Brine:
- ½ C. brown sugar
- ½ C. kosher salt
- 5 C. water
- 2 (12-oz.) bottles beer
- 8 chicken drumsticks
- For Coating:
- ¼ C. olive oil
- ½ C. BBQ rub
- 1 tbsp. fresh parsley, minced
- 1 tbsp. fresh chives, minced
- ¾ C. BBQ sauce
- ¼ C. beer

Directions:
1. For brine: in a bucket, dissolve brown sugar and kosher salt in water and beer.
2. Place the chicken drumsticks in brine and refrigerate, covered for about 3 hours.
3. Set the temperature of Traeger Grill to 275 degrees F and preheat with closed lid for 15 minutes.
4. Remove chicken drumsticks from brine and rinse under cold running water.
5. With paper towels, pat dry chicken drumsticks.
6. Coat drumsticks with olive oil and rub with BBQ rub evenly.
7. Sprinkle the drumsticks with parsley and chives.
8. Arrange the chicken drumsticks onto the grill and cook for about 45 minutes.
9. Meanwhile, in a bowl, mix together BBQ sauce and beer.
10. Remove from grill and coat the drumsticks with BBQ sauce evenly.
11. Cook for about 15 minutes more.
12. Serve immediately.

Nutrition Info:
- Calories per serving: 448; Carbohydrates: 20.5g; Protein: 47.2g; Fat: 16.1g; Sugar: 14.9g; Sodium: 9700mg; Fiber: 0.2g

Beer Can Chicken

Servings: 6
Cooking Time: 1 Hour And 15 Minutes
Ingredients:
- 5-pound chicken
- 1/2 cup dry chicken rub
- 1 can beer

Directions:
1. Preheat your wood pellet grill on smoke for 5 minutes with the lid open.
2. The lid must then be closed and then preheated up to 450 degrees Fahrenheit
3. Pour out half of the beer then shove the can in the chicken and use the legs like a tripod.
4. Place the chicken on the grill until the internal temperature reaches 165°F.
5. Remove from the grill and let rest for 20 minutes before serving. Enjoy.

Nutrition Info:

- Calories: 882 Cal Fat: 51 g Carbohydrates: 2 g Protein: 94 g Fiber: 0 g

Buffalo Chicken Flatbread

Servings: 6
Cooking Time: 30 Minutes
Ingredients:
- 6 mini pita bread
- 1-1/2 cups buffalo sauce
- 4 cups chicken breasts, cooked and cubed
- 3 cups mozzarella cheese
- Blue cheese for drizzling

Directions:
1. Preheat the wood pellet grill to 375-400°F.
2. Place the breads on a flat surface and evenly spread sauce over all of them.
3. Toss the chicken with the remaining buffalo sauce and place it on the pita breads.
4. Top with cheese then place the breads on the grill but indirectly from the heat. Close the grill lid.
5. Cook for 7 minutes or until the cheese has melted and the edges are toasty.
6. Remove from grill and drizzle with blue cheese. Serve and enjoy.

Nutrition Info:
- Calories: 254 Cal Fat: 13 g Carbohydrates: 4 g Protein: 33 g Fiber: 3 g

Special Occasion's Dinner Cornish Hen

Servings: 4
Cooking Time: 1 Hour
Ingredients:
- 4 Cornish game hens
- 4 fresh rosemary sprigs
- 4 tbsp. butter, melted
- 4 tsp. chicken rub

Directions:
1. Set the temperature of Traeger Grill to 375 degrees F and preheat with closed lid for 15 minutes.
2. With paper towels, pat dry the hens.
3. Tuck the wings behind the backs and with kitchen strings, tie the legs together.
4. Coat the outside of each hen with melted butter and sprinkle with rub evenly.
5. Stuff the cavity of each hen with a rosemary sprig.
6. Place the hens onto the grill and cook for about 50-60 minutes.
7. Remove the hens from grill and place onto a platter for about 10 minutes.
8. Cut each hen into desired-sized pieces and serve.

Nutrition Info:
- Calories per serving: 430; Carbohydrates: 2.1g; Protein: 25.4g; Fat: 33g; Sugar: 0g; Sodium: 331mg; Fiber: 0.7g

Hellfire Chicken Wings

Servings: 6
Cooking Time: 40 Minutes
Ingredients:
- 3 pounds chicken wings, tips removed
- 2 tablespoons olive oil
- For the Rub:
- 1 teaspoon onion powder
- 1 teaspoon salt
- 1 teaspoon garlic powder
- 1 tablespoon paprika
- 1 teaspoon ground black pepper
- 1 teaspoon celery seed
- 1 teaspoon cayenne pepper
- 2 teaspoons brown sugar
- For the Sauce:
- 4 jalapeno peppers, sliced crosswise
- 8 tablespoons butter, unsalted
- 1/2 cup hot sauce
- 1/2 cup cilantro leaves

Directions:
1. Switch on the Traeger grill, fill the grill hopper with hickory flavored wood pellets, power the grill on by using the control panel, select 'smoke' on the temperature dial, or set the temperature to 350 degrees F and let it preheat for a minimum of 15 minutes.
2. Prepare the chicken wings and for this, remove tips from the wings, cut each chicken wing through the joint into two pieces, and then place in a large bowl.
3. Prepare the rub and for this, take a small bowl, place all of its ingredients in it and then stir until combined.
4. Sprinkle prepared rub on the chicken wings and then toss until well coated.
5. Meanwhile,
6. When the grill has preheated, open the lid, place chicken wings on the grill grate, shut the grill and smoke for 40 minutes until golden brown and skin have turned crisp, turning halfway.
7. Meanwhile, prepare the sauce and for this, take a small saucepan, place it over medium-low heat, add butter in it and when it melts, add jalapeno and cook for 4 minutes.

8. Then stir in hot sauce and cilantro until mixed and remove the pan from heat.
9. When done, transfer chicken wings to a dish, top with prepared sauce, toss until coated, and then serve.
Nutrition Info:
- InfoCalories: 250 Cal ;Fat: 15 g ;Carbs: 11 g ;Protein: 19 g ;Fiber: 1 g

Roasted Chicken With Pimenton Potatoes

Servings: 16
Cooking Time: 1 Hour
Ingredients:
- 2 whole chicken
- 6 clove garlic, minced
- 2 tablespoons salt
- 3 tablespoons pimento (smoked paprika)
- 3 tablespoons extra virgin olive oil
- 2 bunch fresh thyme
- 3 pounds Yukon gold potatoes

Directions:
1. Season the whole chicken with garlic, salt, paprika, olive oil, and thyme. Massage the chicken to coat all surface of the chicken with the spices. Tie the legs together with a string. Place in a baking dish and place the potatoes on the side. Season the potatoes with salt and olive oil.
2. Allow the chicken to rest in the fridge for 4 hours.
3. When ready to cook, fire the Traeger Grill to 3000F. Use preferred wood pellets. Close the grill lid and preheat for 15 minutes.
4. Place the chicken and potatoes in the grill and cook for 1 hour until a thermometer inserted in the thickest part of the chicken comes out clean.
5. Remove from the grill and allow to rest before carving.
Nutrition Info:
- InfoCalories per serving: 210; Protein: 26.1g; Carbs: 15.3g; Fat: 4.4g Sugar: 0.7g

Cajun Chicken

Servings: 4
Cooking Time: 30 Minutes
Ingredients:
- 2 lb. chicken wings
- Poultry dry rub
- Cajun seasoning

Directions:
1. Season the chicken wings with the dry rub and Cajun seasoning.
2. Preheat the Traeger to 350 degrees F for 15 minutes while the lid is closed.
3. Grill for 30 minutes, flipping twice.
4. Tips: You can also smoke the chicken before grilling.

Maple And Bacon Chicken

Servings: 7
Cooking Time: 1 And ½ Hours
Ingredients:
- 4 boneless and skinless chicken breast
- Salt as needed
- Fresh pepper
- 12 slices bacon, uncooked
- 1cup maple syrup
- ½ cup melted butter
- 1teaspoon liquid smoke

Directions:
1. Preheat your smoker to 250 degrees Fahrenheit
2. Season the chicken with pepper and salt
3. Wrap the breast with 3 bacon slices and cover the entire surface
4. Secure the bacon with toothpicks
5. Take a medium-sized bowl and stir in maple syrup, butter, liquid smoke, and mix well
6. Reserve 1/3rd of this mixture for later use
7. Submerge the chicken breast into the butter mix and coat them well
8. Place a pan in your smoker and transfer the chicken to your smoker
9. Smoker for 1 to 1 and a ½ hours
10. Brush the chicken with reserved butter and smoke for 30 minutes more until the internal temperature reaches 165 degrees Fahrenheit
11. Enjoy!
Nutrition Info:
- Calories: 458 Fats: 20g Carbs: 65g Fiber: 1g

Christmas Dinner Goose

Servings: 12
Cooking Time: 3 Hours
Ingredients:
- 1½ C. kosher salt
- 1 C. brown sugar
- 20 C. water
- 1 (12-lb.) whole goose, giblets removed
- 1 naval orange, cut into 6 wedges
- 1 large onion, cut into 8 wedges
- 2 bay leaves
- ¼ C. juniper berries, crushed

- 12 black peppercorns
- Salt and freshly ground black pepper, to taste
- 1 apple, cut into 6 wedges
- 2-3 fresh parsley sprigs

Directions:
1. Trim off any loose neck skin.
2. Then, trim the first two joints off the wings.
3. Wash the goose under cold running water and with paper towels, pat dry it.
4. With the tip of a paring knife, prick the goose all over the skin.
5. In a large pitcher, dissolve kosher salt and brown sugar in water.
6. Squeeze 3 orange wedges into brine.
7. Add goose, 4 onion wedges, bay leaves, juniper berries and peppercorns in brine and refrigerate for 24 hours.
8. Set the temperature of Traeger Grill to 350 degrees F and preheat with closed lid for 15 minutes.
9. Remove the goose from brine and with paper towels, pat dry completely.
10. Season the in and outside of goose with salt and black pepper evenly.
11. Stuff the cavity with apple wedges, herbs, remaining orange and onion wedges.
12. With kitchen strings, tie the legs together loosely.
13. Place the goose onto a rack arranged in a shallow roasting pan.
14. Arrange the goose on grill and cook for about 1 hour.
15. With a basting bulb, remove some of the fat from the pan and cook for about 1 hour.
16. Again, remove excess fat from the pan and cook for about ½-1 hour more.
17. Remove goose from grill and place onto a cutting board for about 20 minutes before carving.
18. With a sharp knife, cut the goose into desired-sized pieces and serve.

Nutrition Info:
- Calories per serving: 907; Carbohydrates: 23.5g; Protein: 5.6g; Fat: 60.3g; Sugar: 19.9g; Sodium: 8000mg; Fiber: 1.1g

Traeger Smoked Cornish Hens

Servings: 6
Cooking Time: 1 Hour
Ingredients:
- 6 Cornish hens
- 3 tbsp canola oil
- 6 tbsp rub

Directions:
1. Preheat your Traeger to 2750F.
2. Meanwhile, rub the hens with canola oil then with your favorite rub.
3. Place the hens on the grill with the breast side down. Smoke for 30 minutes.
4. Flip the hens and increase the Traeger temperature to 4000F. Cook until the internal temperature reaches 1650F.
5. Remove the hens from the grill and let rest for 10 minutes before serving.

Nutrition Info:
- InfoCalories 696, Total fat 50g, Saturated fat 13g, Total carbs 1g, Net carbs 1g Protein 57g, Sugars 0g, Fiber 0g, Sodium 165mg

Smoked Airline Chicken

Servings: 4
Cooking Time: 1 To 2 Hours
Ingredients:
- 2 boneless chicken breasts with drumettes attached
- ½ cup soy sauce
- ½ cup teriyaki sauce
- ¼ cup canola oil
- ¼ cup white vinegar
- 1 tablespoon minced garlic
- ¼ cup chopped scallions
- 2 teaspoons freshly ground black pepper
- 1 teaspoon ground mustard

Directions:
1. Place the chicken in a baking dish.
2. In a bowl, whisk together the soy sauce, teriyaki sauce, canola oil, vinegar, garlic, scallions, pepper and ground mustard, then pour this marinade over the chicken, coating both sides.
3. Refrigerate the chicken in marinade for 4 hours, turning over every hour.
4. When ready to smoke the chicken, supply your smoker with wood pellets and follow the manufacturer's specific start-up procedure. Preheat, with the lid closed, to 250°F.
5. Remove the chicken from the marinade but do not rinse. Discard the marinade.
6. Arrange the chicken directly on the grill, close the lid, and smoke for 1 hour 30 minutes to 2 hours, or until a meat thermometer inserted in the thickest part of the meat reads 165°F.
7. Let the meat rest for 3 minutes before serving.

Roasted Whole Chicken

Servings: 6 To 8
Cooking Time: 1 To 2 Hours
Ingredients:
- 1 whole chicken
- 2 tablespoons olive oil
- 1 batch Chicken Rub

Directions:
1. Supply your smoker with wood pellets and follow the manufacturer's specific start-up procedure. Preheat the grill, with the lid closed, to 375°F.
2. Coat the chicken all over with olive oil and season it with the rub. Using your hands, work the rub into the meat.
3. Place the chicken directly on the grill grate and smoke until its internal temperature reaches 170°F.
4. Remove the chicken from the grill and let it rest for 10 minutes, before carving and serving.

Rosemary Orange Chicken

Servings: 6
Cooking Time: 45 Minutes
Ingredients:
- 4 pounds chicken, backbone removed
- For the Marinade:
- 2 teaspoons salt
- 3 tablespoons chopped rosemary leaves
- 2 teaspoons Dijon mustard
- 1 orange, zested
- 1/4 cup olive oil
- ¼ cup of orange juice

Directions:
1. Prepare the chicken and for this, rinse the chicken, pat dry with paper towels and then place in a large baking dish.
2. Prepare the marinade and for this, take a medium bowl, place all of its ingredients in it and whisk until combined.
3. Cover chicken with the prepared marinade, cover with a plastic wrap, and then marinate for a minimum of 2 hours in the refrigerator, turning halfway.
4. When ready to cook, switch on the Traeger grill, fill the grill hopper with flavored wood pellets, power the grill on by using the control panel, select 'smoke' on the temperature dial, or set the temperature to 350 degrees F and let it preheat for a minimum of 5 minutes.
5. When the grill has preheated, open the lid, place chicken on the grill grate skin-side down, shut the grill and smoke for 45 minutes until well browned, and the internal temperature reaches 165 degrees F.
6. When done, transfer chicken to a cutting board, let it rest for 10 minutes, cut it into slices, and then serve.

Nutrition Info:
- InfoCalories: 258 Cal ;Fat: 17.4 g ;Carbs: 5.2 g ;Protein: 19.3 g ;Fiber: 0.3 g

Glazed Chicken Thighs

Servings: 4
Cooking Time: 30 Minutes
Ingredients:
- 2 garlic cloves, minced
- ¼ C. honey
- 2 tbsp. soy sauce
- ¼ tsp. red pepper flakes, crushed
- 4 (5-oz.) skinless, boneless chicken thighs
- 2 tbsp. olive oil
- 2 tsp. sweet rub
- ¼ tsp. red chili powder
- Freshly ground black pepper, to taste

Directions:
1. Set the temperature of Traeger Grill to 400 degrees F and preheat with closed lid for 15 minutes.
2. In a small bowl, add garlic, honey, soy sauce and red pepper flakes and with a wire whisk, beat until well combined.
3. Coat chicken thighs with oil and season with sweet rub, chili powder and black pepper generously.
4. Arrange the chicken drumsticks onto the grill and cook for about 15 minutes per side.
5. In the last 4-5 minutes of cooking, coat the thighs with garlic mixture.
6. Serve immediately.

Nutrition Info:
- Calories per serving: 309; Carbohydrates: 18.7g; Protein: 32.3g; Fat: 12.1g; Sugar: 17.6g; Sodium: 504mg; Fiber: 0.2g

Herb Roasted Turkey

Servings: 12
Cooking Time: 3 Hours And 30 Minutes
Ingredients:
- 14 pounds turkey, cleaned
- 2 tablespoons chopped mixed herbs
- Pork and poultry rub as needed
- 1/4 teaspoon ground black pepper
- 3 tablespoons butter, unsalted, melted
- 8 tablespoons butter, unsalted, softened
- 2 cups chicken broth

Directions:

1. Clean the turkey by removing the giblets, wash it inside out, pat dry with paper towels, then place it on a roasting pan and tuck the turkey wings by tiring with butcher's string.
2. Switch on the Traeger grill, fill the grill hopper with hickory flavored wood pellets, power the grill on by using the control panel, select 'smoke' on the temperature dial, or set the temperature to 325 degrees F and let it preheat for a minimum of 15 minutes.
3. Meanwhile, prepared herb butter and for this, take a small bowl, place the softened butter in it, add black pepper and mixed herbs and beat until fluffy.
4. Place some of the prepared herb butter underneath the skin of turkey by using a handle of a wooden spoon, and massage the skin to distribute butter evenly.
5. Then rub the exterior of the turkey with melted butter, season with pork and poultry rub, and pour the broth in the roasting pan.
6. When the grill has preheated, open the lid, place roasting pan containing turkey on the grill grate, shut the grill and smoke for 3 hours and 30 minutes until the internal temperature reaches 165 degrees F and the top has turned golden brown.
7. When done, transfer turkey to a cutting board, let it rest for 30 minutes, then carve it into slices and serve.

Nutrition Info:
- InfoCalories: 154.6 Cal ;Fat: 3.1 g ;Carbs: 8.4 g ;Protein: 28.8 g ;Fiber: 0.4 g

Wood Pellet Grilled Chicken Kabobs

Servings: 6
Cooking Time: 12 Minutes
Ingredients:
- 1/2 cup olive oil
- 2 tbsp white vinegar
- 1 tbsp lemon juice
- 1-1/2 tbsp salt
- 1/2 tbsp pepper, coarsely ground
- 2 tbsp chives, freshly chopped
- 1-1/2 tbsp thyme, freshly chopped
- 2 tbsp Italian parsley freshly chopped
- 1tbsp garlic, minced
- Kabobs
- 1 each orange, red, and yellow pepper
- 1-1/2 pounds chicken breast, boneless and skinless
- 12 mini mushrooms

Directions:
1. In a mixing bowl, add all the marinade ingredients and mix well. Toss the chicken and mushrooms in the marinade then refrigerate for 30 minutes.
2. Meanwhile, soak the skewers in hot water. Remove the chicken from the fridge and start assembling the kabobs.
3. Preheat your wood pellet to 450°F.
4. Grill the kabobs in the wood pellet for 6 minutes, flip them and grill for 6 more minutes.
5. Remove from the grill and let rest. Heat up the naan bread on the grill for 2 minutes.
6. Serve and enjoy.

Nutrition Info:
- Calories: 165 Cal Fat: 13 g Carbohydrates: 1 g Protein: 33 g Fiber: 0 g

Chinese Inspired Duck Legs

Servings: 8
Cooking Time: 1 Hour 10 Minutes
Ingredients:
- For Glaze:
- ¼ C. fresh orange juice
- ¼ C. orange marmalade
- ¼ C. mirin
- 2 tbsp. hoisin sauce
- ½ tsp. red pepper flakes, crushed
- For Duck:
- 1 tsp. kosher salt
- ¾ tsp. freshly ground black pepper
- ¾ tsp. Chinese five-spice powder
- 8 (6-oz.) duck legs

Directions:
1. Set the temperature of Traeger Grill to 235 degrees F and preheat with closed lid for 15 minutes.
2. Forb glaze: in a small pan, add all ingredients over medium-high heat and bring to gentle boil, stirring continuously.
3. Remove from heat and set aside.
4. For rub: in a small bowl, mix together salt, black pepper and five-spice powder.
5. Rub the duck legs with spice rub evenly.
6. Place the duck legs onto the grill, skin side up and cook for about 50 minutes.
7. Coat the duck legs with glaze ad cook for about 20 minutes, flipping and coating with glaze after every 5 minutes.

Nutrition Info:
- Calories per serving: 303; Carbohydrates: 0.1g; Protein: 49.5g; Fat: 10.2g; Sugar: 0g; Sodium: 474mg; Fiber: 0.1g

Wood Pellet Smoked Cornish Hens

Servings: 6
Cooking Time: 1 Hour
Ingredients:
- 6 Cornish hens
- 3 tbsp avocado oil
- 6 tbsp rub of choice

Directions:
1. Fire up the wood pellet and preheat it to 275°F.
2. Rub the hens with oil then coat generously with rub. Place the hens on the grill with the chest breast side down.
3. Smoke for 30 minutes. Flip the hens and increase the grill temperature to 400°F. Cook until the internal temperature reaches 165°F.
4. Remove from the grill and let rest for 10 minutes before serving. Enjoy.

Nutrition Info:
- Calories: 696 Cal Fat: 50 g Carbohydrates: 1 g Protein: 57 g Fiber: 0 g

Turkey Legs

Servings: 4
Cooking Time: 5 Hours
Ingredients:
- 4 turkey legs
- For the Brine:
- 1/2 cup curing salt
- 1 tablespoon whole black peppercorns
- 1 cup BBQ rub
- 1/2 cup brown sugar
- 2 bay leaves
- 2 teaspoons liquid smoke
- 16 cups of warm water
- 4 cups ice
- 8 cups of cold water

Directions:
1. Prepare the brine and for this, take a large stockpot, place it over high heat, pour warm water in it, add peppercorn, bay leaves, and liquid smoke, stir in salt, sugar, and BBQ rub and bring it to a boil.
2. Remove pot from heat, bring it to room temperature, then pour in cold water, add ice cubes and let the brine chill in the refrigerator.
3. Then add turkey legs in it, submerge them completely, and let soak for 24 hours in the refrigerator.
4. After 24 hours, remove turkey legs from the brine, rinse well and pat dry with paper towels.
5. When ready to cook, switch on the Traeger grill, fill the grill hopper with hickory flavored wood pellets, power the grill on by using the control panel, select 'smoke' on the temperature dial, or set the temperature to 250 degrees F and let it preheat for a minimum of 15 minutes.
6. When the grill has preheated, open the lid, place turkey legs on the grill grate, shut the grill, and smoke for 5 hours until nicely browned and the internal temperature reaches 165 degrees F.
7. Serve immediately.

Nutrition Info:
- InfoCalories: 416 Cal ;Fat: 13.3 g ;Carbs: 0 g ;Protein: 69.8 g ;Fiber: 0 g

Sweet Sriracha Bbq Chicken

Servings: 5
Cooking Time: 1 And ½-2 Hours
Ingredients:
- 1 cup sriracha
- ½ cup butter
- ½ cup molasses
- ½ cup ketchup
- ¼ cup firmly packed brown sugar
- 1 teaspoon salt
- 1 teaspoon fresh ground black pepper
- 1 whole chicken, cut into pieces
- ½ teaspoon fresh parsley leaves, chopped

Directions:
1. Preheat your smoker to 250 degrees Fahrenheit using cherry wood
2. Take a medium saucepan and place it over low heat, stir in butter, sriracha, ketchup, molasses, brown sugar, mustard, pepper and salt and keep stirring until the sugar and salt dissolves
3. Divide the sauce into two portions
4. Brush the chicken half with the sauce and reserve the remaining for serving
5. Make sure to keep the sauce for serving on the side, and keep the other portion for basting
6. Transfer chicken to your smoker rack and smoke for about 1 and a ½ to 2 hours until the internal temperature reaches 165 degrees Fahrenheit
7. Sprinkle chicken with parsley and serve with reserved BBQ sauce
8. Enjoy!

Nutrition Info:
- Calories: 148 Fats: 0.6g Carbs: 10g Fiber: 1g

Buttered Thanksgiving Turkey

Servings: 12 To 14
Cooking Time: 5 To 6 Hours
Ingredients:
- 1 whole turkey (make sure the turkey is not pre-brined)
- 2 batches Garlic Butter Injectable
- 3 tablespoons olive oil
- 1 batch Chicken Rub
- 2 tablespoons butter

Directions:
1. Supply your smoker with wood pellets and follow the manufacturer's specific start-up procedure. Preheat the grill, with the lid closed, to 180°F.
2. Inject the turkey throughout with the garlic butter injectable. Coat the turkey with olive oil and season it with the rub. Using your hands, work the rub into the meat and skin.
3. Place the turkey directly on the grill grate and smoke for 3 or 4 hours (for an 8- to 12-pound turkey, cook for 3 hours; for a turkey over 12 pounds, cook for 4 hours), basting it with butter every hour.
4. Increase the grill's temperature to 375°F and continue to cook until the turkey's internal temperature reaches 170°F.
5. Remove the turkey from the grill and let it rest for 10 minutes, before carving and serving.

Authentic Holiday Turkey Breast

Servings: 6
Cooking Time: 4 Hours
Ingredients:
- ½ C. honey
- ¼ C. dry sherry
- 1 tbsp. butter
- 2 tbsp. fresh lemon juice
- Salt, to taste
- 1 (3-3½-pound) skinless, boneless turkey breast

Directions:
1. In a small pan, place honey, sherry and butter over low heat and cook until the mixture becomes smooth, stirring continuously.
2. Remove from heat and stir in lemon juice and salt. Set aside to cool.
3. Transfer the honey mixture and turkey breast in a sealable bag.
4. Seal the bag and shake to coat well.
5. Refrigerate for about 6-10 hours.
6. Set the temperature of Traeger Grill to 225-250 degrees F and preheat with closed lid for 15 minutes.
7. Place the turkey breast onto the grill and cook for about 2½-4 hours or until desired doneness.
8. Remove turkey breast from grill and place onto a cutting board for about 15-20 minutes before slicing.
9. With a sharp knife, cut the turkey breast into desired-sized slices and serve.

Nutrition Info:
- Calories per serving: 443; Carbohydrates: 23.7g; Protein: 59.2g; Fat: 11.4g; Sugar: 23.4g; Sodium: 138mg; Fiber: 0.1g

Smoked Fried Chicken

Servings: 6
Cooking Time: 3 Hours
Ingredients:
- 3.5 lb. chicken
- Vegetable oil
- Salt and pepper to taste
- 2 tablespoons hot sauce
- 1 quart buttermilk
- 2 tablespoons brown sugar
- 1 tablespoon poultry dry rub
- 2 tablespoons onion powder
- 2 tablespoons garlic powder
- 2 1/2 cups all-purpose flour
- Peanut oil

Directions:
1. Set the Traeger wood pellet grill to 200 degrees F.
2. Preheat it for 15 minutes while the lid is closed.
3. Drizzle chicken with vegetable oil and sprinkle with salt and pepper.
4. Smoke chicken for 2 hours and 30 minutes.
5. In a bowl, mix the hot sauce, buttermilk and sugar.
6. Soak the smoked chicken in the mixture.
7. Cover and refrigerate for 1 hour.
8. In another bowl, mix the dry rub, onion powder, garlic powder and flour.
9. Coat the chicken with the mixture.
10. Heat the peanut oil in a pan over medium heat.
11. Fry the chicken until golden and crispy.
12. Tips: Drain chicken on paper towels before serving.

Smoked Turkey Breast

Servings: 2 To 4
Cooking Time: 1 To 2 Hours
Ingredients:
- 1 (3-pound) turkey breast
- Salt
- Freshly ground black pepper
- 1 teaspoon garlic powder

Directions:
1. Supply your smoker with wood pellets and follow the manufacturer's specific start-up procedure. Preheat the grill, with the lid closed, to 180°F.
2. Season the turkey breast all over with salt, pepper, and garlic powder.
3. Place the breast directly on the grill grate and smoke for 1 hour.
4. Increase the grill's temperature to 350°F and continue to cook until the turkey's internal temperature reaches 170°F. Remove the breast from the grill and serve immediately.

Bbq Sauce Smothered Chicken Breasts

Servings: 4
Cooking Time: 30 Minutes
Ingredients:
- 1 tsp. garlic, crushed
- ¼ C. olive oil
- 1 tbsp. Worcestershire sauce
- 1 tbsp. sweet mesquite seasoning
- 4 chicken breasts
- 2 tbsp. regular BBQ sauce
- 2 tbsp. spicy BBQ sauce
- 2 tbsp. honey bourbon BBQ sauce

Directions:
1. Set the temperature of Traeger Grill to 450 degrees F and preheat with closed lid for 15 minutes.
2. In a large bowl, mix together garlic, oil, Worcestershire sauce and mesquite seasoning.
3. Coat chicken breasts with seasoning mixture evenly.
4. Place the chicken breasts onto the grill and cook for about 20-30 minutes.
5. Meanwhile, in a bowl, mix together all 3 BBQ sauces.
6. In the last 4-5 minutes of cooking, coat breast with BBQ sauce mixture.
7. Serve hot.

Nutrition Info:
- Calories per serving: 421; Carbohydrates: 10.1g; Protein: 41,2g; Fat: 23.3g; Sugar: 6.9g; Sodium: 763mg; Fiber: 0.2g

Skinny Smoked Chicken Breasts

Servings: 4 To 6
Cooking Time: 1 Hour 25 Minutes
Ingredients:
- 2½ pounds boneless, skinless chicken breasts
- Salt
- Freshly ground black pepper

Directions:
1. Supply your smoker with wood pellets and follow the manufacturer's specific start-up procedure. Preheat the grill, with the lid closed, to 180°F.
2. Season the chicken breasts all over with salt and pepper.
3. Place the breasts directly on the grill grate and smoke for 1 hour.
4. Increase the grill's temperature to 325°F and continue to cook until the chicken's internal temperature reaches 170°F. Remove the breasts from the grill and serve immediately.

Wood Pellet Sheet Pan Chicken Fajitas

Servings: 10
Cooking Time: 10 Minutes
Ingredients:
- 2 tbsp oil
- 2 tbsp chile margarita seasoning
- 1 tbsp salt
- 1/2 tbsp onion powder
- 1/2 tbsp garlic, granulated
- 2-pound chicken breast, thinly sliced
- 1 red bell pepper, seeded and sliced
- 1 orange bell pepper
- 1 onion, sliced

Directions:
1. Preheat the wood pellet to 450°F. Meanwhile, mix oil and seasoning then toss the chicken and the peppers. Line a sheet pan with foil then place it in the preheated grill. Let it heat for 10 minutes with the grill's lid closed. Open the grill and place the chicken with the veggies on the pan in a single layer. Cook for 10 minutes or until the chicken is cooked and no longer pink. Remove from grill and serve with tortilla or your favorite fixings.

Nutrition Info:
- Calories: 211 Cal Fat: 6 g Carbohydrates: 5 g   Protein: 29 g Fiber: 1 g

Paprika Chicken

Servings: 7
Cooking Time: 2 – 4 Hours
Ingredients:
- 4-6 chicken breast
- 4 tablespoons olive oil
- 2 tablespoons smoked paprika
- ½ tablespoon salt
- ¼ teaspoon pepper
- 2 teaspoons garlic powder
- 2 teaspoons garlic salt
- 2 teaspoons pepper
- 1 teaspoon cayenne pepper
- 1 teaspoon rosemary

Directions:
1. Preheat your smoker to 220 degrees Fahrenheit using your favorite wood Pellets
2. Prepare your chicken breast according to your desired shapes and transfer to a greased baking dish
3. Take a medium bowl and add spices, stir well
4. Press the spice mix over chicken and transfer the chicken to smoker
5. Smoke for 1-1 and a ½ hours
6. Turn-over and cook for 30 minutes more
7. Once the internal temperature reaches 165 degrees Fahrenheit
8. Remove from the smoker and cover with foil
9. Allow it to rest for 15 minutes
10. Enjoy!

Nutrition Info:
- Calories: 237 Fats: 6.1g Carbs: 14g Fiber: 3g

Smoked Chicken Drumsticks

Servings: 5
Cooking Time: 2 Hours 30 Minutes
Ingredients:
- 10 chicken drumsticks
- 2 tsp garlic powder
- 1 tsp salt
- 1 tsp onion powder
- 1/2 tsp ground black pepper
- ½ tsp cayenne pepper
- 1 tsp brown sugar
- 1/3 cup hot sauce
- 1 tsp paprika
- ½ tsp thyme

Directions:
1. In a large mixing bowl, combine the garlic powder, sugar, hot sauce, paprika, thyme, cayenne, salt, and ground pepper. Add the drumsticks and toss to combine.
2. Cover the bowl and refrigerate for 1 hour.
3. Remove the drumsticks from the marinade and let them sit for about 1 hour until they are at room temperature.
4. Arrange the drumsticks into a rack.
5. Start your pellet grill on smoke, leaving the lid open for 5 minutes for the fire to start.
6. Close the lid and preheat grill to 250°F, using hickory or apple hardwood pellets.
7. Place the rack on the grill and smoke drumsticks for 2 hours, 30 minutes, or until the drumsticks' internal temperature reaches 180°F.
8. Remove drumsticks from heat and let them rest for a few minutes.
9. Serve.

Nutrition Info:
- Calories: 167 Total Fat: 5.4 g Saturated Fat: 1.4 g Cholesterol: 81 mg Sodium: 946 mg Total Carbohydrate: 2.6 g Dietary Fiber: 0.5 g Total Sugars: 1.3 g Protein: 25.7 g

Smoked And Fried Chicken Wings

Servings: 6
Cooking Time: 2 Hours
Ingredients:
- 3 pounds chicken wings
- 1 tbsp Goya adobo all-purpose seasoning
- Sauce of your choice

Directions:
1. Fire up your wood pellet grill and set it to smoke.
2. Meanwhile, coat the chicken wings with adobo all-purpose seasoning. Place the chicken on the grill and smoke for 2 hours.
3. Remove the wings from the grill.
4. Preheat oil to 375°F in a frying pan. Drop the wings in batches and let fry for 5 minutes or until the skin is crispy.
5. Drain the oil and proceed with drizzling preferred sauce
6. Drain oil and drizzle preferred sauce
7. Enjoy.

Nutrition Info:
- Calories: 755 Cal Fat: 55 g Carbohydrates: 24 g Protein: 39 g Fiber: 1 g

Wood-fired Chicken Breasts

Servings: 2 To 4
Cooking Time: 45 Minutes
Ingredients:
- 2 (1-pound) bone-in, skin-on chicken breasts
- 1 batch Chicken Rub

Directions:
1. Supply your smoker with wood pellets and follow the manufacturer's specific start-up procedure. Preheat the grill, with the lid closed, to 350°F.
2. Season the chicken breasts all over with the rub. Using your hands, work the rub into the meat.
3. Place the breasts directly on the grill grate and smoke until their internal temperature reaches 170°F. Remove the breasts from the grill and serve immediately.

Thanksgiving Dinner Turkey

Servings: 16
Cooking Time: 4 Hours
Ingredients:
- ½ lb. butter, softened
- 2 tbsp. fresh thyme, chopped
- 2 tbsp. fresh rosemary, chopped
- 6 garlic cloves, crushed
- 1 (20-lb.) whole turkey, neck and giblets removed
- Salt and freshly ground black pepper, to taste

Directions:
1. Set the temperature of Traeger Grill to 300 degrees F and preheat with closed lid for 15 minutes, using charcoal.
2. In a bowl, place butter, fresh herbs, garlic, salt and black pepper and mix well.
3. With your fingers, separate the turkey skin from breast to create a pocket.
4. Stuff the breast pocket with ¼-inch thick layer of butter mixture.
5. Season the turkey with salt and black pepper evenly.
6. Arrange the turkey onto the grill and cook for 3-4 hours.
7. Remove the turkey from grill and place onto a cutting board for about 15-20 minutes before carving.
8. With a sharp knife, cut the turkey into desired-sized pieces and serve.

Nutrition Info:
- Calories per serving: 965; Carbohydrates: 0.6g; Protein: 106.5g; Fat: 52g; Sugar: 0g; Sodium: 1916mg; Fiber: 0.2g

Wood Pellet Grilled Buffalo Chicken

Servings: 6
Cooking Time: 20 Minutes
Ingredients:
- 5 chicken breasts, boneless and skinless
- 2 tbsp homemade bbq rub
- 1 cup homemade Cholula buffalo sauce

Directions:
1. Preheat the wood pellet grill to 400°F.
2. Slice the chicken into long strips and season with bbq rub.
3. Place the chicken on the grill and paint both sides with buffalo sauce.
4. Cook for 4 minutes with the grill closed. Cook while flipping and painting with buffalo sauce every 5 minutes until the internal temperature reaches 165°F.
5. Remove from the grill and serve when warm. Enjoy.

Nutrition Info:
- InfoCalories 176, Total fat 4g, Saturated fat 1g, Total carbs 1g, Net carbs 1g, Protein 32g, Sugar 1g, Fiber 0g, Sodium: 631mg

Hickory Smoked Chicken

Servings: 4
Cooking Time: 30 Minutes
Ingredients:
- 4 chicken breasts
- ¼ cup olive oil
- 1 teaspoon pressed garlic
- 1 tablespoon Worcestershire sauce
- Kirkland Sweet Mesquite Seasoning as needed
- 1 button Traeger Honey Bourbon Sauce

Directions:
1. Place all ingredients in a bowl except for the Bourbon sauce. Massage the chicken until all parts are coated with the seasoning.
2. Allow to marinate in the fridge for 4 hours.
3. Once ready to cook, fire the Traeger Grill to 3500F. Use Hickory wood pellets and close the lid. Preheat for 15 minutes.
4. Place the chicken directly into the grill grate and cook for 30 minutes. Flip the chicken halfway through the cooking time.
5. Five minutes before the cooking time ends, brush all surfaces of the chicken with the Honey Bourbon Sauce.
6. Serve immediately.

Nutrition Info:
- InfoCalories per serving: 622; Protein: 60.5g; Carbs: 1.1g; Fat: 40.3g Sugar: 0.4g

Traeger Grilled Buffalo Chicken Legs

Servings: 8
Cooking Time: 1 Hour 15 Minutes;
Ingredients:
- 12 chicken legs
- 1/2 tbsp salt
- 1 tbsp buffalo seasoning
- 1 cup Buffalo sauce

Directions:
1. Preheat your Traeger to 3250F.
2. Toss the chicken legs in salt and seasoning then place them on the preheated grill.
3. Grill for 40 minutes turning twice through the cooking.
4. Increase the heat and cook for 10 more minutes. Brush the chicken legs and brush with buffalo sauce. Cook for an additional 10 minutes or until the internal temperature reaches 1650F.
5. Remove from the Traeger and brush with more buffalo sauce.
6. Serve with blue cheese, celery, and hot ranch.

Nutrition Info:
- InfoCalories 956, Total fat 47g, Saturated fat 13g, Total carbs 1g, Net carbs 1g Protein 124g, Sugars 0g, Fiber 0g, Sodium 1750mg

Traeger Asian Miso Chicken Wings

Servings: 6
Cooking Time: 25 Minutes
Ingredients:
- 2 lb chicken wings
- 3/4 cup soy
- 1/2 cup pineapple juice
- 1 tbsp sriracha
- 1/8 cup miso
- 1/8 cup gochujang
- 1/2 cup water
- 1/2 cup oil
- Togarashi

Directions:
1. Preheat the Traeger to 3750F
2. Combine all the ingredients except togarashi in a zip lock bag. Toss until the chicken wings are well coated. Refrigerate for 12 hours
3. Pace the wings on the grill grates and close the lid. Cook for 25 minutes or until the internal temperature reaches 1650F
4. Remove the wings from the Traeger and sprinkle Togarashi.
5. Serve when hot and enjoy.

Nutrition Info:
- InfoCalories 703, Total fat 56g, Saturated fat 14g, Total carbs 24g, Net carbs 23g Protein 27g, Sugars 6g, Fiber 1g, Sodium 1156mg

Traeger Chicken Breast

Servings: 6
Cooking Time: 15 Minutes
Ingredients:
- 3 chicken breasts
- 1 tbsp avocado oil
- 1/4 tbsp garlic powder
- 1/4 tbsp onion powder
- 3/4 tbsp salt
- 1/4 tbsp pepper

Directions:
1. Preheat your Traeger to 3750F
2. Cut the chicken breast into halves lengthwise then coat with avocado oil.
3. Season with garlic powder, onion powder, salt, and pepper.
4. Place the chicken on the grill and cook for 7 minutes on each side or until the internal temperature reaches 1650F

Nutrition Info:
- InfoCalories 120, Total fat 4g, Saturated fat 1g, Total carbs 0g, Net carbs 0g Protein 19g, Sugars 0g, Fiber 0g, Sodium 309mg

Smoked Chicken With Apricot Bbq Glaze

Servings: 6
Cooking Time: 30 Minutes
Ingredients:
- 2 whole chicken, halved
- 4 tablespoon Traeger Chicken Rub
- 1 cup Trager Apricot BBQ Sauce

Directions:
1. Massage the chicken with the chicken rub. Allow to marinate for 2 hours in the fridge.
2. When ready to cook, fire the Traeger Grill to 3500F. Use preferred wood pellets. Close the grill lid and preheat for 15 minutes.
3. Place the chicken on the grill grate and grill for 15 minutes on each side. Baste the chicken with Apricot BBQ glaze.
4. Once cooked, allow to rest for 10 minutes before slicing.

Nutrition Info:
- InfoCalories per serving: 304; Protein: 49g; Carbs: 10.2g; Fat: 6.5g Sugar: 8.7g

Barbecue Chicken Wings

Servings: 4
Cooking Time: 15 Minutes
Ingredients:
- Fresh chicken wings
- Salt to taste
- Pepper to taste
- Garlic powder
- Onion powder
- Cayenne
- Paprika
- Seasoning salt
- Bbq sauce to taste

Directions:
1. Preheat the wood pellet grill to low.
2. In a mixing bowl, mix all the seasoning ingredients then toss the chicken wings until well coated.
3. Place the wings on the grill and cook for 20 minutes or until the wings are fully cooked.
4. Let rest to cool for 5 minutes then toss with bbq sauce.
5. Serve with orzo and salad. Enjoy.

Nutrition Info:
- InfoCalories 311, Total fat 22g, Saturated fat 4g, Total carbs 22g, Net carbs 19g, Protein 22g, Sugar 12g, Fiber 3g, Sodium: 1400mg

Fish And Seafood Recipes

Dijon-smoked Halibut

Servings: 6
Cooking Time: 2 Hours
Ingredients:
- 4 (6-ounce) halibut steaks
- ¼ cup extra-virgin olive oil
- 2 teaspoons kosher salt
- 1 teaspoon freshly ground black pepper
- ½ cup mayonnaise
- ½ cup sweet pickle relish
- ¼ cup finely chopped sweet onion
- ¼ cup chopped roasted red pepper
- ¼ cup finely chopped tomato
- ¼ cup finely chopped cucumber
- 2 tablespoons Dijon mustard
- 1 teaspoon minced garlic

Directions:
1. Rub the halibut steaks with the olive oil and season on both sides with the salt and pepper. Transfer to a plate, cover with plastic wrap, and refrigerate for 4 hours.
2. Supply your smoker with wood pellets and follow the manufacturer's specific start-up procedure. Preheat, with the lid closed, to 200°F.
3. Remove the halibut from the refrigerator and rub with the mayonnaise.
4. Put the fish directly on the grill grate, close the lid, and smoke for 2 hours, or until opaque and an instant-read thermometer inserted in the fish reads 140°F.
5. While the fish is smoking, combine the pickle relish, onion, roasted red pepper, tomato, cucumber, Dijon mustard, and garlic in a medium bowl. Refrigerate the mustard relish until ready to serve.
6. Serve the halibut steaks hot with the mustard relish.

Cajun-blackened Shrimp

Servings: 4
Cooking Time: 20 Minutes
Ingredients:
- 1 pound peeled and deveined shrimp, with tails on
- 1 batch Cajun Rub
- 8 tablespoons (1 stick) butter
- ¼ cup Worcestershire sauce

Directions:
1. Supply your smoker with wood pellets and follow the manufacturer's specific start-up procedure. Preheat the grill, with the lid closed, to 450°F and place a cast-iron skillet on the grill grate. Wait about 10 minutes after your grill has reached temperature, allowing the skillet to get hot.
2. Meanwhile, season the shrimp all over with the rub.

3. When the skillet is hot, place the butter in it to melt. Once the butter melts, stir in the Worcestershire sauce.
4. Add the shrimp and gently stir to coat. Smoke-braise the shrimp for about 10 minutes per side, until opaque and cooked through. Remove the shrimp from the grill and serve immediately.

Spicy Shrimps Skewers

Servings: 4
Cooking Time: 6 Minutes
Ingredients:
- 2 pounds shrimp, peeled, and deveined
- For the Marinade:
- 6 ounces Thai chilies
- 6 cloves of garlic, peeled
- 1 ½ teaspoon sugar
- 2 tablespoons Napa Valley rub
- 1 ½ tablespoon white vinegar
- 3 tablespoons olive oil

Directions:
1. Prepare the marinade and for this, place all of its ingredients in a food processor and then pulse for 1 minute until smooth.
2. Take a large bowl, place shrimps on it, add prepared marinade, toss until well coated, and let marinate for a minimum of 30 minutes in the refrigerator.
3. When ready to cook, switch on the Traeger grill, fill the grill hopper with apple-flavored wood pellets, power the grill on by using the control panel, select 'smoke' on the temperature dial, or set the temperature to 450 degrees F and let it preheat for a minimum of 5 minutes.
4. Meanwhile, remove shrimps from the marinade and then thread onto skewers.
5. When the grill has preheated, open the lid, place shrimps' skewers on the grill grate, shut the grill and smoke for 3 minutes per side until firm.
6. When done, transfer shrimps' skewers to a dish and then serve.

Nutrition Info:
- InfoCalories: 187.2 Cal ;Fat: 2.7 g ;Carbs: 2.7 g ;Protein: 23.2 g ;Fiber: 0.2 g

Traeger Grilled Lingcod

Servings: 6
Cooking Time: 15 Minutes
Ingredients:
- 2 lb lingcod fillets
- 1/2 tbsp salt
- 1/2 tbsp white pepper
- 1/4 tbsp cayenne pepper
- Lemon wedges

Directions:
1. Preheat your Traeger to 3750F.
2. Place the lingcod on a parchment paper or on a grill mat.
3. Season the fish with salt, pepper, and top with lemon wedges.
4. Cook the fish for 15 minutes or until the internal temperature reaches 1450F.

Nutrition Info:
- InfoCalories 245, Total fat 2g, Saturated fat 0g, Total carbs 2g, Net carbs 0g Protein 52g, Sugars 1g, Fiber 1g, Sodium 442mg

Oysters In The Shell

Servings: 4
Cooking Time: 20 Minutes
Ingredients:
- 8 medium oysters, unopened, in the shell, rinsed and scrubbed
- 1 batch Lemon Butter Mop for Seafood

Directions:
1. Supply your smoker with wood pellets and follow the manufacturer's specific start-up procedure. Preheat the grill, with the lid closed, to 375°F.
2. Place the unopened oysters directly on the grill grate and grill for about 20 minutes, or until the oysters are done and their shells open.
3. Discard any oysters that do not open. Shuck the remaining oysters, transfer them to a bowl, and add the mop. Serve immediately.

Grilled Shrimp Scampi

Servings: 4
Cooking Time: 10 Minutes
Ingredients:
- 1 lb raw shrimp, tail on
- 1/2 cup salted butter, melted
- 1/4 cup white wine, dry
- 1/2 tbsp fresh garlic, chopped
- 1 tbsp lemon juice
- 1/2 tbsp garlic powder
- 1/2 tbsp salt

Directions:
1. Preheat your wood pellet grill to 400°F with a cast iron inside.
2. In a mixing bowl, mix butter, wine, garlic, and juice then pour in the cast iron. Let the mixture mix for 4 minutes.

3. Sprinkle garlic and salt on the shrimp then place it on the cast iron. Grill for 10 minutes with the lid closed.
4. Remove the shrimp from the grill and serve when hot. Enjoy.

Nutrition Info:
- InfoCalories 298, Total fat 24g, Saturated fat 15g, Total Carbs 2g, Net Carbs 2g, Protein 16g, Sugar 0g, Fiber 0g, Sodium: 1091mg, Potassium 389mg

Jerk Shrimp

Servings: 12
Cooking Time: 6 Minutes

Ingredients:
- 2 pounds shrimp, peeled, deveined
- 3 tablespoons olive oil
- For the Spice Mix:
- 1 teaspoon garlic powder
- 1 teaspoon of sea salt
- 1/4 teaspoon ground cayenne
- 1 tablespoon brown sugar
- 1/8 teaspoon smoked paprika
- 1 tablespoon smoked paprika
- 1/4 teaspoon ground thyme
- 1 lime, zested

Directions:
1. Switch on the Traeger grill, fill the grill hopper with flavored wood pellets, power the grill on by using the control panel, select 'smoke' on the temperature dial, or set the temperature to 450 degrees F and let it preheat for a minimum of 5 minutes.
2. Meanwhile, prepare the spice mix and for this, take a small bowl, place all of its ingredients in it and stir until mixed.
3. Take a large bowl, place shrimps in it, sprinkle with prepared spice mix, drizzle with oil and toss until well coated.
4. When the grill has preheated, open the lid, place shrimps on the grill grate, shut the grill and smoke for 3 minutes per side until firm and thoroughly cooked.
5. When done, transfer shrimps to a dish and then serve.

Nutrition Info:
- InfoCalories: 131 Cal ;Fat: 4.3 g ;Carbs: 0 g ;Protein: 22 g ;Fiber: 0 g

Wood Pellet Rockfish

Servings: 6
Cooking Time: 20 Minutes

Ingredients:
- 6 rockfish fillets
- 1 lemon, sliced
- 3/4 tbsp Himalayan salt
- 2 tbsp fresh dill, chopped
- 1/2 tbsp garlic powder
- 1/2 tbsp onion powder
- 6 tbsp butter

Directions:
1. Preheat your wood pellet grill to 375°F.
2. Place the rockfish in a baking dish and season with salt, dill, garlic, and onion.
3. Place butter on top of the fish then close the lid. Cook for 20 minutes or until the fish is no longer translucent.
4. Remove from grill and let sit for 5 minutes before serving. enjoy.

Nutrition Info:
- InfoCalories 270, Total fat 17g, Saturated fat 9g, Total Carbs 2g, Net Carbs 0g, Protein 28g, Sugar 0g, Fiber 0g, Sodium: 381mg

Super-tasty Trout

Servings: 8
Cooking Time: 5 Hours

Ingredients:
- 1 (7-lb.) whole lake trout, butterflied
- ½ C. kosher salt
- ½ C. fresh rosemary, chopped
- 2 tsp. lemon zest, grated finely

Directions:
1. Rub the trout with salt generously and then, sprinkle with rosemary and lemon zest.
2. Arrange the trout in a large baking dish and refrigerate for about 7-8 hours.
3. Remove the trout from baking dish and rinse under cold running water to remove the salt.
4. With paper towels, pat dry the trout completely.
5. Arrange a wire rack in a sheet pan.
6. Place the trout onto the wire rack, skin side down and refrigerate for about 24 hours.
7. Set the temperature of Traeger Grill to 180 degrees F and preheat with closed lid for 15 minutes, using charcoal.
8. Place the trout onto the grill and cook for about 2-4 hours or until desired doneness.
9. Remove the trout from grill and place onto a cutting board for about 5 minutes before serving.

Nutrition Info:
- Calories per serving: 633; Carbohydrates: 2.4g; Protein: 85.2g; Fat: 31.8g; Sugar: 0g; Sodium: 5000mg; Fiber: 1.6g

Grilled Blackened Salmon

Servings: 4
Cooking Time: 30 Minutes
Ingredients:
- 4 salmon fillet
- Blackened dry rub
- Italian seasoning powder

Directions:
1. Season salmon fillets with dry rub and seasoning powder.
2. Grill in the Traeger wood pellet grill at 325 degrees F for 10 to 15 minutes per side.
3. Tips: You can also drizzle salmon with lemon juice

Cod With Lemon Herb Butter

Servings: 4
Cooking Time: 15 Minutes
Ingredients:
- 4 tablespoons butter
- 1 clove garlic, minced
- 1 tablespoon tarragon, chopped
- 1 tablespoon lemon juice
- 1 teaspoon lemon zest
- Salt and pepper to taste
- 1 lb. cod fillet

Directions:
1. Preheat the Traeger wood pellet grill to high for 15 minutes while the lid is closed.
2. In a bowl, mix the butter, garlic, tarragon, lemon juice and lemon zest, salt and pepper.
3. Place the fish in a baking pan.
4. Spread the butter mixture on top.
5. Bake the fish for 15 minutes.
6. Tips: You can also use other white fish fillet for this recipe.

Citrus Salmon

Servings: 6
Cooking Time: 30 Minutes
Ingredients:
- 2 (1-lb.) salmon fillets
- Salt and freshly ground black pepper, to taste
- 1 tbsp. seafood seasoning
- 2 lemons, sliced
- 2 limes, sliced

Directions:
1. Set the temperature of Traeger Grill to 225 degrees F and preheat with closed lid for 15 minutes.
2. Season the salmon fillets with salt, black pepper and seafood seasoning evenly.
3. Place the salmon fillets onto the grill and top each with lemon and lime slices evenly.
4. Cook for about 30 minutes.
5. Remove the salmon fillets from grill and serve hot.

Nutrition Info:
- Calories per serving: 327; Carbohydrates: 1g; Protein: 36.1g; Fat: 19.8g; Sugar: 0.2g; Sodium: 237mg; Fiber: 0.3g

Hot-smoked Salmon

Servings: 4
Cooking Time: 4 To 6 Hours
Ingredients:
- 1 (2-pound) half salmon fillet
- 1 batch Dill Seafood Rub

Directions:
1. Supply your smoker with wood pellets and follow the manufacturer's specific start-up procedure. Preheat the grill, with the lid closed, to 180°F.
2. Season the salmon all over with the rub. Using your hands, work the rub into the flesh.
3. Place the salmon directly on the grill grate, skin-side down, and smoke until its internal temperature reaches 145°F. Remove the salmon from the grill and serve immediately.

Octopus With Lemon And Oregano

Servings: 4
Cooking Time: 1 Hour And 30 Minutes
Ingredients:
- 3 lemons
- 3 pounds cleaned octopus, thawed if frozen
- 6 cloves garlic, peeled
- 4 sprigs fresh oregano
- 2 bay leaves
- Salt and pepper
- 3 tablespoons good-quality olive oil
- Minced fresh oregano for garnish

Directions:
1. Halve one of the lemons. Put the octopus, garlic, oregano sprigs, bay leaves, a large pinch of salt, and lemon halves in a large pot with enough water to cover by a couple of inches. Bring to a boil, adjust the heat so the liquid bubbles gently but steadily, and cook, occasionally turning with tongs, until the octopus is tender 30 to 90 minutes. (Check with the tip of a sharp knife; it should go in smoothly.) Drain; discard the seasonings. (You can cover and refrigerate the octopus for up to 24 hours.)

2. Start the coals or heat a gas grill for direct hot cooking. Make sure the grates are clean.
3. Squeeze the juice 1 of the remaining lemons and whisk it with the oil and salt and pepper to taste. Cut the octopus into large serving pieces and toss with the oil mixture.
4. Put the octopus on the grill directly over the fire. Cover the grill and cook until heated through and charred, 4 to 5 minutes per side. Cut the remaining lemon in wedges. Transfer the octopus to a platter, sprinkle with minced oregano, and serve with the lemon wedges.

Nutrition Info:
- Calories: 139 Fats: 1.8 g Cholesterol: 0 mg Carbohydrates: 3.7 g Fiber: 0 g Sugars: 0 g Proteins: 25.4 g

Citrus-smoked Trout

Servings: 6
Cooking Time: 1 To 2 Hours
Ingredients:
- 6 to 8 skin-on rainbow trout, cleaned and scaled
- 1 gallon orange juice
- ½ cup packed light brown sugar
- ¼ cup salt
- 1 tablespoon freshly ground black pepper
- Nonstick spray, oil, or butter, for greasing
- 1 tablespoon chopped fresh parsley
- 1 lemon, sliced

Directions:
1. Fillet the fish and pat dry with paper towels.
2. Pour the orange juice into a large container with a lid and stir in the brown sugar, salt, and pepper.
3. Place the trout in the brine, cover, and refrigerate for 1 hour.
4. Cover the grill grate with heavy-duty aluminum foil. Poke holes in the foil and spray with cooking spray (see Tip).
5. Supply your smoker with wood pellets and follow the manufacturer's specific start-up procedure. Preheat, with the lid closed, to 225°F.
6. Remove the trout from the brine and pat dry. Arrange the fish on the foil-covered grill grate, close the lid, and smoke for 1 hour 30 minutes to 2 hours, or until flaky.
7. Remove the fish from the heat. Serve garnished with the fresh parsley and lemon slices.

Cajun Seasoned Shrimp

Servings: 4
Cooking Time: 16-20 Minutes
Ingredients:
- 20 pieces of jumbo Shrimp
- 1/2 teaspoon of Cajun seasoning
- 1 tablespoon of Canola oil
- 1 teaspoon of magic shrimp seasoning

Directions:
1. Take a large bowl and add canola oil, shrimp, and seasonings.
2. Mix well for fine coating.
3. Now put the shrimp on skewers.
4. Put the grill grate inside the grill and set a timer to 8 minutes at high for preheating.
5. Once the grill is preheated, open the unit and place the shrimp skewers inside.
6. Cook the shrimp for 2 minutes.
7. Open the unit to flip the shrimp and cook for another 2 minutes at medium.
8. Own done, serve.

Nutrition Info:
- Calories: 382 Total Fat: 7.4g Saturated Fat: 0g Cholesterol: 350mg Sodium: 2208mg Total Carbohydrate: 23.9g Dietary Fiber 2.6g Total Sugars: 2.6g Protein: 50.2g

Halibut In Parchment

Servings: 4
Cooking Time: 15 Minutes
Ingredients:
- 16 asparagus spears, trimmed, sliced into 1/2-inch pieces
- 2 ears of corn kernels
- 4 ounces halibut fillets, pin bones removed
- 2 lemons, cut into 12 slices
- Salt as needed
- Ground black pepper as needed
- 2 tablespoons olive oil
- 2 tablespoons chopped parsley

Directions:
1. Switch on the Traeger grill, fill the grill hopper with flavored wood pellets, power the grill on by using the control panel, select 'smoke' on the temperature dial, or set the temperature to 450 degrees F and let it preheat for a minimum of 5 minutes.
2. Meanwhile, cut out 18-inch long parchment paper, place a fillet in the center of each parchment, season with salt and black pepper, and then drizzle with oil.
3. Cover each fillet with three lemon slices, overlapping slightly, sprinkle one-fourth of asparagus and corn on each fillet, season with some salt and black pepper, and seal the fillets and vegetables tightly to prevent steam from escaping the packet.
4. When the grill has preheated, open the lid, place fillet packets on the grill grate, shut the grill and smoke for 15

minutes until packets have turned slightly brown and puffed up.
5. When done, transfer packets to a dish, let them stand for 5 minutes, then cut 'X' in the center of each packet, carefully uncover the fillets an vegetables, sprinkle with parsley, and then serve.
Nutrition Info:
- InfoCalories: 186.6 Cal ;Fat: 2.8 g ;Carbs: 14.2 g ;Protein: 25.7 g ;Fiber: 4.1 g

Traeger Rockfish

Servings: 6
Cooking Time: 20 Minutes
Ingredients:
- 6 rockfish fillets
- 1 lemon, sliced
- 3/4 tbsp salt
- 2 tbsp fresh dill, chopped
- 1/2 tbsp garlic powder
- 1/2 tbsp onion powder
- 6 tbsp butter

Directions:
1. Preheat your Traeger to 4000F.
2. Season the fish with salt, dill, garlic and onion powder on both sides then place it in a baking dish.
3. Place a pat of butter and a lemon slice on each fillet. Place the baking dish in the Traeger and close the lid.
4. Cook for 20 minutes or until the fish is no longer translucent and is flaky.
5. Remove from Traeger and let rest for 5 minutes before serving.

Nutrition Info:
- InfoCalories 270, Total fat 17g, Saturated fat 9g, Total carbs 2g, Net carbs 2g Protein 28g, Sugars 0g, Fiber 0g, Sodium 381mg

Bbq Oysters

Servings: 4-6
Cooking Time: 16 Minutes
Ingredients:
- Shucked oysters - 12
- Unsalted butter - 1 lb.
- Chopped green onions - 1 bunch
- Honey Hog BBQ Rub or Meat Church "The Gospel" - 1 tbsp
- Minced green onions - ½ bunch
- Seasoned breadcrumbs - ½ cup
- Cloves of minced garlic - 2
- Shredded pepper jack cheese - 8 oz
- Traeger Heat and Sweet BBQ sauce

Directions:
1. Preheat the pellet grill for about 10-15 minutes with the lid closed.
2. To make the compound butter, wait for the butter to soften. Then combine the butter, onions, BBQ rub, and garlic thoroughly.
3. Lay the butter evenly on plastic wrap or parchment paper. Roll it up in a log shape and tie the ends with butcher's twine. Place these in the freezer to solidify for an hour. This butter can be used on any kind of grilled meat to enhance its flavor. Any other high-quality butter can also replace this compound butter.
4. Shuck the oysters, keeping the juice in the shell.
5. Sprinkle all the oysters with breadcrumbs and place them directly on the grill. Allow them to cook for 5 minutes. You will know they are cooked when the oysters begin to curl slightly at the edges.
6. Once they are cooked, put a spoonful of the compound butter on the oysters. Once the butter melts, you can add a little bit of pepper jack cheese to add more flavor to them.
7. The oysters must not be on the grill for longer than 6 minutes, or you risk overcooking them. Put a generous squirt of the BBQ sauce on all the oysters. Also, add a few chopped onions.
8. Allow them to cool for a few minutes and enjoy the taste of the sea!

Nutrition Info:
- Info Carbohydrates: 2.5 g Protein: 4.7 g Fat: 1.1 g Sodium: 53 mg Cholesterol: 25 mg

Grilled Tilapia

Servings: 6
Cooking Time: 2o Minutes
Ingredients:
- 2 tsp dried parsley
- ½ tsp garlic powder
- 1 tsp cayenne pepper
- ½ tsp ground black pepper
- ½ tsp thyme
- ½ tsp dried basil
- ½ tsp oregano
- 3 tbsp olive oil
- ½ tsp lemon pepper
- 1 tsp kosher salt
- 1 lemon (juiced)
- 6 tilapia fillets
- 1 ½ tsp creole seafood seasoning

Directions:

1. In a mixing bowl, combine spices
2. Brush the fillets with oil and lemon juice.
3. Liberally, season all sides of the tilapia fillets with the seasoning mix.
4. Preheat your grill to 325°F
5. Place a non-stick BBQ grilling try on the grill and arrange the tilapia fillets onto it.
6. Grill for 15 to 20 minutes
7. Remove fillets and cool down

Nutrition Info:
- Calories: 176 Cal Fat: 9.6 g Carbohydrates: 1.5 g Protein: 22.3 g Fiber: 0.5 g

Grilled Lingcod

Servings: 6
Cooking Time: 15 Minutes

Ingredients:
- 2 lb lingcod fillets
- 1/2 tbsp salt
- 1/2 tbsp white pepper
- 1/4 tbsp cayenne
- Lemon wedges

Directions:
1. Preheat the wood pellet grill to 375°F.
2. Place the lingcod on a parchment paper and season it with salt, white pepper, cayenne pepper then top with the lemon.
3. Place the fish on the grill and cook for 15 minutes or until the internal temperature reaches 145°F.
4. Serve and enjoy.

Nutrition Info:
- InfoCalories 245, Total fat 2g, Saturated fat 0g, Total Carbs 2g, Net Carbs 1g, Protein 52g, Sugar 1g, Fiber 1g, Sodium: 442mg, Potassium 649mg

Grilled Rainbow Trout

Servings: 6
Cooking Time: 2 Hours

Ingredients:
- 6 rainbow trout, cleaned, butterfly
- For the Brine:
- 1/4 cup salt
- 1 tablespoon ground black pepper
- 1/2 cup brown sugar
- 2 tablespoons soy sauce
- 16 cups water

Directions:

1. Prepare the brine and for this, take a large container, add all of its ingredients in it, stir until sugar has dissolved, then add trout and let soak for 1 hour in the refrigerator.
2. When ready to cook, switch on the Traeger grill, fill the grill hopper with oak flavored wood pellets, power the grill on by using the control panel, select 'smoke' on the temperature dial, or set the temperature to 225 degrees F and let it preheat for a minimum of 15 minutes.
3. Meanwhile, remove trout from the brine and pat dry with paper towels.
4. When the grill has preheated, open the lid, place trout on the grill grate, shut the grill and smoke for 2 hours until thoroughly cooked and tender.
5. When done, transfer trout to a dish and then serve.

Nutrition Info:
- InfoCalories: 250 Cal ;Fat: 12 g ;Carbs: 1.4 g ;Protein: 33 g ;Fiber: 0.3 g

Smoked Shrimp

Servings: 4
Cooking Time: 10 Minutes

Ingredients:
- 4 tablespoons olive oil
- 1 tablespoon Cajun seasoning
- 2 cloves garlic, minced
- 1 tablespoon lemon juice
- Salt to taste
- 2 lb. shrimp, peeled and deveined

Directions:
1. Combine all the ingredients in a sealable plastic bag.
2. Toss to coat evenly.
3. Marinate in the refrigerator for 4 hours.
4. Set the Traeger wood pellet grill to high.
5. Preheat it for 15 minutes while the lid is closed.
6. Thread shrimp onto skewers.
7. Grill for 4 minutes per side.
8. Tips: Soak skewers first in water if you are using wooden skewers.

Barbeque Shrimp

Servings: 6
Cooking Time: 8 Minutes
Ingredients:
- 2-pound raw shrimp (peeled and deveined)
- ¼ cup extra virgin olive oil
- ½ tsp paprika
- ½ tsp red pepper flakes
- 2 garlic cloves (minced)
- 1 tsp cumin
- 1 lemon (juiced)
- 1 tsp kosher salt
- 1 tbsp chili paste
- Bamboo or wooden skewers (soaked for 30 minutes, at least)

Directions:
1. Combine the pepper flakes, cumin, lemon, salt, chili, paprika, garlic and olive oil. Add the shrimp and toss to combine.
2. Transfer the shrimp and marinade into a zip-lock bag and refrigerate for 4 hours.
3. Let shrimp rest in room temperature after pulling it out from marinade
4. Start your grill on smoke, leaving the lid opened for 5 minutes, or until fire starts. Use hickory wood pellet.
5. Keep lid unopened and preheat the grill to "high" for 15 minutes.
6. Thread shrimps onto skewers and arrange the skewers on the grill grate.
7. Smoke shrimps for 8 minutes, 4 minutes per side.
8. Serve and enjoy.

Nutrition Info:
- Calories: 267 Cal Fat: 11.6 g Carbohydrates: 4.9 g Protein: 34.9 g Fiber:0.4 g

Blackened Salmon

Servings: 4
Cooking Time: 30 Minutes
Ingredients:
- 2 lb. salmon, fillet, scaled and deboned
- 2 tablespoons olive oil
- 4 tablespoons sweet dry rub
- 1 tablespoon cayenne pepper
- 2 cloves garlic, minced

Directions:
1. Turn on your wood pellet grill.
2. Set it to 350 degrees F.
3. Brush the salmon with the olive oil.
4. Sprinkle it with the dry rub, cayenne pepper, and garlic.
5. Grill for 5 minutes per side.

Nutrition Info:
- InfoCalories: 460Fat: 23 gCholesterol: 140 mgCarbohydrates: 7 g Fiber: 5 g Sugars: 2 g Protein: 50 g

Grilled Salmon

Servings: 4
Cooking Time: 25 Minutes
Ingredients:
- 1 (2-pound) half salmon fillet
- 3 tablespoons mayonnaise
- 1 batch Dill Seafood Rub

Directions:
1. Supply your smoker with wood pellets and follow the manufacturer's specific start-up procedure. Preheat the grill, with the lid closed, to 325°F.
2. Using your hands, rub the salmon fillet all over with the mayonnaise and sprinkle it with the rub.
3. Place the salmon directly on the grill grate, skin-side down, and grill until its internal temperature reaches 145°F. Remove the salmon from the grill and serve immediately.

Cajun Catfish

Servings: 6
Cooking Time: 15 Minutes
Ingredients:
- 2½ pounds catfish fillets
- 2 tablespoons olive oil
- 1 batch Cajun Rub

Directions:
1. Supply your smoker with wood pellets and follow the manufacturer's specific start-up procedure. Preheat the grill, with the lid closed, to 300°F.
2. Coat the catfish fillets all over with olive oil and season with the rub. Using your hands, work the rub into the flesh.
3. Place the fillets directly on the grill grate and smoke until their internal temperature reaches 145°F. Remove the catfish from the grill and serve immediately

Wood Pellet Teriyaki Smoked Shrimp

Servings: 6
Cooking Time: 10 Minutes
Ingredients:
- 1 lb tail-on shrimp, uncooked
- 1/2 tbsp onion powder
- 1/2 tbsp salt
- 1/2 tbsp Garlic powder
- 4 tbsp Teriyaki sauce
- 4 tbsp sriracha mayo
- 2 tbsp green onion, minced

Directions:
1. Peel the shrimps leaving the tails then wash them removing any vein left over. Drain and pat with a paper towel to drain.
2. Preheat the wood pellet to 450°F
3. Season the shrimp with onion, salt, and garlic then place it on the grill to cook for 5 minutes on each side.
4. Remove the shrimp from the grill and toss it with teriyaki sauce. Serve garnished with mayo and onions. Enjoy.

Nutrition Info:
- InfoCalories 87, Total fat 0g, Saturated fat 0g, Total Carbs 2g, Net Carbs 2g, Protein 16g, Sugar 1g, Fiber 0g, Sodium: 1241mg

Barbecued Shrimp

Servings: 4
Cooking Time: 10 Minutes
Ingredients:
- 1 pound peeled and deveined shrimp, with tails on
- 2 tablespoons olive oil
- 1 batch Dill Seafood Rub

Directions:
1. Soak wooden skewers in water for 30 minutes.
2. Supply your smoker with wood pellets and follow the manufacturer's specific start-up procedure. Preheat the grill, with the lid closed, to 375°F.
3. Thread 4 or 5 shrimp per skewer.
4. Coat the shrimp all over with olive oil and season each side of the skewers with the rub.
5. Place the skewers directly on the grill grate and grill the shrimp for 5 minutes per side. Remove the skewers from the grill and serve immediately.

Wood Pellet Smoked Buffalo Shrimp

Servings: 6
Cooking Time: 5 Minutes
Ingredients:
- 1 lb raw shrimps peeled and deveined
- 1/2 tbsp salt
- 1/4 tbsp garlic salt
- 1/4 tbsp garlic powder
- 1/4 tbsp onion powder
- 1/2 cup buffalo sauce

Directions:
1. Preheat the wood pellet grill to 450°F.
2. Coat the shrimp with both salts, garlic and onion powders.
3. Place the shrimp in a grill and cook for 3 minutes on each side.
4. Remove from the grill and toss in buffalo sauce. Serve with cheese, celery and napkins. Enjoy.

Nutrition Info:
- InfoCalories 57, Total fat 1g, Saturated fat 0g, Total Carbs 1g, Net Carbs 1g, Protein 10g, Sugar 0g, Fiber 0g, Sodium: 1106mg, Potassium 469mg.

Halibut With Garlic Pesto

Servings: 4
Cooking Time: 10 Minutes
Ingredients:
- 4 halibut fillets
- 1 cup olive oil
- Salt and pepper to taste
- 1/4 cup garlic, chopped
- 1/4 cup pine nuts

Directions:
1. Set the Traeger wood pellet grill to smoke.
2. Establish fire for 5 minutes.
3. Set temperature to high.
4. Place a cast iron on a grill.
5. Season fish with salt and pepper.
6. Add fish to the pan.
7. Drizzle with a little oil.
8. Sear for 4 minutes per side.
9. Prepare the garlic pesto by pulsing the remaining ingredients in the food processor until smooth.
10. Serve fish with garlic pesto.
11. Tips: You can also use other white fish fillets for this recipe.

Peppercorn Tuna Steaks

Servings: 3
Cooking Time: 10 Minutes
Ingredients:
- ¼ cup of salt
- 2 pounds yellowfin tuna
- ¼ cup Dijon mustard
- Freshly ground black pepper
- 2 tablespoons peppercorn

Directions:
1. Take a large-sized container and dissolve salt in warm water (enough water to cover fish)
2. Transfer tuna to the brine and cover, refrigerate for 8 hours
3. Preheat your smoker to 250 degrees Fahrenheit with your preferred wood
4. Remove tuna from bring and pat it dry
5. Transfer to grill pan and spread Dijon mustard all over
6. Season with pepper and sprinkle peppercorn on top
7. Transfer tuna to smoker and smoker for 1 hour
8. Enjoy!

Nutrition Info:
- Calories: 707 Fats: 57g Carbs: 10g Fiber: 2g

Cider Salmon

Servings: 4
Cooking Time: 1 Hour
Ingredients:
- 1 ½ pound salmon fillet, skin-on, center-cut, pin bone removed
- For the Brine:
- 4 juniper berries, crushed
- 1 bay leaf, crumbled
- 1 piece star anise, broken
- 1 1/2 cups apple cider
- For the Cure:
- 1/2 cup salt
- 1 teaspoon ground black pepper
- 1/4 cup brown sugar
- 2 teaspoons barbecue rub

Directions:
1. Prepare the brine and for this, take a large container, add all of its ingredients in it, stir until mixed, then add salmon and let soak for a minimum of 8 hours in the refrigerator.
2. Meanwhile, prepare the cure and for this, take a small bowl, place all of its ingredients in it and stir until combined.
3. After 8 hours, remove salmon from the brine, then take a baking dish, place half of the cure in it, top with salmon skin-side down, sprinkle remaining cure on top, cover with plastic wrap and let it rest for 1 hour in the refrigerator.
4. When ready to cook, switch on the Traeger grill, fill the grill hopper with oak flavored wood pellets, power the grill on by using the control panel, select 'smoke' on the temperature dial, or set the temperature to 200 degrees F and let it preheat for a minimum of 5 minutes.
5. Meanwhile, remove salmon from the cure, pat dry with paper towels, and then sprinkle with black pepper.
6. When the grill has preheated, open the lid, place salmon on the grill grate, shut the grill, and smoke for 1 hour until the internal temperature reaches 150 degrees F.
7. When done, transfer salmon to a cutting board, let it rest for 5 minutes, then remove the skin and serve.

Nutrition Info:
- InfoCalories: 233 Cal ;Fat: 14 g ;Carbs: 0 g ;Protein: 25 g ;Fiber: 0 g

Grilled Herbed Tuna

Servings: 6
Cooking Time: 10 Minutes
Ingredients:
- 6 tuna steaks
- 1 tablespoon lemon zest
- 1 tablespoon fresh thyme, chopped
- 1 tablespoon fresh parsley, chopped
- Garlic salt to taste

Directions:
1. Sprinkle the tuna steaks with lemon zest, herbs and garlic salt.
2. Cover with foil.
3. Refrigerate for 4 hours.
4. Grill for 3 minutes per side.
5. Tips: Take the fish out of the refrigerator 30 minutes before cooking.

Sriracha Salmon

Servings: 4
Cooking Time: 25 Minutes
Ingredients:
- 3-pound salmon, skin on
- For the Marinade:
- 1 teaspoon lime zest
- 1 tablespoon minced garlic
- 1 tablespoon grated ginger
- Sea salt as needed
- Ground black pepper as needed
- 1/4 cup maple syrup
- 2 tablespoons soy sauce

- 2 tablespoons Sriracha sauce
- 1 tablespoon toasted sesame oil
- 1 tablespoon rice vinegar
- 1 teaspoon toasted sesame seeds

Directions:

1. Prepare the marinade and for this, take a small bowl, place all of its ingredients in it, stir until well combined, and then pour the mixture into a large plastic bag.
2. Add salmon in the bag, seal it, turn it upside down to coat salmon with the marinade and let it marinate for a minimum of 2 hours in the refrigerator.
3. When ready to cook, switch on the Traeger grill, fill the grill hopper with flavored wood pellets, power the grill on by using the control panel, select 'smoke' on the temperature dial, or set the temperature to 450 degrees F and let it preheat for a minimum of 5 minutes.
4. Meanwhile, take a large baking sheet, line it with parchment paper, place salmon on it skin-side down and then brush with the marinade.
5. When the grill has preheated, open the lid, place baking sheet containing salmon on the grill grate, shut the grill and smoke for 25 minutes until thoroughly cooked.
6. When done, transfer salmon to a dish and then serve.

Nutrition Info:

- InfoCalories: 360 Cal ;Fat: 21 g ;Carbs: 28 g ;Protein: 16 g ;Fiber: 1.5 g

Wood-fired Halibut

Servings: 4
Cooking Time: 20 Minutes

Ingredients:

- 1 pound halibut fillet
- 1 batch Dill Seafood Rub

Directions:

1. Supply your smoker with wood pellets and follow the manufacturer's specific start-up procedure. Preheat the grill, with the lid closed, to 325°F.
2. Sprinkle the halibut fillet on all sides with the rub. Using your hands, work the rub into the meat.
3. Place the halibut directly on the grill grate and grill until its internal temperature reaches 145°F. Remove the halibut from the grill and serve immediately.

Traeger Lobster Tail

Servings: 2
Cooking Time: 15 Minutes

Ingredients:

- 10 oz lobster tail
- 1/4 tbsp old bay seasoning
- 1/4 tbsp Himalayan salt
- 2 tbsp butter, melted
- 1 tbsp fresh parsley, chopped

Directions:

1. Preheat your Traeger to 4500F.
2. Slice the tail down the middle then season it with bay seasoning and salt.
3. Place the tails directly on the grill with the meat side down. Grill for 15 minutes or until the internal temperature reaches 1400F.
4. Remove from the Traeger and drizzle with butter.
5. Serve when hot garnished with parsley.

Nutrition Info:

- InfoCalories 305, Total fat 14g, Saturated fat 8g, Total carbs 5g, Net carbs 5g Protein 38g, Sugars 0g, Fiber 0g, Sodium 684mg

Wine Infused Salmon

Servings: 4
Cooking Time: 5 Hours

Ingredients:

- 2 C. low-sodium soy sauce
- 1 C. dry white wine
- 1 C. water
- ½ tsp. Tabasco sauce
- 1/3 C. sugar
- ¼ C. salt
- ½ tsp. garlic powder
- ½ tsp. onion powder
- Freshly ground black pepper, to taste
- 4 (6-oz.) salmon fillets

Directions:

1. In a large bowl, add all ingredients except salmon and stir until sugar is dissolved.
2. Add salmon fillets and coat with brine well.
3. Refrigerate, covered overnight.
4. Remove salmon from bowl and rinse under cold running water.
5. With paper towels, pat dry the salmon fillets.
6. Arrange a wire rack in a sheet pan.
7. Place the salmon fillets onto wire rack, skin side down and set aside to cool for about 1 hour.
8. Set the temperature of Traeger Grill to 165 degrees F and preheat with closed lid for 15 minutes, using charcoal.
9. Place the salmon fillets onto the grill, skin side down and cook for about 3-5 hours or until desired doneness.
10. Remove the salmon fillets from grill and serve hot.

Nutrition Info:

- Calories per serving: 377; Carbohydrates: 26.3g; Protein: 41.1g; Fat: 10.5g; Sugar: 25.1g; Sodium: 14000mg; Fiber: 0g

Charleston Crab Cakes With Remoulade

Servings: 4
Cooking Time: 45 Minutes
Ingredients:
- 1¼ cups mayonnaise
- ¼ cup yellow mustard
- 2 tablespoons sweet pickle relish, with its juices
- 1 tablespoon smoked paprika
- 2 teaspoons Cajun seasoning
- 2 teaspoons prepared horseradish
- 1 teaspoon hot sauce
- 1 garlic clove, finely minced
- 2 pounds fresh lump crabmeat, picked clean
- 20 butter crackers (such as Ritz brand), crushed
- 2 tablespoons Dijon mustard
- 1 cup mayonnaise
- 2 tablespoons freshly squeezed lemon juice
- 1 tablespoon salted butter, melted
- 1 tablespoon Worcestershire sauce
- 1 tablespoon Old Bay seasoning
- 2 teaspoons chopped fresh parsley
- 1 teaspoon ground mustard
- 2 eggs, beaten
- ¼ cup extra-virgin olive oil, divided

Directions:
1. For the remoulade:
2. In a small bowl, combine the mayonnaise, mustard, pickle relish, paprika, Cajun seasoning, horseradish, hot sauce, and garlic.
3. Refrigerate until ready to serve.
4. For the crab cakes:
5. Supply your smoker with wood pellets and follow the manufacturer's specific start-up procedure. Preheat, with the lid closed, to 375°F.
6. Spread the crabmeat on a foil-lined baking sheet and place over indirect heat on the grill, with the lid closed, for 30 minutes.
7. Remove from the heat and let cool for 15 minutes.
8. While the crab cools, combine the crushed crackers, Dijon mustard, mayonnaise, lemon juice, melted butter, Worcestershire sauce, Old Bay, parsley, ground mustard, and eggs until well incorporated.
9. Fold in the smoked crabmeat, then shape the mixture into 8 (1-inch-thick) crab cakes.
10. In a large skillet or cast-iron pan on the grill, heat 2 tablespoons of olive oil. Add half of the crab cakes, close the lid, and smoke for 4 to 5 minutes on each side, or until crispy and golden brown.
11. Remove the crab cakes from the pan and transfer to a wire rack to drain. Pat them to remove any excess oil.
12. Repeat steps 6 and 7 with the remaining oil and crab cakes.
13. Serve the crab cakes with the remoulade.

Wood Pellet Grilled Scallops

Servings: 4
Cooking Time: 15 Minutes
Ingredients:
- 2 lb sea scallops, dried with a paper towel
- 1/2 tbsp garlic salt
- 2 tbsp kosher salt
- 4 tbsp salted butter
- Squeeze lemon juice

Directions:
1. Preheat the wood pellet grill to 400°F with the cast pan inside.
2. Sprinkle with both salts, pepper on both sides of the scallops.
3. Place the butter on the cast iron then add the scallops. Close the lid and cook for 8 minutes.
4. Flip the scallops and close the lid once more. Cook for 8 more minutes.
5. Remove the scallops from the grill and give a lemon squeeze. Serve immediately and enjoy.

Nutrition Info:
- InfoCalories 177, Total fat 7g, Saturated fat 4g, Total Carbs 6g, Net Carbs 6g, Protein 23g, Sugar 0g, Fiber 0g, Sodium: 1430mg, Potassium 359mg

Teriyaki Smoked Shrimp

Servings: 6
Cooking Time: 20 Minutes
Ingredients:
- Uncooked shrimp - 1 lb.
- Onion powder - ½ tbsp
- Garlic powder - ½ tbsp
- Teriyaki sauce - 4 tbsp
- Mayo - 4 tbsp
- Minced green onion - 2 tbsp
- Salt - ½ tbsp

Directions:

1. Remove the shells from the shrimp and wash thoroughly.
2. Preheat the wood pellet grill to 450 degrees.
3. Season with garlic powder, onion powder, and salt.
4. Cook the shrimp for 5-6 minutes on each side.
5. Once cooked, remove the shrimp from the grill and garnish it with spring onion, teriyaki sauce, and mayo.

Nutrition Info:
- Info   Carbohydrates: 2 g Protein: 16 g Sodium: 1241 mg Cholesterol: 190 mg

Juicy Smoked Salmon

Servings: 5
Cooking Time: 50 Minutes

Ingredients:
- ½ cup of sugar
- 2 tablespoon salt
- 2 tablespoons crushed red pepper flakes
- ½ cup fresh mint leaves, chopped
- ¼ cup brandy
- 1(4 pounds) salmon, bones removed
- 2cups alder wood pellets, soaked in water

Directions:
1. Take a medium-sized bowl and add brown sugar, crushed red pepper flakes, mint leaves, salt, and brandy until a paste forms
2. Rub the paste all over your salmon and wrap the salmon with a plastic wrap
3. Allow them to chill overnight
4. Preheat your smoker to 220 degrees Fahrenheit and add wood Pellets
5. Transfer the salmon to the smoker rack and cook smoke for 45 minutes
6. Once the salmon has turned red-brown and the flesh flakes off easily, take it out and serve!

Nutrition Info:
- Calories: 370 Fats: 28g Carbs: 1g Fiber: 0g

Cajun Smoked Catfish

Servings: 4
Cooking Time: 2 Hours

Ingredients:
- 4 catfish fillets (5 ounces each)
- ½ cup Cajun seasoning
- 1 tsp ground black pepper
- 1 tbsp smoked paprika
- 1 /4 tsp cayenne pepper
- 1 tsp hot sauce
- 1 tsp granulated garlic
- 1 tsp onion powder
- 1 tsp thyme
- 1 tsp salt or more to taste
- 2 tbsp chopped fresh parsley

Directions:
1. Pour water into the bottom of a square or rectangular dish. Add 4 tbsp salt. Arrange the catfish fillets into the dish. Cover the dish and refrigerate for 3 to 4 hours.
2. Combine the paprika, cayenne, hot sauce, onion, salt, thyme, garlic, pepper and Cajun seasoning in a mixing bowl.
3. Remove the fish from the dish and let it sit for a few minutes, or until it is at room temperature. Pat the fish fillets dry with a paper towel.
4. Rub the seasoning mixture over each fillet generously.
5. Start your grill on smoke, leaving the lid opened for 5 minutes, or until fire starts.
6. Keep lid unopened and preheat to 200°F, using mesquite hardwood pellets.
7. Arrange the fish fillets onto the grill grate and close the grill. Cook for about 2 hours, or until the fish is flaky.
8. Remove the fillets from the grill and let the fillets rest for a few minutes to cool.
9. Serve and garnish with chopped fresh parsley.

Nutrition Info:
- Calories: 204 Cal Fat: 11.1 g   Carbohydrates: 2.7 g Protein: 22.9 g Fiber: 0.6 g

Lively Flavored Shrimp

Servings: 6
Cooking Time: 30 Minutes

Ingredients:
- 8 oz. salted butter, melted
- ¼ C. Worcestershire sauce
- ¼ C. fresh parsley, chopped
- 1 lemon, quartered
- 2 lb. jumbo shrimp, peeled and deveined
- 3 tbsp. BBQ rub

Directions:
1. In a metal baking pan, add all ingredients except for shrimp and BBQ rub and mix well.
2. Season the shrimp with BBQ rub evenly.
3. Add the shrimp in the pan with butter mixture and coat well.
4. Set aside for about 20-30 minutes.
5. Set the temperature of Traeger Grill to 250 degrees F and preheat with closed lid for 15 minutes.
6. Place the pan onto the grill and cook for about 25-30 minutes.
7. Remove the pan from grill and serve hot.

Nutrition Info:

- Calories per serving: 462; Carbohydrates: 4.7g; Protein: 34.9g; Fat: 33.3g; Sugar: 2.1g; Sodium: 485mg; Fiber: 0.2g

Buttered Crab Legs

Servings: 4
Cooking Time: 10 Minutes
Ingredients:
- 12 tablespoons butter
- 1 tablespoon parsley, chopped
- 1 tablespoon tarragon, chopped
- 1 tablespoon chives, chopped
- 1 tablespoon lemon juice
- 4 lb. king crab legs, split in the center

Directions:
1. Set the Traeger wood pellet grill to 375 degrees F.
2. Preheat it for 15 minutes while lid is closed.
3. In a pan over medium heat, simmer the butter, herbs and lemon juice for 2 minutes.
4. Place the crab legs on the grill.
5. Pour half of the sauce on top.
6. Grill for 10 minutes.
7. Serve with the reserved butter sauce.
8. Tips: You can also use shrimp for this recipe.

Grilled King Crab Legs

Servings: 4
Cooking Time: 25 Minutes
Ingredients:
- 4 pounds king crab legs (split)
- 4 tbsp lemon juice
- 2 tbsp garlic powder
- 1 cup butter (melted)
- 2 tsp brown sugar
- 2 tsp paprika
- Black pepper (depends to your liking)

Directions:
1. In a mixing bowl, combine the lemon juice, butter, sugar, garlic, paprika and pepper.
2. Arrange the split crab on a baking sheet, split side up. Drizzle ¾ of the butter mixture over the crab legs. Configure your pellet grill for indirect cooking and preheat it to 225°F, using mesquite wood pellets.
3. Arrange the crab legs onto the grill grate, shell side down. Cover the grill and cook 25 minutes.
4. Remove the crab legs from the grill. Serve and top with the remaining butter mixture.

Nutrition Info:
- Calories: 480 Cal Fat: 53.2 g Carbohydrates: 6.1 g Protein: 88.6 g Fiber: 1.2 g

Smoked Scallops

Servings: 6
Cooking Time: 15 Minutes
Ingredients:
- 2 pounds sea scallops
- 4 tbsp salted butter
- 2 tbsp lemon juice
- ½ tsp ground black pepper
- 1 garlic clove (minced)
- 1 kosher tsp salt
- 1 tsp freshly chopped tarragon

Directions:
1. Let the scallops dry using paper towels and drizzle all sides with salt and pepper to season
2. Place you're a cast iron pan in your grill and preheat the grill to 400°F with lid closed for 15 minutes.
3. Combine the butter and garlic in hot cast iron pan. Add the scallops and stir. Close grill lid and cook for 8 minutes. Flip the scallops and cook for an additional 7 minutes.
4. Remove the scallop from heat and let it rest for a few minutes.
5. Stir in the chopped tarragon. Serve and top with lemon juice.

Nutrition Info:
- Calories: 204 Cal Fat: 8.9 g Carbohydrates: 4 g Protein: 25.6 g Fiber: 0.1 g

Chilean Sea Bass

Servings: 6
Cooking Time: 40 Minutes
Ingredients:
- 4 sea bass fillets, skinless, each about 6 ounces
- Chicken rub as needed
- 8 tablespoons butter, unsalted
- 2 tablespoons chopped thyme leaves
- Lemon slices for serving
- For the Marinade:
- 1 lemon, juiced
- 4 teaspoons minced garlic
- 1 tablespoon chopped thyme
- 1 teaspoon blackened rub
- 1 tablespoon chopped oregano
- 1/4 cup oil

Directions:
1. Prepare the marinade and for this, take a small bowl, place all of its ingredients in it, stir until well combined, and then pour the mixture into a large plastic bag.

2. Add fillets in the bag, seal it, turn it upside down to coat fillets with the marinade and let it marinate for a minimum of 30 minutes in the refrigerator.

3. When ready to cook, switch on the Traeger grill, fill the grill hopper with apple-flavored wood pellets, power the grill on by using the control panel, select 'smoke' on the temperature dial, or set the temperature to 325 degrees F and let it preheat for a minimum of 15 minutes.

4. Meanwhile, take a large baking pan and place butter on it.

5. When the grill has preheated, open the lid, place baking pan on the grill grate, and wait until butter melts.

6. Remove fillets from the marinade, pour marinade into the pan with melted butter, then season fillets with chicken rubs until coated on all sides, then place them into the pan, shut the grill and cook for 30 minutes until internal temperature reaches 160 degrees F, frequently basting with the butter sauce.

7. When done, transfer fillets to a dish, sprinkle with thyme and then serve with lemon slices.

Nutrition Info:
- InfoCalories: 232 Cal ;Fat: 12.2 g ;Carbs: 0.8 g ;Protein: 28.2 g ;Fiber: 0.1 g

Halibut

Servings: 4
Cooking Time: 3o Minutes
Ingredients:
- 1-pound fresh halibut filet (cut into 4 equal sizes)
- 1 tbsp fresh lemon juice
- 2 garlic cloves (minced)
- 2 tsp soy sauce
- ½ tsp ground black pepper
- ½ tsp onion powder
- 2 tbsp honey
- ½ tsp oregano
- 1 tsp dried basil
- 2 tbsp butter (melted)
- Maple syrup for serving

Directions:
1. Combine the lemon juice, honey, soy sauce, onion powder, oregano, dried basil, pepper and garlic.
2. Brush the halibut filets generously with the filet the mixture. Wrap the filets with aluminum foil and refrigerate for 4 hours.
3. Remove the filets from the refrigerator and let them sit for about 2 hours, or until they are at room temperature.
4. Activate your wood pellet grill on smoke, leaving the lid opened for 5 minutes or until fire starts.
5. The lid must not be opened for it to be preheated and reach 275°F 15 minutes, using fruit wood pellets.
6. Place the halibut filets directly on the grill grate and smoke for 30 minutes
7. Remove the filets from the grill and let them rest for 10 minutes.
8. Serve and top with maple syrup to taste

Nutrition Info:
- Calories: 180 Cal Fat: 6.3 g Carbohydrates: 10 g Protein: 20.6 g Fiber: 0.3 g

Spicy Shrimp

Servings: 4
Cooking Time: 10 Minutes
Ingredients:
- 3 tablespoons olive oil
- 6 cloves garlic
- 2 tablespoons chicken dry rub
- 6 oz. chili
- 1 1/2 tablespoons white vinegar
- 1 1/2 teaspoons sugar
- 2 lb. shrimp, peeled and deveined

Directions:
1. Add olive oil, garlic, dry rub, chili, vinegar and sugar in a food processor.
2. Blend until smooth.
3. Transfer mixture to a bowl.
4. Stir in shrimp.
5. Cover and refrigerate for 30 minutes.
6. Preheat the Traeger wood pellet grill to hit for 15 minutes while the lid is closed.
7. Thread shrimp onto skewers.
8. Grill for 3 minute per side.
9. Tips: You can also add vegetables to the skewers.

Seared Tuna Steaks

Servings: 2
Cooking Time: 10 Minutes
Ingredients:
- 2 (1½- to 2-inch-thick) tuna steaks
- 2 tablespoons olive oil
- Salt
- Freshly ground black pepper

Directions:
1. Supply your smoker with wood pellets and follow the manufacturer's specific start-up procedure. Preheat the grill, with the lid closed, to 500°F.
2. Rub the tuna steaks all over with olive oil and season both sides with salt and pepper.

3. Place the tuna steaks directly on the grill grate and grill for 3 to 5 minutes per side, leaving a pink center. Remove the tuna steaks from the grill and serve immediately.

Lobster Tails

Servings: 4
Cooking Time: 35 Minutes
Ingredients:
- 2 lobster tails, each about 10 ounces
- For the Sauce:
- 2 tablespoons chopped parsley
- 1/4 teaspoon garlic salt
- 1 teaspoon paprika
- 1/4 teaspoon ground black pepper
- 1/4 teaspoon old bay seasoning
- 8 tablespoons butter, unsalted
- 2 tablespoons lemon juice

Directions:
1. Switch on the Traeger grill, fill the grill hopper with flavored wood pellets, power the grill on by using the control panel, select 'smoke' on the temperature dial, or set the temperature to 450 degrees F and let it preheat for a minimum of 15 minutes.
2. Meanwhile, prepare the sauce and for this, take a small saucepan, place it over medium-low heat, add butter in it and when it melts, add remaining ingredients for the sauce and stir until combined, set aside until required.
3. Prepare the lobster and for this, cut the shell from the middle to the tail by using kitchen shears and then take the meat from the shell, keeping it attached at the base of the crab tail.
4. Then butterfly the crab meat by making a slit down the middle, then place lobster tails on a baking sheet and pour 1 tablespoon of sauce over each lobster tail, reserve the remaining sauce.
5. When the grill has preheated, open the lid, place crab tails on the grill grate, shut the grill and smoke for 30 minutes until opaque.
6. When done, transfer lobster tails to a dish and then serve with the remaining sauce.

Nutrition Info:
- InfoCalories: 290 Cal ;Fat: 22 g ;Carbs: 1 g ;Protein: 20 g ;Fiber: 0.3 g

Traeger Smoked Shrimp

Servings: 6
Cooking Time: 10 Minutes
Ingredients:
- 1 lb tail-on shrimp, uncooked
- 1/2 tbsp onion powder
- 1/2 tbsp garlic powder
- 1/2 tbsp salt
- 4 tbsp teriyaki sauce
- 2 tbsp green onion, minced
- 4 tbsp sriracha mayo

Directions:
1. Peel the shrimp shells leaving the tail on then wash well and rise.
2. Drain well and pat dry with a paper towel.
3. Preheat your Traeger to 4500F.
4. Season the shrimp with onion powder, garlic powder, and salt. Place the shrimp in the Traeger and cook for 6 minutes on each side.
5. Remove the shrimp from the Traeger and toss with teriyaki sauce then garnish with onions and mayo.

Nutrition Info:
- InfoCalories 87, Total fat 0g, Saturated fat 0g, Total carbs 2g, Net carbs 2g Protein 16g, Sugars 0g, Fiber 0g, Sodium 1241mg

Grilled Shrimp Kabobs

Servings: 4
Cooking Time: 10 Minutes
Ingredients:
- 1 lb. colossal shrimp, peeled and deveined
- 2 tbsp. oil
- 1/2 tbsp. garlic salt
- 1/2 tbsp. salt
- 1/8 tbsp. pepper
- 6 skewers

Directions:
1. Preheat your Traeger to 3750F.
2. Pat the shrimp dry with a paper towel.
3. In a mixing bowl, mix oil, garlic salt, salt, and pepper
4. Toss the shrimp in the mixture until well coated.
5. Skewer the shrimps and cook in the Traeger with the lid closed for 4 minutes.
6. Open the lid, flip the skewers and cook for another 4 minutes or until the shrimp is pink and the flesh is opaque.
7. Serve.

Nutrition Info:
- InfoCalories 325, Total fat 0g, Saturated fat 0g, Total carbs 0g, Net carbs 0g Protein 20g, Sugars 0g, Fiber 0g, Sodium 120mg

Grilled Lobster Tail

Servings: 4
Cooking Time: 15 Minutes
Ingredients:
- 2 (8 ounces each) lobster tails
- 1/4 tsp old bay seasoning
- ½ tsp oregano
- 1 tsp paprika
- Juice from one lemon
- 1/4 tsp Himalayan salt
- 1/4 tsp freshly ground black pepper
- 1/4 tsp onion powder
- 2 tbsp freshly chopped parsley
- ¼ cup melted butter

Directions:
1. Slice the tail in the middle with a kitchen shear. Pull the shell apart slightly and run your hand through the meat to separate the meat partially
2. Combine the seasonings
3. Drizzle lobster tail with lemon juice and season generously with the seasoning mixture.
4. Preheat your wood pellet smoker to 450°F, using apple wood pellets.
5. Place the lobster tail directly on the grill grate, meat side down. Cook for about 15 minutes.
6. The tails must be pulled off and it must cool down for a few minutes
7. Drizzle melted butter over the tails.
8. Serve and garnish with fresh chopped parsley.

Nutrition Info:
- Calories: 146 Cal Fat: 11.7 g Carbohydrates: 2.1 g Protein: 9.3 g Fiber: 0.8 g

Traeger Salmon With Togarashi

Servings: 3
Cooking Time: 20 Minutes
Ingredients:
- 1 salmon fillet
- 1/4 cup olive oil
- 1/2 tbsp kosher salt
- 1 tbsp Togarashi seasoning

Directions:
1. Preheat your Traeger to 4000F.
2. Place the salmon on a sheet lined with non-stick foil with the skin side down.
3. Rub the oil into the meat then sprinkle salt and Togarashi.
4. Place the salmon on the grill and cook for 20 minutes or until the internal temperature reaches 1450F with the lid closed.
5. Remove from the Traeger and serve when hot.

Nutrition Info:
- InfoCalories 119, Total fat 10g, Saturated fat 2g, Total carbs 0g, Net carbs 0g Protein 0g, Sugars 0g, Fiber 0g, Sodium 720mg

No-fuss Tuna Burgers

Servings: 6
Cooking Time: 15 Minutes
Ingredients:
- 2 lb. tuna steak
- 1 green bell pepper, seeded and chopped
- 1 white onion, chopped
- 2 eggs
- 1 tsp. soy sauce
- 1 tbsp. blackened Saskatchewan rub
- Salt and freshly ground black pepper, to taste

Directions:
1. Set the temperature of Traeger Grill to 500 degrees F and preheat with closed lid for 15 minutes.
2. In a bowl, add all the ingredients and mix until well combined.
3. With greased hands, make patties from mixture.
4. Place the patties onto the grill close to the edges and cook for about 10-15 minutes, flipping once halfway through.
5. Serve hot.

Nutrition Info:
- Calories per serving: 313; Carbohydrates: 3.4g; Protein: 47.5g; Fat: 11g; Sugar: 1.9g; Sodium: 174mg; Fiber: 0.7g

Grilled Teriyaki Salmon

Servings: 4
Cooking Time: 30 Minutes
Ingredients:
- 1 salmon fillet
- 1/8 cup olive oil
- 1/2 tbsp salt
- 1/4 tbsp pepper
- 1/4 tbsp garlic salt
- 1/4 cup butter, sliced
- 1/4 teriyaki sauce
- 1 tbsp sesame seeds

Directions:
1. Preheat the grill to 400°F.
2. Place the salmon fillet on a non-stick foil sheet. Drizzle the salmon with oil, seasonings, and butter on top.
3. Pace the foil tray on the grill and close the lid. Cook for 8 minutes then open the lid.
4. Brush the salmon with teriyaki sauce and repeat after every 5 minutes until all sauce is finished. The internal temperature should be 145°F.
5. Remove the salmon from the grill and sprinkle with sesame seeds.
6. Serve and enjoy with your favorite side dish.

Nutrition Info:
- InfoCalories 296, Total fat 25g, Saturated fat 10g, Total Carbs 3g, Net Carbs 3g, Protein 14g, Sugar 3g, Fiber 0g, Sodium: 1179mg, Potassium 459mg

Enticing Mahi-mahi

Servings: 4
Cooking Time: 10 Minutes
Ingredients:
- 4 (6-oz.) mahi-mahi fillets
- 2 tbsp. olive oil
- Salt and freshly ground black pepper, to taste

Directions:
1. Set the temperature of Traeger Grill to 350 degrees F and preheat with closed lid for 15 minutes.
2. Coat fish fillets with olive oil and season with salt and black pepper evenly.
3. Place the fish fillets onto the grill and cook for about 5 minutes per side.
4. Remove the fish fillets from grill and serve hot.

Nutrition Info:
- Calories per serving: 195; Carbohydrates: 0g; Protein: 31.6g; Fat: 7g; Sugar: 0g; Sodium: 182mg; Fiber: 0g

Grilled Shrimp

Servings: 4
Cooking Time: 15 Minutes
Ingredients:
- Jumbo shrimp peeled and cleaned - 1 lb.
- Oil - 2 tbsp
- Salt - ½ tbsp
- Skewers - 4-5
- Pepper - ⅛ tbsp
- Garlic salt - ½ tbsp

Directions:
1. Preheat the wood pellet grill to 375 degrees.
2. Mix all the ingredients in a small bowl.
3. After washing and drying the shrimp, mix it well with the oil and seasonings.
4. Add skewers to the shrimp and set the bowl of shrimp aside.
5. Open the skewers and flip them.
6. Cook for 4 more minutes. Remove when the shrimp is opaque and pink.

Nutrition Info:
- Carbohydrates: 1.3 g Protein: 19 g Fat: 1.4 g Sodium: 805 mg Cholesterol: 179 mg

Vegetable & Vegetarian Recipes

Smoked Pumpkin Soup

Servings: 6
Cooking Time: 1 Hour And 33 Minutes
Ingredients:
- 5 pounds pumpkin, seeded and sliced
- 3 tablespoons butter
- 1 onion, diced
- 2 cloves garlic, minced
- 1 tablespoon brown sugar
- 1 teaspoon paprika
- ¼ teaspoon ground cinnamon
- ¼ teaspoon ground nutmeg
- ½ cup apple cider
- 5 cups broth
- ½ cup cream

Directions:
1. Fire the Traeger Grill to 1800F. Use desired wood pellets when cooking. Close the lid and preheat for 15 minutes.
2. Place the pumpkin on the grill grate and smoke for an hour or until tender. Allow to cool.
3. Melt the butter in a large saucepan over medium heat and sauté the onion and garlic for 3 minutes. Stir in the rest of the ingredients including the smoked pumpkin. Cook for another 30 minutes.
4. Transfer to a blender and pulse until smooth.

Nutrition Info:
- InfoCalories per serving: 246; Protein: 8.8g; Carbs: 32.2g; Fat: 11.4g Sugar: 15.5g

Baked Cheesy Corn Pudding

Servings: 6
Cooking Time: 30 Minutes
Ingredients:
- 3 cloves of garlic, chopped
- 3 tablespoons butter
- 3 cups whole corn kernels
- 8 ounces cream cheese
- 1 cup cheddar cheese
- 1 cup parmesan cheese
- 1 tablespoon salt
- ½ tablespoon black pepper
- ½ cup dry breadcrumbs
- 1 cup mozzarella cheese, grated
- 1 tablespoon thyme, minced

Directions:
1. Fire the Traeger Grill to 3500F. Use desired wood pellets when cooking. Close the lid and preheat for 15 minutes.
2. In a large saucepan, sauté the garlic and butter for 2 minutes until fragrant. Add the corn, cheddar cheese, parmesan cheese, salt, and pepper. Heat until the corn is melted then pour into a baking dish.
3. In a small bowl, combine the breadcrumbs, mozzarella cheese, and thyme.
4. Spread the cheese and bread crumb mixture on top of the corn mixture.
5. Place the baking dish on the grill grate and cook for 25 minutes.
6. Allow to rest before removing from the mold.

Nutrition Info:
- InfoCalories per serving: 523; Protein: 29.4g; Carbs: 34g; Fat: 31.2g Sugar: 10.8g

Wood Pellet Cold Smoked Cheese

Servings: 10
Cooking Time: 2 Minutes
Ingredients:
- Ice
- 1 aluminum pan, full-size and disposable
- 1 aluminum pan, half-size and disposable
- Toothpicks
- A block of cheese

Directions:
1. Preheat the wood pellet to 165°F wit the lid closed for 15 minutes.
2. Place the small pan in the large pan. Fill the surrounding of the small pan with ice.
3. Place the cheese in the small pan on top of toothpicks then place the pan on the grill and close the lid.
4. Smoke cheese for 1 hour, flip the cheese, and smoke for 1 more hour with the lid closed.
5. Remove the cheese from the grill and wrap it in parchment paper. Store in the fridge for 2 3 days for the smoke flavor to mellow.
6. Remove from the fridge and serve. Enjoy.

Nutrition Info:
- InfoCalories 1910, Total fat 7g, Saturated fat 6g, Total Carbs 2g, Net Carbs 2g, Protein 6g, Sugar 1g, Fiber 0g, Sodium: 340mg, Potassium 0mg

Grilled Corn With Honey & Butter

Servings: 4
Cooking Time: 10 Minutes
Ingredients:
- 6 pieces corn
- 2 tablespoons olive oil
- 1/2 cup butter
- 1/2 cup honey
- 1 tablespoon smoked salt
- Pepper to taste

Directions:
1. Preheat the wood pellet grill to high for 15 minutes while the lid is closed.
2. Brush the corn with oil and butter.
3. Grill the corn for 10 minutes, turning from time to time.
4. Mix honey and butter.
5. Brush corn with this mixture and sprinkle with smoked salt and pepper.
6. Tips: Slice off the kernels and serve as side dish to a main course.

Caldereta Stew

Servings: 12
Cooking Time: 4 Hours
Ingredients:
- 2lb. chuck roast, sliced into cubes
- 2tablespoons olive oil
- 1carrot, sliced into cubes
- 2potatoes, sliced into cubes
- 4garlic cloves, chopped
- 2tablespoons tomato paste
- 2cups tomato sauce
- 2red bell peppers, sliced into strips
- 2green bell peppers, sliced into strips
- 2cups of water
- 1/2 cup cheddar cheese, grated
- 1/4 cup liver spread
- Salt to taste

Directions:
1. Put the beef in a cast iron pan.
2. Place this in the smoking cabinet.
3. Open the side dampers and sear slide.
4. Set the temperature to 375 degrees F.
5. Smoke the beef for 1 hour and 30 minutes.
6. Flip the beef and smoke for another 1 hour and 30 minutes.
7. Add a Dutch oven on top of the grill.
8. Pour in the olive oil.
9. Add the carrots and potatoes.
10. Cook for 5 minutes.
11. Stir in the garlic and cook for 1 minute.
12. Transfer the beef to the Dutch oven.
13. Stir in the tomato paste, tomato sauce, bell peppers, and water.
14. Bring to a boil.
15. Reduce temperature to 275 degrees F.
16. Simmer for 1 hour.
17. Add the cheese and liver.
18. Season with the salt.

Nutrition Info:
- Calories: 191.1 Fat: 9.3 g Cholesterol: 34 mg Carbohydrates: 15.4 g Fiber: 1.8 g Sugars: 1.3 g Protein: 11.3 g

Roasted Root Vegetables

Servings: 6
Cooking Time: 45 Minutes
Ingredients:
- 1 large red onion, peeled
- 1 bunch of red beets, trimmed, peeled
- 1 large yam, peeled
- 1 bunch of golden beets, trimmed, peeled
- 1 large parsnips, peeled
- 1 butternut squash, peeled
- 1 large carrot, peeled
- 6 garlic cloves, peeled
- 3 tablespoons thyme leaves
- Salt as needed
- 1 cinnamon stick
- Ground black pepper as needed
- 3 tablespoons olive oil
- 2 tablespoons honey

Directions:
1. Switch on the Traeger grill, fill the grill hopper with hickory flavored wood pellets, power the grill on by using the control panel, select 'smoke' on the temperature dial, or set the temperature to 450 degrees F and let it preheat for a minimum of 15 minutes.
2. Meanwhile, cut all the vegetables into ½-inch pieces, place them in a large bowl, add garlic, thyme, and cinnamon, drizzle with oil and toss until mixed.
3. Take a large cookie sheet, line it with foil, spread with vegetables, and then season with salt and black pepper.
4. When the grill has preheated, open the lid, place prepared cookie sheet on the grill grate, shut the grill and smoke for 45 minutes until tender.

5. When done, transfer vegetables to a dish, drizzle with honey, and then serve.

Nutrition Info:
- InfoCalories: 164 Cal ;Fat: 4 g ;Carbs: 31.7 g ;Protein: 2.7 g ;Fiber: 6.4 g

Grilled Artichokes

Servings: 6

Cooking Time: 15 Minutes

Ingredients:
- 3 large artichokes, blanched and halved
- 3 + 3 tablespoons olive oil
- Salt and pepper to taste
- 1 cup mayonnaise
- 1 cup yogurt
- 2 tablespoons parsley, chopped
- 2 tablespoons capers
- Lemon juice to taste

Directions:

1. Fire the Traeger Grill to 5000F. Use desired wood pellets when cooking. Close the lid and preheat for 15 minutes.

2. Brush the artichokes with 3 tablespoons of olive oil. Season with salt and pepper to taste.

3. Place on the grill grate and cook for 15 minutes.

4. Allow to cool before slicing.

5. Once cooled, slice the artichokes and place in a bowl.

6. In another bowl, mix together the mayonnaise, yogurt, parsley, capers, and lemon juice. Season with salt and pepper to taste. Mix until well-combined.

7. Pour sauce over the artichokes.

8. Toss to coat.

Nutrition Info:
- InfoCalories per serving: 257; Protein: 6.7g; Carbs: 13.2 g; Fat: 20.9g Sugar: 3.7g

Smoked Tomato And Mozzarella Dip

Servings: 4

Cooking Time: 1 Hour

Ingredients:
- 8ounces smoked mozzarella cheese, shredded
- 8ounces Colby cheese, shredded
- ½ cup parmesan cheese, grated
- 1cup sour cream
- 1cup sun-dried tomatoes
- 1and ½ teaspoon salt
- 1teaspoon fresh ground pepper
- 1teaspoon dried basil
- 1teaspoon dried oregano
- 1teaspoon red pepper flakes
- 1garlic clove, minced
- ½ teaspoon onion powder
- French toast, serving

Directions:

1. Preheat your smoker to 275 degrees Fahrenheit using your preferred wood

2. Take a large bowl and stir in the cheeses, tomatoes, pepper, salt, basil, oregano, red pepper flakes, garlic, onion powder and mix well

3. Transfer the mix to a small metal pan and transfer to a smoker

4. Smoke for 1 hour

5. Serve with toasted French bread

6. Enjoy!

Nutrition Info:
- Calories: 174 Fats: 11g Carbs: 15g Fiber: 2g

Smoked Pickles

Servings: 6

Cooking Time: 15 Minutes

Ingredients:
- 1-quart water
- ¼ cup sugar
- ½ quart white vinegar
- ½ cup salt
- ½ teaspoon peppercorns
- 1 ½ teaspoons celery seeds
- 1 ½ teaspoons coriander seeds
- 1 teaspoon mustard seeds
- 8 cloves of garlic, minced
- 1 bunch dill weed
- 12 small cucumbers

Directions:

1. Place the water, sugar, vinegar, salt, and peppercorns in a saucepan. Bring to a boil over medium flame.

2. Transfer to a bowl and allow to cool. Add in the rest of the ingredients.

3. Allow the cucumber to soak in the brine for at least 3 days.

4. When ready to cook, fire the Traeger Grill to 5000F. Use desired wood pellets when cooking. Close the lid and preheat for 15 minutes.

5. Pat dry the cucumber with paper towel and place on the grill grate. Smoke for 15 minutes.

Nutrition Info:
- InfoCalories per serving: 67; Protein: 2.4g; Carbs: 12.9g; Fat: 1.1g Sugar:8.5 g

Wood Pellet Grilled Zucchini Squash Spears

Servings: 5
Cooking Time: 10 Minutes
Ingredients:
- 4 zucchini, cleaned and ends cut
- 2 tbsp olive oil
- 1 tbsp sherry vinegar
- 2 thyme, leaves pulled
- Salt and pepper to taste

Directions:
1. Cut the zucchini into halves then cut each half thirds.
2. Add the rest of the ingredients in a ziplock bag with the zucchini pieces. Toss to mix well.
3. Preheat the wood pellet temperature to 350°F with the lid closed for 15 minutes.
4. Remove the zucchini from the bag and place them on the grill grate with the cut side down.
5. Cook for 4 minutes per side or until the zucchini are tender.
6. Remove from grill and serve with thyme leaves. Enjoy.

Nutrition Info:
- InfoCalories 74, Total fat 5.4g, Saturated fat 0.5g, Total Carbs 6.1g, Net Carbs 3.8g, Protein 2.6g, Sugar 3.9g, Fiber 2.3g, Sodium: 302mg, Potassium 599mg

Grilled Zucchini

Servings: 6
Cooking Time: 10 Minutes
Ingredients:
- 4 medium zucchini
- 2 tablespoons olive oil
- 1 tablespoon sherry vinegar
- 2 sprigs of thyme, leaves chopped
- ½ teaspoon salt
- 1/3 teaspoon ground black pepper

Directions:
1. Switch on the Traeger grill, fill the grill hopper with oak flavored wood pellets, power the grill on by using the control panel, select 'smoke' on the temperature dial, or set the temperature to 350 degrees F and let it preheat for a minimum of 5 minutes.
2. Meanwhile, cut the ends of each zucchini, cut each in half and then into thirds and place in a plastic bag.
3. Add remaining ingredients, seal the bag, and shake well to coat zucchini pieces.
4. When the grill has preheated, open the lid, place zucchini on the grill grate, shut the grill and smoke for 4 minutes per side.
5. When done, transfer zucchini to a dish, garnish with more thyme and then serve.

Nutrition Info:
- InfoCalories: 74 Cal ;Fat: 5.4 g ;Carbs: 6.1 g ;Protein: 2.6 g ;Fiber: 2.3 g

Potluck Salad With Smoked Cornbread

Servings: 6
Cooking Time: 35 To 45 Minutes
Ingredients:
- 1 cup all-purpose flour
- 1 cup yellow cornmeal
- 1 tablespoon sugar
- 2 teaspoons baking powder
- 1 teaspoon salt
- 1 cup milk
- 1 egg, beaten, at room temperature
- 4 tablespoons (½ stick) unsalted butter, melted and cooled
- Nonstick cooking spray or butter, for greasing
- ½ cup milk
- ½ cup sour cream
- 2 tablespoons dry ranch dressing mix
- 1 pound bacon, cooked and crumbled
- 3 tomatoes, chopped
- 1 bell pepper, chopped
- 1 cucumber, seeded and chopped
- 2 stalks celery, chopped (about 1 cup)
- ½ cup chopped scallions

Directions:
1. For the cornbread:
2. In a medium bowl, combine the flour, cornmeal, sugar, baking powder, and salt.
3. In a small bowl, whisk together the milk and egg. Pour in the butter, then slowly fold this mixture into the dry ingredients.
4. Supply your smoker with wood pellets and follow the manufacturer's specific start-up procedure. Preheat, with the lid closed, to 375°F.
5. Coat a cast iron skillet with cooking spray or butter.
6. Pour the batter into the skillet, place on the grill grate, close the lid, and smoke for 35 to 45 minutes, or until the cornbread is browned and pulls away from the side of the skillet.

7. Remove the cornbread from the grill and let cool, then coarsely crumble.
8. For the salad:
9. In a small bowl, whisk together the milk, sour cream, and ranch dressing mix.
10. In a medium bowl, combine the crumbled bacon, tomatoes, bell pepper, cucumber, celery, and scallions.
11. In a large serving bowl, layer half of the crumbled cornbread, half of the bacon-veggie mixture, and half of the dressing. Toss lightly.
12. Repeat the layering with the remaining cornbread, bacon-veggie mixture, and dressing. Toss again.
13. Refrigerate the salad for at least 1 hour. Serve cold.

Twice-smoked Potatoes

Servings: 16
Cooking Time: 1 Hour 35 Minutes
Ingredients:
- 8 Idaho, Russet, or Yukon Gold potatoes
- 1 (12-ounce) can evaporated milk, heated
- 1 cup (2 sticks) butter, melted
- ½ cup sour cream, at room temperature
- 1 cup grated Parmesan cheese
- ½ pound bacon, cooked and crumbled
- ¼ cup chopped scallions
- Salt
- Freshly ground black pepper
- 1 cup shredded Cheddar cheese

Directions:
1. Supply your smoker with wood pellets and follow the manufacturer's specific start-up procedure. Preheat, with the lid closed, to 400°F.
2. Poke the potatoes all over with a fork. Arrange them directly on the grill grate, close the lid, and smoke for 1 hour and 15 minutes, or until cooked through and they have some give when pinched.
3. Let the potatoes cool for 10 minutes, then cut in half lengthwise.
4. Into a medium bowl, scoop out the potato flesh, leaving ¼ inch in the shells; place the shells on a baking sheet.
5. Using an electric mixer on medium speed, beat the potatoes, milk, butter, and sour cream until smooth.
6. Stir in the Parmesan cheese, bacon, and scallions, and season with salt and pepper.
7. Generously stuff each shell with the potato mixture and top with Cheddar cheese.
8. Place the baking sheet on the grill grate, close the lid, and smoke for 20 minutes, or until the cheese is melted.

Vegan Smoked Carrot Dogs

Servings: 2
Cooking Time: 35 Minutes
Ingredients:
- 4 carrots, thick
- 2 tbsp avocado oil
- 1/2 tbsp garlic powder
- 1 tbsp liquid smoke
- Pepper to taste
- Kosher salt to taste

Directions:
1. Preheat your Traeger to 425oF then line a parchment paper on a baking sheet.
2. Peel the carrots to resemble a hot dog. Round the edges when peeling.
3. Whisk together oil, garlic powder, liquid smoke, pepper and salt in a bowl, small.
4. Now place carrots on the baking sheet and pour the mixture over. Roll your carrots in the mixture to massage seasoning and oil into them. Use fingertips.
5. Roast the carrots in the Traeger until fork tender for about 35 minutes. Brush the carrots using the marinade mixture every 5 minutes.
6. Remove and place into hot dog buns then top with hot dog toppings of your choice.
7. Serve and enjoy!

Nutrition Info:
- InfoCalories 76, Total fat 1.8g, Saturated 0.4g, Total 14.4g, Net carbs 10.6g, Protein 1.5g, Sugar 6.6g, Fiber 3.8g, Sodium 163mg, Potassium 458mg

Roasted Peach Salsa

Servings: 6
Cooking Time: 10 Minutes
Ingredients:
- 6 whole peaches, pitted and halved
- 3 tomatoes, chopped
- 2 whole onions, chopped
- ½ cup cilantro, chopped
- 2 cloves garlic, minced
- 5 teaspoons apple cider vinegar
- ½ teaspoon salt
- ¼ teaspoon black pepper
- 2 tablespoons olive oil

Directions:
1. Fire the Traeger Grill to 3000F. Use desired wood pellets when cooking. Close the lid and preheat for 15 minutes.

2. Place the peaches on the grill grate and cook for 5 minutes on each side. Remove from the grill and allow to rest for 5 minutes.

3. Place the peaches, tomatoes, onion, and cilantro in a salad bowl. On a smaller bowl, stir in the garlic, apple cider vinegar, salt, pepper, and olive oil. Stir until well-combined. Pour into the salad and toss to coat.

Nutrition Info:

- InfoCalories per serving: 155 ; Protein: 3.1g; Carbs: 27.6 g; Fat: 5.1g Sugar: 20g

Roasted Sheet Pan Vegetables

Servings: 6

Cooking Time: 20 Minutes

Ingredients:

- 1 small purple cauliflower, cut into florets
- 1 small yellow cauliflower, cut into florets
- 4 cups butternut squash
- 2 cups mushroom, fresh
- 3 tablespoons extra virgin olive oil
- 2 teaspoons salt
- 2 teaspoons black pepper

Directions:

1. Fire the Traeger Grill to 3500F. Use desired wood pellets when cooking. Close the lid and preheat for 15 minutes.

2. Place the vegetables in a baking tray and season with olive oil, salt, and pepper. Toss to coat all vegetables.

3. Place in the grill and cook for 20 minutes. Make sure to shake the tray halfway through the cooking time for even cooking.

Nutrition Info:

- InfoCalories per serving: 101; Protein: 3.8g; Carbs: 16.9g; Fat: 3.5g Sugar: 4.4g

Smoked Baked Beans

Servings: 12

Cooking Time: 3 Hours

Ingredients:

- 1 medium yellow onion diced
- 3 jalapenos
- 56 oz pork and beans
- 3/4 cup barbeque sauce
- 1/2 cup dark brown sugar
- 1/4 cup apple cider vinegar
- 2 tbsp Dijon mustard
- 2 tbsp molasses

Directions:

1. Preheat the smoker to 250°F. Pour the beans along with all the liquid in a pan. Add brown sugar, barbeque sauce, Dijon mustard, apple cider vinegar, and molasses. Stir. Place the pan on one of the racks. Smoke for 3 hours until thickened. Remove after 3 hours. Serve

Nutrition Info:

- Calories: 214 Cal Fat: 2 g Carbohydrates: 42 g Protein: 7 g Fiber: 7 g

Smoked Hummus

Servings: 6

Cooking Time: 20 Minutes

Ingredients:

- 1 ½ cups chickpeas, rinsed and drained
- ¼ cup tahini
- 1 tablespoon garlic, minced
- 2 tablespoons extra virgin olive oil
- 1 teaspoon salt
- 4 tablespoons lemon juice

Directions:

1. Fire the Traeger Grill to 3500F. Use desired wood pellets when cooking. Close the lid and preheat for 15 minutes.

2. Spread the chickpeas on a sheet tray and place on the grill grate. Smoke for 20 minutes.

3. Let the chickpeas cool at room temperature.

4. Place smoked chickpeas in a blender or food processor. Add in the rest of the ingredients. Pulse until smooth.

5. Serve with roasted vegetables if desired.

Nutrition Info:

- InfoCalories per serving: 271; Protein: 12.1g; Carbs: 34.8g; Fat: 10.4g Sugar: 5.7g

Traeger Smoked Mushrooms

Servings: 2

Cooking Time: 45 Minutes

Ingredients:

- 4 cups whole baby portobello, cleaned
- 1 tbsp canola oil
- 1 tbsp onion powder
- 1 tbsp garlic, granulated
- 1 tbsp salt
- 1 tbsp pepper

Directions:

1. Place all the ingredients in a bowl, mix, and combine.

2. Set your Traeger to 180oF.

3. Place the mushrooms on the grill directly and smoke for about 30 minutes.

4. Increase heat to high and cook the mushroom for another 15 minutes.
5. Serve warm and enjoy!

Nutrition Info:
- InfoCalories 118, Total fat 7.6g, Saturated fat 0.6g, Total carbs 10.8g, Net carbs 8.3g, Protein 5.4g, Sugars 3.7g, Fiber 2.5g, Sodium 3500mg, Potassium 536mg

Bunny Dogs With Sweet And Spicy Jalapeño Relish

Servings: 8
Cooking Time: 35 To 40 Minutes
Ingredients:
- 8 hot dog-size carrots, peeled
- ¼ cup honey
- ¼ cup yellow mustard
- Nonstick cooking spray or butter, for greasing
- Salt
- Freshly ground black pepper
- 8 hot dog buns
- Sweet and Spicy Jalapeño Relish

Directions:
1. Prepare the carrots by removing the stems and slicing in half lengthwise.
2. In a small bowl, whisk together the honey and mustard.
3. Supply your smoker with wood pellets and follow the manufacturer's specific start-up procedure. Preheat, with the lid closed, to 375°F.
4. Line a baking sheet with aluminum foil and coat with cooking spray.
5. Brush the carrots on both sides with the honey mustard and season with salt and pepper; put on the baking sheet.
6. Place the baking sheet on the grill grate, close the lid, and smoke for 35 to 40 minutes, or until tender and starting to brown.
7. To serve, lightly toast the hot dog buns on the grill and top each with two slices of carrot and some relish.

Smoked Healthy Cabbage

Servings: 5
Cooking Time: 2 Hours
Ingredients:
- 1head cabbage, cored
- 4tablespoons butter
- 2tablespoons rendered bacon fat
- 1chicken bouillon cube
- 1teaspoon fresh ground black pepper
- 1garlic clove, minced

Directions:
1. Preheat your smoker to 240 degrees Fahrenheit using your preferred wood
2. Fill the hole of your cored cabbage with butter, bouillon cube, bacon fat, pepper and garlic
3. Wrap the cabbage in foil about two-thirds of the way up
4. Make sure to leave the top open
5. Transfer to your smoker rack and smoke for 2 hours
6. Unwrap and enjoy!

Nutrition Info:
- Calories: 231 Fats: 10g Carbs: 26g Fiber: 1g

Blt Pasta Salad

Servings: 6
Cooking Time: 35 To 45 Minutes
Ingredients:
- 1 pound thick-cut bacon
- 16 ounces bowtie pasta, cooked according to package directions and drained
- 2 tomatoes, chopped
- ½ cup chopped scallions
- ½ cup Italian dressing
- ½ cup ranch dressing
- 1 tablespoon chopped fresh basil
- 1 teaspoon salt
- 1 teaspoon freshly ground black pepper
- 1 teaspoon garlic powder
- 1 head lettuce, cored and torn

Directions:
1. Supply your smoker with wood pellets and follow the manufacturer's specific start-up procedure. Preheat, with the lid closed, to 225°F.
2. Arrange the bacon slices on the grill grate, close the lid, and cook for 30 to 45 minutes, flipping after 20 minutes, until crisp.
3. Remove the bacon from the grill and chop.
4. In a large bowl, combine the chopped bacon with the cooked pasta, tomatoes, scallions, Italian dressing, ranch dressing, basil, salt, pepper, and garlic powder. Refrigerate until ready to serve.
5. Toss in the lettuce just before serving to keep it from wilting.

Smoked Mushrooms

Servings: 6
Cooking Time: 10 Minutes
Ingredients:
- 4 cups baby portobello, whole and cleaned
- 1 tablespoon canola oil
- 1 teaspoon onion powder
- 1 teaspoon garlic powder
- Salt and pepper to taste

Directions:
1. Place all ingredients in a bowl and toss to coat the mushrooms with the seasoning.
2. Fire the Traeger Grill to 3500F. Use desired wood pellets when cooking. Close the lid and preheat for 15 minutes.
3. Place mushrooms on the grill grate and smoke for 10 minutes. Make sure to flip the mushrooms halfway through the cooking time.
4. Remove from the grill and serve.

Nutrition Info:
- InfoCalories per serving: 62; Protein: 5.2g; Carbs: 6.6g; Fat: 2.9g Sugar: 0.3g

Smoked Deviled Eggs

Servings: 4 To 6
Cooking Time: 50 Minutes
Ingredients:
- 6 large eggs
- 1 slice bacon
- 1/4 cup mayonnaise
- 1 tsp Dijon mustard
- 1 tsp apple cider vinegar
- 1/4 tsp paprika
- Pinch of kosher salt
- 1 tbsp chives, chopped

Directions:
1. Preheat pellet grill to 180°F and turn smoke setting on, if applicable.
2. Bring a pot of water to a boil. Add eggs and hard boil eggs for about 12 minutes.
3. Remove eggs from pot and place them into an ice-water bath. Once eggs have cooled completely, peel them and slice in half lengthwise.
4. Place sliced eggs on grill, yolk side up. Smoke for 30 to 45 minutes, depending on how much smoky flavor you want.
5. While eggs smoke, cook bacon until it's crispy.
6. Remove eggs from the grill and allow to cool on a plate.
7. Remove the yolks and place all of them in a small bowl. Place the egg whites on a plate.
8. Mash yolks with a fork and add mayonnaise, mustard, apple cider vinegar, paprika, and salt. Stir until combined.
9. Spoon a scoop of yolk mixture back into each egg white.
10. Sprinkle paprika, chives, and crispy bacon bits to garnish. Serve and enjoy!

Nutrition Info:
- Calories: 140 Fat: 12 g Cholesterol: 190 mg Carbohydrate: 1 g Fiber: 0 Sugar: 0 Protein: 6 g

Roasted Vegetable Medley

Servings: 4 To 6
Cooking Time: 50 Minutes
Ingredients:
- 2 medium potatoes, cut to 1 inch wedges
- 2 red bell peppers, cut into 1 inch cubes
- 1 small butternut squash, peeled and cubed to 1 inch cube
- 1 red onion, cut to 1 inch cubes
- 1 cup broccoli, trimmed
- 2 tbsp olive oil
- 1 tbsp balsamic vinegar
- 1 tbsp fresh rosemary, minced
- 1 tbsp fresh thyme, minced
- 1 tsp kosher salt
- 1 tsp ground black pepper

Directions:
1. Preheat pellet grill to 425°F.
2. In a large bowl, combine potatoes, peppers, squash, and onion.
3. In a small bowl, whisk together olive oil, balsamic vinegar, rosemary, thyme, salt, and pepper.
4. Pour marinade over vegetables and toss to coat. Allow resting for about 15 minutes.
5. Place marinated vegetables into a grill basket, and place a grill basket on the grill grate. Cook for about 30-40 minutes, occasionally tossing in the grill basket.
6. Remove veggies from grill and transfer to a serving dish. Allow to cool for 5 minutes, then serve and enjoy!

Nutrition Info:
- Calories: 158.6 Fat: 7.4 g Cholesterol: 0 Carbohydrate: 22 g Fiber: 7.2 g Sugar: 3.1 g Protein: 5.2 g

Grilled Sugar Snap Peas

Servings: 4
Cooking Time: 10 Minutes

Ingredients:
- 2-pound sugar snap peas, ends trimmed
- ½ teaspoon garlic powder
- 1 teaspoon salt
- 2/3 teaspoon ground black pepper
- 2 tablespoons olive oil

Directions:
1. Switch on the Traeger grill, fill the grill hopper with apple-flavored wood pellets, power the grill on by using the control panel, select 'smoke' on the temperature dial, or set the temperature to 450 degrees F and let it preheat for a minimum of 15 minutes.
2. Meanwhile, take a medium bowl, place peas in it, add garlic powder and oil, season with salt and black pepper, toss until mixed and then spread on the sheet pan.
3. When the grill has preheated, open the lid, place the prepared sheet pan on the grill grate, shut the grill and smoke for 10 minutes until slightly charred.
4. Serve straight away.

Nutrition Info:
- InfoCalories: 91 Cal ;Fat: 5 g ;Carbs: 9 g ;Protein: 4 g ;Fiber: 3 g

Mexican Street Corn With Chipotle Butter

Servings: 4
Cooking Time: 12 To 14 Minutes

Ingredients:
- 4 ears corn
- ½ cup sour cream
- ½ cup mayonnaise
- ¼ cup chopped fresh cilantro, plus more for garnish
- Chipotle Butter, for topping
- 1 cup grated Parmesan cheese

Directions:
1. Supply your smoker with wood pellets and follow the manufacturer's specific start-up procedure. Preheat, with the lid closed, to 450°F.
2. Shuck the corn, removing the silks and cutting off the cores.
3. Tear four squares of aluminum foil large enough to completely cover an ear of corn.
4. In a medium bowl, combine the sour cream, mayonnaise, and cilantro. Slather the mixture all over the ears of corn.
5. Wrap each ear of corn in a piece of foil, sealing tightly. Place on the grill, close the lid, and smoke for 12 to 14 minutes.
6. Remove the corn from the foil and place in a shallow baking dish. Top with chipotle butter, the Parmesan cheese, and more chopped cilantro.
7. Serve immediately.

Split Pea Soup With Mushrooms

Servings: 4
Cooking Time: 35 Minutes

Ingredients:
- 2tbsp. Olive Oil
- 3Garlic cloves, minced
- 3tbsp. Parsley, fresh and chopped
- 2Carrots chopped
- 1.2/3 cup Green Peas
- 9cups Water
- 2tsp. Salt
- 1/4 tsp. Black Pepper
- 1lb. Portobello Mushrooms
- 1Bay Leaf
- 2Celery Ribs, chopped
- 1Onion quartered
- 1/2 tsp. Thyme, dried
- 6tbsp. Parmesan Cheese, grated

Directions:
1. First, keep oil, onion, and garlic in the blender pitcher.
2. Next, select the 'saute' button.
3. Once sautéed, stir in the rest of the ingredients, excluding parsley and cheese.
4. Then, press the 'hearty soup' button.
5. Finally, transfer the soup among the serving bowls and garnish it with parsley and cheese.

Nutrition Info:
- Calories: 61 Fat: 1.1 g Total Carbs: 10 g Fiber: 1.9 g Sugar: 3.2 g Protein: 3.2 g Cholesterol: 0

Ramen Soup

Servings: 2
Cooking Time: 35 Minutes
Ingredients:
- 4cups Chicken Stock
- 1tbsp. Extra Virgin Olive Oil
- 2Baby Bok Choy Head, leaves torn
- 1Shallot, chopped into 1-inch piece
- 3oz. Ramen, dried
- 4Garlic cloves
- 1tsp. Sesame Oil, toasted
- 2tsp. Ginger, fresh
- One bunch of Green Onion, sliced thinly
- 1cup Chicken, cooked and cut into 1-inch cubes

Directions:
1. First, keep the olive oil, shallot, garlic, and ginger in the blender pitcher.
2. After that, press the 'saute' button.
3. Next, stir in the chicken, green onions, chicken stock, and sesame oil into it.
4. Now, select the 'hearty soup' button.
5. Then, three minutes before the program ends, spoon in the ramen noodles and baby bok choy.
6. Check the chicken's internal temperature and ensure it is 165 ° F and if it is, then transfer the soup to the serving bowls.
7. Serve immediately and enjoy it.

Nutrition Info:
- Calories: 190 Fat: 8g Total Carbs: 25g Fiber: 1 g Sugar: 0.5 g Protein: 3 g Cholesterol: 2.5 mg

Chicken Tortilla Soup

Servings: 4
Cooking Time: 35 Minutes
Ingredients:
- 1/2 cup Black Beans, canned
- 1Jalapeno Pepper, halved and seeds removed
- 1-1/2 cup Chicken Stock
- 2Carrots, sliced into ¼-inch pieces
- 1/2 of 1 Onion, peeled and halved
- 1/2 cup Corn
- 3 Garlic cloves
- 14-1/2 oz. Fire Roasted Tomatoes
- 1/4 cup Cilantro Leaves
- 10 oz. Chicken Breast, diced into ½ inch
- For the seasoning mix:
- 1/4 tsp. Chipotle
- 1tsp. Cuminutes
- 1/2 tsp. Sea Salt
- 1/2 tsp. Smoked Paprika

Directions:
1. Place pepper, carrots, onion, garlic cloves, and cilantro in the blender pitcher.
2. Pulse the mixture for 3 minutes and then pour the chicken stock to it.
3. Pulse again for another 3 minutes.
4. Next, stir in the remaining ingredients and press the 'hearty soup' button.
5. Finally, transfer to the serving bowl.

Nutrition Info:
- Calories: 260 Fat: 4 g Total Carbs: 40 g Fiber: 5.9 g Sugar: 8 g Protein: 14 g Cholesterol: 20 mg

Smoked Balsamic Potatoes And Carrots

Servings: 6
Cooking Time: 10 Minutes
Ingredients:
- 2 large carrots, peeled and chopped roughly
- 2 large Yukon Gold potatoes, peeled and wedged
- 5 tablespoons olive oil
- 5 tablespoons balsamic vinegar
- Salt and pepper to taste

Directions:
1. Fire the Traeger Grill to 4000F. Use desired wood pellets when cooking. Close the lid and preheat for 15 minutes.
2. Place all ingredients in a bowl and toss to coat the vegetables with the seasoning.
3. Place on a baking tray lined with foil.
4. Place on the grill grate and close the lid. Cook for 30 minutes.

Nutrition Info:
- InfoCalories per serving: 219; Protein: 2.9g; Carbs: 27g; Fat: 11.4g Sugar:4.5 g

Grilled Zucchini Squash

Servings: 6
Cooking Time: 10 Minutes
Ingredients:
- 3 medium zucchinis, sliced into ¼ inch thick lengthwise
- 2 tablespoons olive oil
- 1 tablespoon sherry vinegar
- 2 thyme leaves, pulled
- Salt and pepper to taste

Directions:
1. Fire the Traeger Grill to 3500F. Use desired wood pellets when cooking. Close the lid and preheat for 15 minutes.
2. Place zucchini in a bowl and all ingredients. Gently massage the zucchini slices to coat with the seasoning.
3. Place the zucchini on the grill grate and cook for 5 minutes on each side.

Nutrition Info:
- InfoCalories per serving: 44; Protein: 0.3 g; Carbs: 0.9 g; Fat: 4g Sugar: 0.1g

Whole Roasted Cauliflower With Garlic Parmesan Butter

Servings: 5
Cooking Time: 45 Minutes
Ingredients:
- 1/4 cup olive oil
- Salt and pepper to taste
- 1 cauliflower, fresh
- 1/2 cup butter, melted
- 1/4 cup parmesan cheese, grated
- 2 garlic cloves, minced
- 1/2 tbsp parsley, chopped

Directions:
1. Preheat the wood pellet grill with the lid closed for 15 minutes.
2. Meanwhile, brush the cauliflower with oil then season with salt and pepper.
3. Place the cauliflower in a cast iron and place it on a grill grate.
4. Cook for 45 minutes or until the cauliflower is golden brown and tender.
5. Meanwhile, mix butter, cheese, garlic, and parsley in a mixing bowl.
6. In the last 20 minutes of cooking, add the butter mixture.
7. Remove the cauliflower from the grill and top with more cheese and parsley if you desire. Enjoy.

Nutrition Info:
- InfoCalories 156, Total fat 11.1g, Saturated fat 3.4g, Total Carbs 8.8g, Net Carbs 5.1g, Protein 8.2g, Sugar 0g, Fiber 3.7g, Sodium: 316mg, Potassium 468.2mg

Wood Pellet Grilled Mexican Street Corn

Servings: 6
Cooking Time: 25 Minutes
Ingredients:
- 6 ears of corn on the cob, shucked
- 1 tbsp olive oil
- Kosher salt and pepper to taste
- 1/4 cup mayo
- 1/4 cup sour cream
- 1 tbsp garlic paste
- 1/2 tbsp chili powder
- Pinch of ground red pepper
- 1/2 cup cotija cheese, crumbled
- 1/4 cup cilantro, chopped
- 6 lime wedges

Directions:
1. Brush the corn with oil and sprinkle with salt.
2. Place the corn on a wood pellet grill set at 350°F. Cook for 25 minutes as you turn it occasionally.
3. Meanwhile mix mayo, cream, garlic, chili, and red pepper until well combined.
4. When the corn is cooked remove from the grill, let it rest for some minutes then brush with the mayo mixture.
5. Sprinkle cotija cheese, more chili powder, and cilantro. Serve with lime wedges. Enjoy.

Nutrition Info:
- InfoCalories 144, Total fat 5g, Saturated fat 2g, Total Carbs 10g, Net Carbs 10g, Protein 0g, Sugar 0g, Fiber 0g, Sodium: 136mg, Potassium 173mg

Wood Pellet Grilled Vegetables

Servings: 8
Cooking Time: 15 Minutes
Ingredients:
- 1 veggie tray
- 1/4 cup vegetable oil
- 2 tbsp veggie seasoning

Directions:
1. Preheat the wood pellet grill to 375°F
2. Toss the vegetables in oil then place on a sheet pan.
3. Sprinkle with veggie seasoning then place on the hot grill.
4. Grill for 15 minutes or until the veggies are cooked.

5. Let rest then serve. Enjoy.
Nutrition Info:
- InfoCalories 44, Total fat 5g, Saturated fat 0g, Total Carbs 1g, Net Carbs 1g, Protein 0g, Sugar 0g, Fiber 0g, Sodium: 36mg, Potassium 10mg

Grilled Sweet Potato Planks

Servings: 8
Cooking Time: 30 Minutes
Ingredients:
- 5 sweet potatoes, sliced into planks
- 1 tablespoon olive oil
- 1 teaspoon onion powder
- Salt and pepper to taste

Directions:
1. Set the Traeger wood pellet grill to high.
2. Preheat it for 15 minutes while the lid is closed.
3. Coat the sweet potatoes with oil.
4. Sprinkle with onion powder, salt and pepper.
5. Grill the sweet potatoes for 15 minutes.
6. Tips: Grill for a few more minutes if you want your sweet potatoes crispier.

Smoked Mashed Red Potatoes

Servings: 8
Cooking Time: 30 Minutes
Ingredients:
- 8 large potatoes
- Salt and pepper to taste
- ½ cup heavy cream
- ¼ cup butter

Directions:
1. Fire the Traeger Grill to 1800F. Use desired wood pellets when cooking. Close the lid and preheat for 15 minutes.
2. Slice the potatoes into half and season with salt and pepper to taste. Place on a baking tray.
3. Place the tray with the potatoes on the grill grate and cook for 30 minutes. Be sure to flip the potatoes halfway through the cooking time.
4. Once cooked, remove from the grill and place on a bowl. Add the rest of the ingredients and mash until well-combined.

Nutrition Info:
- InfoCalories per serving: 363 ; Protein: 7.8g; Carbs: 65.2g; Fat: 8.9g Sugar: 3.4g

Salt-crusted Baked Potatoes

Servings: 6
Cooking Time: 40 Minutes
Ingredients:
- 6 russet potatoes, scrubbed and dried
- 3 tablespoons oil
- 1 tablespoons salt
- Butter as needed
- Sour cream as needed

Directions:
1. Fire the Traeger Grill to 4000F. Use desired wood pellets when cooking. Close the lid and preheat for 15 minutes.
2. In a large bowl, coat the potatoes with oil and salt. Place seasoned potatoes on a baking tray.
3. Place the tray with potatoes on the grill grate.
4. Close the lid and grill for 40 minutes.
5. Serve with butter and sour cream.

Nutrition Info:
- InfoCalories per serving: 363; Protein: 8g; Carbs: 66.8g; Fat: 8.6g Sugar: 2.3g

Smoked Eggs

Servings: 12
Cooking Time: 30 Minutes
Ingredients:
- 12 hardboiled eggs, peeled and rinsed

Directions:
1. Supply your smoker with wood pellets and follow the manufacturer's specific start-up procedure. Preheat the grill, with the lid closed, to 120°F.
2. Place the eggs directly on the grill grate and smoke for 30 minutes. They will begin to take on a slight brown sheen.
3. Remove the eggs and refrigerate for at least 30 minutes before serving. Refrigerate any leftovers in an airtight container for 1 or 2 weeks.

Easy Smoked Vegetables

Servings: 6
Cooking Time: 1 ½ Hour
Ingredients:
- 1 cup of pecan wood chips
- 1 ear fresh corn, silk strands removed, and husks, cut corn into 1-inch pieces
- 1 medium yellow squash, 1/2-inch slices
- 1 small red onion, thin wedges
- 1 small green bell pepper, 1-inch strips
- 1 small red bell pepper, 1-inch strips
- 1 small yellow bell pepper, 1-inch strips
- 1 cup mushrooms, halved
- 2 tbsp vegetable oil

- Vegetable seasonings

Directions:
1. Take a large bowl and toss all the vegetables together in it. Sprinkle it with seasoning and coat all the vegetables well with it.
2. Place the wood chips and a bowl of water in the smoker.
3. Preheat the smoker at 100°F or ten minutes.
4. Put the vegetables in a pan and add to the middle rack of the electric smoker.
5. Smoke for thirty minutes until the vegetable becomes tender.
6. When done, serve, and enjoy.

Nutrition Info:
- Calories: 97 Cal Fat: 5 g Carbohydrates: 11 g Protein: 2 g Fiber: 3 g

Roasted Okra

Servings: 4
Cooking Time: 30 Minutes

Ingredients:
- Nonstick cooking spray or butter, for greasing
- 1 pound whole okra
- 2 tablespoons extra-virgin olive oil
- 2 teaspoons seasoned salt
- 2 teaspoons freshly ground black pepper

Directions:
1. Supply your smoker with wood pellets and follow the manufacturer's specific start-up procedure. Preheat, with the lid closed, to 400°F. Alternatively, preheat your oven to 400°F.
2. Line a shallow rimmed baking pan with aluminum foil and coat with cooking spray.
3. Arrange the okra on the pan in a single layer. Drizzle with the olive oil, turning to coat. Season on all sides with the salt and pepper.
4. Place the baking pan on the grill grate, close the lid, and smoke for 30 minutes, or until crisp and slightly charred. Alternatively, roast in the oven for 30 minutes.
5. Serve hot.

Coconut Bacon

Servings: 2
Cooking Time: 30 Minutes

Ingredients:
- 3 1/2 cups flaked coconut
- 1 tbsp pure maple syrup
- 1 tbsp water
- 2 tbsp liquid smoke
- 1 tbsp soy sauce
- 1 tsp smoked paprika (optional)

Directions:
1. Preheat the smoker at 325°F.
2. Take a large mixing bowl and combine liquid smoke, maple syrup, soy sauce, and water.
3. Pour flaked coconut over the mixture. Add it to a cooking sheet.
4. Place in the middle rack of the smoker.
5. Smoke it for 30 minutes and every 7-8 minutes, keep flipping the sides.
6. Serve and enjoy.

Nutrition Info:
- Calories: 1244 Cal Fat: 100 g Carbohydrates: 70 g Protein: 16 g Fiber: 2 g

Garlic And Herb Smoke Potato

Servings: 6
Cooking Time: 2 Hours

Ingredients:
- 1.5 pounds bag of Gemstone Potatoes
- 1/4 cup Parmesan, fresh grated
- For the Marinade
- 2 tbsp olive oil
- 6 garlic cloves, freshly chopped
- 1/2 tsp dried oregano
- 1/2 tsp dried basil
- 1/2 tsp dried dill
- 1/2 tsp salt
- 1/2 tsp dried Italian seasoning
- 1/4 tsp ground pepper

Directions:
1. Preheat the smoker to 225°F.
2. Wash the potatoes thoroughly and add them to a sealable plastic bag.
3. Add garlic cloves, basil, salt, Italian seasoning, dill, oregano, and olive oil to the zip lock bag. Shake.
4. Place in the fridge for 2 hours to marinate.
5. Next, take an Aluminum foil and put 2 tbsp of water along with the coated potatoes. Fold the foil so that the potatoes are sealed in
6. Place in the preheated smoker.
7. Smoke for 2 hours
8. Remove the foil and pour the potatoes into a bowl.
9. Serve with grated Parmesan cheese.

Nutrition Info:
- Calories: 146 Cal Fat: 6 g Carbohydrates: 19 g Protein: 4 g Fiber: 2.1 g

Corn Chowder

Servings: 3 To 4
Cooking Time: 35 Minutes

Ingredients:
- 1/4 tsp. Cajun Seasoning
- 2tbsp. Butter, unsalted
- 2tbsp. Parsley, fresh and minced
- 1Onion quartered
- 1/2 cup Celery Stalks, diced
- 1/4 tsp. Sea Salt
- 2Garlic cloves
- 1/4 cup Heavy Cream
- 1/2 cup Carrot, diced
- 3cups Corn Kernels, frozen
- 2-1/2 cups Vegetable Broth
- 1/4 tsp. Black Pepper, grounded
- 1Red Potato, chopped

Directions:
1. To start with, keep butter, onion, and garlic in the pitcher of the blender.
2. After that, press the 'saute' button.
3. Next, stir in all the remaining ingredients to the pitcher and select the 'hearty soup' button.
4. Once the program gets over, transfer the soup to serving bowls and serve immediately.
5. Garnish with parsley leaves.

Nutrition Info:
- Calories: 499 Fat: 40 g Total Carbs: 32 g Fiber: 2.5 g Sugar: 7.3 g Protein: 6.8 g Cholesterol: 120 mg

Grilled Asparagus With Wild Mushrooms

Servings: 4
Cooking Time: 10 Minutes

Ingredients:
- 2 bunches fresh asparagus, trimmed
- 4 cups wild mushrooms, sliced
- 1 large shallots, sliced into rings
- Extra virgin oil as needed
- 2 tablespoons butter, melted

Directions:
1. Fire the Traeger Grill to 5000F. Use desired wood pellets when cooking. Close the lid and preheat for 15 minutes.
2. Place the asparagus, mushrooms, and shallots on a baking tray. Drizzle with oil and butter and season with salt and pepper to taste.
3. Place on a baking tray and cook for 10 minutes. Make sure to give the asparagus a good stir halfway through the cooking time for even browning.

Nutrition Info:
- InfoCalories per serving: 218; Protein: 15.2g; Carbs: 26.6 g; Fat: 10g Sugar: 12.9g

Smokey Roasted Cauliflower

Servings: 4 To 6
Cooking Time: 1 Hour 20 Minutes

Ingredients:
- 1head cauliflower
- cup parmesan cheese
- Spice Ingredients:
- 1tbsp olive oil
- 2cloves garlic, chopped
- 1tsp kosher salt
- 1tsp smoked paprika

Directions:
1. Preheat pellet grill to 180°F. If applicable, set smoke setting to high.
2. Cut cauliflower into bite-size flowerets and place in a grill basket. Place basket on the grill grate and smoke for an hour.
3. Mix spice Ingredients In a small bowl while the cauliflower is smoking. Remove cauliflower from the grill after an hour and let cool.
4. Change grill temperature to 425°F. After the cauliflower has cooled, put cauliflower in a resealable bag, and pour marinade in the bag. Toss to combine in the bag.
5. Place cauliflower back in a grill basket and return to grill. Roast in the grill basket for 10-12 minutes or until the outsides begin to get crispy and golden brown.
6. Remove from grill and transfer to a serving dish. Sprinkle parmesan cheese over the cauliflower and rest for a few minutes so the cheese can melt. Serve and enjoy!

Nutrition Info:
- Calories: 70 Fat: 35 g Cholesterol: 0 Carbohydrate: 7 g Fiber: 3 g Sugar: 3 g Protein: 3 g

Smoked Stuffed Mushrooms

Servings: 12
Cooking Time: 1 Hour 15 Minutes
Ingredients:
- 12-16 white mushrooms, large, cleaned and stems removed
- 1/2 cup parmesan cheese
- 1/2 cup bread crumbs, Italian
- 2 minced garlic cloves
- 2 tbsp fresh parsley, chopped
- 1/4 -1/3 cup olive oil
- Salt and pepper to taste

Directions:
1. Preheat your Traeger 375oF.
2. Remove mushroom very bottom stem then dice the rest into small pieces.
3. Combine mushroom stems, parmesan cheese, bread crumbs, garlic, parsley, 3 tbsp oil, pepper, and salt in a bowl, large. Combine until moist.
4. Layer mushrooms in a pan, disposable, then fill them with the mixture until heaping. Drizzle with more oil.
5. Place the pan on the Traeger grill.
6. Smoke for about 1 hour 20 minutes until filling browns and mushrooms become tender.
7. Remove from Traeger and serve.
8. Enjoy!

Nutrition Info:
- InfoCalories 74, Total fat 6.1g, Saturated fat 1g, Total carbs 4.1g, Net carbs 3.7g, Protein 1.6g, Sugars 0.6g, Fiber 0.4g, Sodium 57mg, Potassium 72mg

Crispy Maple Bacon Brussels Sprouts

Servings: 6
Cooking Time: 1 Hour
Ingredients:
- 1lb brussels sprouts, trimmed and quartered
- 6 slices thick-cut bacon
- 3tbsp maple syrup
- 1tsp olive oil
- 1/2 tsp kosher salt
- 1/2 tsp ground black pepper

Directions:
1. Preheat pellet grill to 425°F.
2. Cut bacon into 1/2 inch thick slices.
3. Place brussels sprouts in a single layer in the cast iron skillet. Drizzle with olive oil and maple syrup, then toss to coat. Sprinkle bacon slices on top then season with kosher salt and black pepper.
4. Place skillet in the pellet grill and roast for about 40 to 45 minutes, or until the brussels sprouts are caramelized and brown.
5. Remove skillet from grill and allow brussels sprouts to cool for about 5 to 10 minutes. Serve and enjoy!

Nutrition Info:
- Calories: 175.3 Fat: 12.1 g Cholesterol: 6.6 mg Carbohydrate: 13.6 g Fiber: 2.9 g Sugar: 7.6 g Protein: 4.8 g

Roasted Hasselback Potatoes

Servings: 6
Cooking Time: 30 Minutes
Ingredients:
- 6 large russet potatoes
- 1-pound bacon
- ½ cup butter
- Salt to taste
- 1 cup cheddar cheese
- 3 whole scallions, chopped

Directions:
1. Fire the Traeger Grill to 3500F. Use desired wood pellets when cooking. Close the lid and preheat for 15 minutes.
2. Place two wooden spoons on either side of the potato and slice the potato into thin strips without completely cutting through the potato.
3. Chop the bacon into small pieces and place in between the cracks or slices of the potatoes.
4. Place potatoes in a cast iron skillet. Top the potatoes with butter, salt, and cheddar cheese.
5. Place the skillet on the grill grate and cook for 30 minutes. Make sure to baste the potatoes with melted cheese 10 minutes before the cooking time ends.

Nutrition Info:
- InfoCalories per serving: 662; Protein: 16.1g; Carbs: 71.5g; Fat: 38g Sugar: 2.3g

Broccoli-cauliflower Salad

Servings: 4
Cooking Time: 25 Minutes
Ingredients:
- 1½ cups mayonnaise
- ½ cup sour cream
- ¼ cup sugar
- 1 bunch broccoli, cut into small pieces
- 1 head cauliflower, cut into small pieces
- 1 small red onion, chopped
- 6 slices bacon, cooked and crumbled (precooked bacon works well)
- 1 cup shredded Cheddar cheese

Directions:
1. In a small bowl, whisk together the mayonnaise, sour cream, and sugar to make a dressing.
2. In a large bowl, combine the broccoli, cauliflower, onion, bacon, and Cheddar cheese.
3. Pour the dressing over the vegetable mixture and toss well to coat.
4. Serve the salad chilled.

Garlic And Rosemary Potato Wedges

Servings: 4
Cooking Time: 1 Hour 30 Minutes
Ingredients:
- 4-6 large russet potatoes, cut into wedges
- ¼ cup olive oil
- 2 garlic cloves, minced
- 2 tablespoons rosemary leaves, chopped
- 2 teaspoon salt
- 1 teaspoon fresh ground black pepper
- 1 teaspoon sugar
- 1 teaspoon onion powder

Directions:
1. Preheat your smoker to 250 degrees Fahrenheit using maple wood
2. Take a large bowl and add potatoes and olive oil
3. Toss well
4. Take another small bowl and stir garlic, salt, rosemary, pepper, sugar, onion powder
5. Sprinkle the mix on all sides of the potato wedge
6. Transfer the seasoned wedge to your smoker rack and smoke for 1 and a ½ hours
7. Serve and enjoy!

Nutrition Info:
- Calories: 291 Fats: 10g Carbs: 46g Fiber: 2g

Traeger Fries With Chipotle Ketchup

Servings: 6
Cooking Time: 10 Minutes
Ingredients:
- 6 Yukon Gold potatoes, scrubbed and cut into thick strips
- 1 tablespoon Traeger Beef Rub
- 1 tablespoon extra-virgin olive oil
- 1 teaspoon onion powder
- 1 teaspoon garlic powder
- ½ cup chipotle peppers, chopped
- 1 cup ketchup
- 1 tablespoon sugar
- 1 tablespoon cumin
- 1 tablespoon chili powder
- 1 whole lime
- 2 tablespoons butter

Directions:
1. Place the potatoes in a bowl and stir in the Traeger Beef Rub, olive oil, onion powder, and garlic powder. Toss to coat the potatoes with the spices.
2. Fire the Traeger Grill to 500ºF. Use desired wood pellets when cooking. Close the lid and preheat for 15 minutes.
3. Place the potatoes on a baking sheet lined with foil.
4. Place on the grill grate and cook for 10 minutes.
5. Meanwhile, place the rest of the ingredients in a small bowl and mix until well-combined.
6. Serve the fries with the chipotle ketchup sauce.

Nutrition Info:
- InfoCalories per serving: 387 ; Protein: 8.6g; Carbs: 79.3g; Fat: 5.6g Sugar: 13.7g

Grilled Corn On The Cob With Parmesan And Garlic

Servings: 6
Cooking Time: 30 Minutes
Ingredients:
- 4 tablespoons butter, melted
- 2 cloves of garlic, minced
- Salt and pepper to taste
- 8 corns, unhusked
- ½ cup parmesan cheese, grated
- 1 tablespoon parsley chopped

Directions:

1. Fire the Traeger Grill to 4500F. Use desired wood pellets when cooking. Close the lid and preheat for 15 minutes.
2. Place butter, garlic, salt, and pepper in a bowl and mix until well combined.
3. Peel the corn husk but do not detach the husk from the corn. Remove the silk. Brush the corn with the garlic butter mixture and close the husks.
4. Place the corn on the grill grate and cook for 30 minutes turning the corn every 5 minutes for even cooking.

Nutrition Info:
- InfoCalories per serving: 272; Protein: 8.8g; Carbs: 38.5g; Fat: 12.3g Sugar: 6.6g

Scampi Spaghetti Squash

Servings: 4
Cooking Time: 40 Minutes
Ingredients:
- 1 spaghetti squash
- 2 tablespoons extra-virgin olive oil
- 1 teaspoon salt
- 1 teaspoon freshly ground black pepper
- 2 teaspoons garlic powder
- 4 tablespoons (½ stick) unsalted butter
- ½ cup white wine
- 1 tablespoon minced garlic
- 2 teaspoons chopped fresh parsley
- 1 teaspoon red pepper flakes
- ½ teaspoon salt
- ½ teaspoon freshly ground black pepper

Directions:
1. For the squash:
2. Supply your smoker with wood pellets and follow the manufacturer's specific start-up procedure. Preheat, with the lid closed, to 375°F.
3. Cut off both ends of the squash, then cut it in half lengthwise. Scoop out and discard the seeds.
4. Rub the squash flesh well with the olive oil and sprinkle on the salt, pepper, and garlic powder.
5. Place the squash cut-side up on the grill grate, close the lid, and smoke for 40 minutes, or until tender
6. For the sauce:
7. On the stove top, in a medium saucepan over medium heat, combine the butter, white wine, minced garlic, parsley, red pepper flakes, salt, and pepper, and cook for about 5 minutes, or until heated through. Reduce the heat to low and keep the sauce warm.
8. Remove the squash from the grill and let cool slightly before shredding the flesh with a fork; discard the skin.
9. Stir the shredded squash into the garlic-wine butter sauce and serve immediately.

Sweet Jalapeño Cornbread

Servings: 12
Cooking Time: 50 Minutes
Ingredients:
- 2/3 cup margarine, softened
- 2/3 cup white sugar
- 2cups cornmeal
- 1.1/3 cups all-purpose flour
- 4tsp baking powder
- 1tsp kosher salt
- 3eggs
- 1.2/3 cups milk
- 1cup jalapeños, deseeded and chopped
- Butter, to line baking dish

Directions:
1. Preheat pellet grill to 400°F.
2. Beat margarine and sugar together in a medium-sized bowl until smooth.
3. In another bowl, combine cornmeal, flour, baking powder, and salt.
4. In a third bowl, combine and whisk eggs and milk.
5. Pour 1/3 of the milk mixture and 1/3 of the flour mixture into the margarine mixture at a time, whisking just until mixed after each pour.
6. Once thoroughly combined, stir in chopped jalapeño.
7. Lightly butter the bottom of the baking dish. Pour cornbread mixture evenly into the baking dish.
8. Place dish on grill grates and close the lid. Cook for about 23-25 minutes, or until thoroughly cooked. The way to test is by inserting a toothpick into the center of the cornbread - it should come out clean once removed.
9. Remove dish from the grill and allow to rest for 10 minutes before slicing and serving.

Nutrition Info:
- Calories: 160 Fat: 6 g Cholesterol: 15 mg Carbohydrate: 25 g Fiber: 10 g Sugar: 0.5 g Protein: 3 g

Wood Pellet Smoked Asparagus

Servings: 4
Cooking Time: 1 Hour
Ingredients:
- 1 bunch fresh asparagus, ends cut
- 2 tbsp olive oil
- Salt and pepper to taste

Directions:
1. Fire up your wood pellet smoker to 230°F
2. Place the asparagus in a mixing bowl and drizzle with olive oil. Season with salt and pepper.
3. Place the asparagus in a tinfoil sheet and fold the sides such that you create a basket.
4. Smoke the asparagus for 1 hour or until soft turning after half an hour.
5. Remove from the grill and serve. Enjoy.

Nutrition Info:
- InfoCalories 43, Total fat 2g, Saturated fat 0g, Total Carbs 4g, Net Carbs 2g, Protein 3g, Sugar 2g, Fiber 2g, Sodium: 148mg

Vegetable Skewers

Servings: 4
Cooking Time: 20 Minutes
Ingredients:
- 2 cups whole white mushrooms
- 2 large yellow squash, peeled, chopped
- 1 cup chopped pineapple
- 1 cup chopped red pepper
- 1 cup halved strawberries
- 2 large zucchini, chopped
- For the Dressing:
- 2 lemons, juiced
- ½ teaspoon ground black pepper
- 1/2 teaspoon sea salt
- 1 teaspoon red chili powder
- 1 tablespoon maple syrup
- 1 tablespoon orange zest
- 2 tablespoons apple cider vinegar
- 1/4 cup olive oil

Directions:
1. Switch on the Traeger grill, fill the grill hopper with flavored wood pellets, power the grill on by using the control panel, select 'smoke' on the temperature dial, or set the temperature to 450 degrees F and let it preheat for a minimum of 5 minutes.
2. Meanwhile, prepared thread vegetables and fruits on skewers alternately and then brush skewers with oil.
3. When the grill has preheated, open the lid, place vegetable skewers on the grill grate, shut the grill, and smoke for 20 minutes until tender and lightly charred.
4. Meanwhile, prepare the dressing and for this, take a small bowl, place all of its ingredients in it and then whisk until combined.
5. When done, transfer skewers to a dish, top with prepared dressing and then serve.

Nutrition Info:
- InfoCalories: 130 Cal ;Fat: 2 g ;Carbs: 20 g ;Protein: 2 g ;Fiber: 0.3 g

Roasted Parmesan Cheese Broccoli

Servings: 3 To 4
Cooking Time: 45 Minutes
Ingredients:
- 3cups broccoli, stems trimmed
- 1tbsp lemon juice
- 1tbsp olive oil
- 2garlic cloves, minced
- 1/2 tsp kosher salt
- 1/2 tsp ground black pepper
- 1tsp lemon zest
- 1/8 cup parmesan cheese, grated

Directions:
1. Preheat pellet grill to 375°F.
2. Place broccoli in a resealable bag. Add lemon juice, olive oil, garlic cloves, salt, and pepper. Seal the bag and toss to combine. Let the mixture marinate for 30 minutes.
3. Pour broccoli into a grill basket. Place basket on grill grates to roast. Grill broccoli for 14-18 minutes, flipping broccoli halfway through. Grill until tender yet a little crispy on the outside.
4. Remove broccoli from grill and place on a serving dish—zest with lemon and top with grated parmesan cheese. Serve immediately and enjoy!

Nutrition Info:
- Calories: 82.6 Fat: 4.6 g Cholesterol: 1.8 mg Carbohydrate: 8.1 g Fiber: 4.6 g Sugar: 0 Protein: 5.5

Southern Slaw

Servings: 10
Cooking Time: 1 Hour And 10 Minutes
Ingredients:
- 1 head cabbage, shredded
- ¼ cup white vinegar
- ¼ cup sugar
- 1 teaspoon paprika
- ½ teaspoon salt
- ½ teaspoon freshly ground black pepper
- 1 cup heavy (whipping) cream

Directions:
1. Place the shredded cabbage in a large bowl.
2. In a small bowl, combine the vinegar, sugar, paprika, salt, and pepper.
3. Pour the vinegar mixture over the cabbage and mix well.
4. Fold in the heavy cream and refrigerate for at least 1 hour before serving.

Feisty Roasted Cauliflower

Servings: 4
Cooking Time: 10 Minutes
Ingredients:
- 1 cauliflower head, cut into florets
- 1 tablespoon oil
- 1 cup parmesan, grated
- 2 garlic cloves, crushed
- ½ teaspoon pepper
- ½ teaspoon salt
- ¼ teaspoon paprika

Directions:
1. Preheat your Smoker to 180 degrees F
2. Transfer florets to smoker and smoke for 1 hour
3. Take a bowl and add all ingredients except cheese
4. Once smoking is done, remove florets
5. Increase temperature to 450 degrees F, brush florets with the brush and transfer to grill
6. Smoke for 10 minutes more
7. Sprinkle cheese on top and let them sit (Lid closed) until cheese melts
8. Serve and enjoy!

Nutrition Info:
- Calories: 45 Fats: 2g Carbs: 7g Fiber: 1g

Other Favorite Recipes

Braised Pork Carnitas

Servings: 6
Cooking Time: 3 Hours
Ingredients:
- 3 lb. pork shoulder, sliced into cubes
- 2 tablespoons pulled pork dry rub
- 1 cup chicken broth
- 2 tablespoons olive oil
- Corn tortillas
- 3 jalapeno pepper, minced
- Cilantro, chopped
- Fresh cheese, crumbled
- Red onion, sliced

Directions:
1. Turn on your wood pellet grill.
2. Set it to 300 degrees F.
3. Sprinkle the pork cubes with the dry rub.
4. Place in a Dutch oven.
5. Pour in the chicken broth.
6. Add the Dutch oven on top of the grill.
7. Open the sear slide.
8. Bring to a boil.
9. Cover the Dutch oven and seal the sear slide.
10. Simmer for 2 hours and 30 minutes.
11. Uncover and open the sear slide.
12. Bring to a boil.
13. Take the Dutch oven off the grill. Set aside.
14. Pour the olive oil into a pan over medium heat.
15. Fry the pork for 10 minutes.
16. Top the corn tortillas with the pork cubes and the rest of the ingredients.

Nutrition Info:
- Calories: 250 Fat: 13 g Cholesterol: 40 mg Carbohydrates: 18 g Fiber: 2 g Sugars: 4 g Protein: 13 g

White Bbq Sauce

Servings: 3 Cups
Cooking Time: 10 Minutes
Ingredients:
- 1 ½ cups mayonnaise
- ⅓ cup plus 2 tablespoons apple-cider vinegar
- 2 tablespoons lemon juice
- 2 tablespoons prepared horseradish
- 1 teaspoon mustard powder
- Kosher salt and freshly ground black pepper, to taste
- cayenne pepper, to taste

Directions:
1. Combine the mayonnaise, vinegar, lemon juice, horseradish and mustard powder in a medium nonreactive bowl, and whisk until smooth.
2. Add salt, pepper and cayenne to taste. Brush on grilled or roasted chicken during the end of the cooking process, and pass remaining sauce at the table.

Grilled Tuna Burger With Ginger Mayonnaise

Servings: 4
Cooking Time: 20 Minutes
Ingredients:
- 1 Tbsp of sesame oil, optional
- 4 Tbsp of ginger, optional
- 4 hamburger buns
- Black pepper, freshly ground
- 2 Tbsp and 1 tsp of soy sauce
- 4 of 5 ounces of tuna steak
- Natural oil
- 1/2 cup of mayonnaise

Directions:
1. Set the grill for direct cooking at 300°F. Use maple pellets for a robust woody taste.
2. Rub soy sauce on the tuna steak and season with pepper.
3. In another bowl, prepare a rub by mixing the ginger, mayonnaise, 1 tsp of soy sauce, and sesame oil.
4. With a brush, apply the rub on the tuna steak then grill for 10 minutes before flipping. Grill the other side for another 10 minutes.
5. Serve immediately with fish between buns. Add mayonnaise and ginger as layers.

Nutrition Info:
- InfoPer Serving: Calories: 220kcal, Protein: 21.5g, Fat: 16g, Carbs: 23g.

Smoked Soy Sauce

Servings: 1
Cooking Time: 1 Hour
Ingredients:
- 100ml soy sauce
- Bradley flavor bisquettes cherry

Directions:
1. Put soy sauce in a heat-resistant bowl, large-mouth.
2. Smoke in a smoker at 158-176oF for about 1 hour. Stir a few times.
3. Remove and cool then put in a bottle. Let sit for one day.
4. Serve and enjoy!

Nutrition Info:
- InfoCalories 110, Total fat 0g, Saturated fat 0g, Total carbs 25g, Net carbs 25g, Protein 2g, Sugar 25g, Fiber 0g, Sodium: 270mg

Grilled Pineapple With Chocolate Sauce

Servings: 6 To 8
Cooking Time: 25 Minutes
Ingredients:
- 1pineapple
- 8 oz bittersweet chocolate chips
- 1/2 cup spiced rum
- 1/2 cup whipping cream
- 2tbsp light brown sugar

Directions:
1. Preheat pellet grill to 400°F.
2. De-skin the pineapple and slice pineapple into 1 in cubes.
3. In a saucepan, combine chocolate chips. When chips begin to melt, add rum to the saucepan. Continue to stir until combined, then add a splash of the pineapple's juice.
4. Add in whipping cream and continue to stir the mixture. Once the sauce is smooth and thickening, lower heat to simmer to keep warm.
5. Thread pineapple cubes onto skewers. Sprinkle skewers with brown sugar.
6. Place skewers on the grill grate. Grill for about 5 minutes per side, or until grill marks begin to develop.
7. Remove skewers from grill and allow to rest on a plate for about 5 minutes. Serve alongside warm chocolate sauce for dipping.

Nutrition Info:
- Calories: 112.6 Fat: 0.5 g Cholesterol: 0 Carbohydrate: 28.8 g Fiber: 1.6 g Sugar: 0.1 g Protein: 0.4 g

Sweet And Spicy Cinnamon Rub

Servings: 1/4 Cup
Cooking Time: 5 Minutes
Ingredients:
- 2 tablespoons light brown sugar
- 1 teaspoon coarse kosher salt
- 1 teaspoon garlic powder
- 1 teaspoon onion powder
- 1 teaspoon sweet paprika
- ½ teaspoon freshly ground black pepper
- ½ teaspoon cayenne pepper
- ½ teaspoon dried oregano leaves
- ½ teaspoon ground ginger
- ½ teaspoon ground cumin
- ¼ teaspoon smoked paprika
- ¼ teaspoon ground cinnamon
- ¼ teaspoon ground coriander
- ¼ teaspoon chili powder

Directions:
1. In a small airtight container or zip-top bag, combine the brown sugar, salt, garlic powder, onion powder, sweet paprika, black pepper, cayenne, oregano, ginger, cumin, smoked paprika, cinnamon, coriander, and chili powder.
2. Close the container and shake to mix. Unused rub will keep in an airtight container for months.

Grilled Clam With Lemon-cayenne Butter

Servings: 2
Cooking Time: 15 Minutes
Ingredients:
- 2 tsp of lemon juice, preferably fresh
- Large pinch of salt (kosher)
- 2 dozen of littleneck clams
- 1 large clove of garlic
- Chives, freshly chopped
- 4 Tbsp of unsalted butter, already melted
- Pinch of cayenne pepper

Directions:
1. Set the grill for direct cooking at 300°F. Use alder wood pellets for mild taste and aroma.
2. Mash garlic and salt with a mortar and pestle to form a paste.
3. Scoop the paste into a small bowl and add cayenne pepper, butter, and lemon.
4. Grill clam over the preheated cooking grid for 5 minutes. When clam is ready, it will open. Carefully transfer opened clam to the bowl containing lemon-cayenne butter. Do not spill the clam-juice when transporting.
5. Gently mix the clam and butter until it is well-combined.
6. Serve immediately with chives.

Nutrition Info:
- InfoPer Serving: Calories: 148kcal, Carbs: 31g, Fat: 19g, Protein: 25g

Smoked Tuna

Servings: 6
Cooking Time: 3 Hours
Ingredients:
- 2 cups water
- 1 cup brown sugar
- 1 cup salt
- 1 tablespoon lemon zest
- 6 tuna fillets

Directions:
1. Mix water, brown sugar, salt and lemon zest in a bowl.
2. Coat the tuna fillets with the mixture.
3. Refrigerate for 6 hours.
4. Rinse the tuna and pat dry with paper towels.
5. Preheat the Traeger wood pellet grill to 180 degrees F for 15 minutes while the lid is closed.
6. Smoke the tuna for 3 hours.
7. Tips: You can also soak tuna in the brine for 24 hours.

Rosemary Chicken Glazed With Balsamic With Bacon Pearl Onions

Servings: 4
Cooking Time: 50 Minutes
Ingredients:
- 2 Tbsp of unsalted butter
- 1 Tbsp of brown sugar, light
- 1 4pounds chicken
- 2 Tbsp of balsamic vinegar
- 1/4 pound of bacon
- 1 Tbsp of thyme, fresh
- 3/4 of pearl onions, frozen

Directions:
1. Rub black pepper and salt all over the chicken, including cavities. Put the chicken on a rack and keep inside the refrigerator for 24 hours.
2. Preheat the grill for direct cooking at 420°F (High). Use mesquite wood pellets for a distinctive, strong woody taste.
3. Mix the vinegar, butter, brown sugar, and thyme in a bowl, then rub it on the chicken with a brush.
4. Put the pearl onion, balsamic mixture, and bacon under the chicken in the roasting pan.

5. Roast the chicken on the preheated grill for 35 minutes. Flip the chicken with a tong and roast for another 15 minutes, or until the internal temperature of the thigh reads 165-1700F.
6. Rest for 5 minutes, then serve the chicken with the bacon and the onion.

Nutrition Info:
- InfoPer Serving: Calories: 390kcal, Protein: 39g, Fat: 48g, Carbs: 53.

Succulent Lamb Chops

Servings: 4 To 6
Cooking Time: 10 To 20 Minutes

Ingredients:
- ½ cup rice wine vinegar
- 1 teaspoon liquid smoke
- 2 tablespoons extra-virgin olive oil
- 2 tablespoons dried minced onion
- 1 tablespoon chopped fresh mint
- 8 (4-ounce) lamb chops
- ½ cup hot pepper jelly
- 1 tablespoon Sriracha
- 1 teaspoon salt
- 1 teaspoon freshly ground black pepper

Directions:
1. In a small bowl, whisk together the rice wine vinegar, liquid smoke, olive oil, minced onion, and mint. Place the lamb chops in an aluminum roasting pan. Pour the marinade over the meat, turning to coat thoroughly. Cover with plastic wrap and marinate in the refrigerator for 2 hours.
2. Supply your smoker with wood pellets and follow the manufacturer's specific start-up procedure. Preheat, with the lid closed, to 165°F, or the "Smoke" setting.
3. On the stove top, in a small saucepan over low heat, combine the hot pepper jelly and Sriracha and keep warm.
4. When ready to cook the chops, remove them from the marinade and pat dry. Discard the marinade.
5. Season the chops with the salt and pepper, then place them directly on the grill grate, close the lid, and smoke for 5 minutes to "breathe" some smoke into them.
6. Remove the chops from the grill. Increase the pellet cooker temperature to 450°F, or the "High" setting. Once the grill is up to temperature, place the chops on the grill and sear, cooking for 2 minutes per side to achieve medium-rare chops. A meat thermometer inserted in the thickest part of the meat should read 145°F. Continue grilling, if necessary, to your desired doneness.
7. Serve the chops with the warm Sriracha pepper jelly on the side.

Smoking Burgers

Servings: 8
Cooking Time: 4o Minutes

Ingredients:
- For the topping:
- 3 apples, peeled and cut into slices
- 75g blueberries
- 25g salted butter
- 2 tablespoons maple syrup
- For the cake:
- 75g butter, cut into cubes
- 75g organic virgin coconut oil, cut into cubes
- 100g cane sugar
- 2 large free-range eggs, beaten
- 75g buckwheat flour
- 75g ground almonds
- ½ teaspoon bicarbonate of soda
- 1 teaspoon baking powder
- 1 teaspoon cinnamon

Directions:
1. Preheat oven to 180°C. Caramelize the apples.
2. Add the blueberries last. Set aside. Place the sugar, butter and coconut oil into a mixing bowl and cream until pale and fluffy.
3. Gradually add the beaten eggs, adding a bit of flour if the mixture begins to curdle. Continue to beat the mixture until fluffy. Fold in the remaining flour, ground almonds, baking powder and cinnamon.
4. Transfer the apple and blueberry mixture into the bottom of a greased Bundt cake mold, leveling well with the back of a spoon. Then pour the cake mixture over the top. Bake for about 40 minutes or until a skewer comes out clean. Leave to cool. Delicious served with Greek yogurt.

Nutrition Info:
- Calories: 275 Cal Fat: 10 g Carbohydrates: 31 g Protein: 14 g Fiber: 4 g

Ginger And Chili Grilled Shrimp

Servings: 6
Cooking Time: 1 Hour 15 Minutes

Ingredients:
- 1 tsp of salt, kosher
- 2 mangos, riped, peeled, and chopped
- 1 Tbsp of fresh ginger, grated
- 2 cloves of garlic, crushed
- 1-1/4 pound of jumbo shrimp, deveined and peeled.
- 2 jalapenos, chopped
- 1/2 cup of buttermilk, low-fat

- 1/2 tsp of black pepper, ground
- 1 lime, small and also cut into wedges (6)

Directions:
1. Set the grill for direct cooking at 150°F. Use hickory wood pellets for a robust taste.
2. Pour the ginger into a bowl, add buttermilk, jalapenos, garlic, pepper, and salt. Mix thoroughly.
3. Put shrimps inside the same bowl, and mix well with a wooden spoon. Allow it to marinate in the refrigerator for an hour
4. Arrange 2 mango chops, 3 shrimps on a water-soaked wooden skewer. Do this for the other 5 skewers.
5. Place shrimp skewers on the grates and grill for 10 minutes, or until the shrimps turn opaque. Serve immediately with the lime wedge

Nutrition Info:
- InfoPer Serving: Calories: 80kcal, Protein: 20g, Fat:1.3g, Carb: 1.2g

Twice Grilled Potatoes

Servings: 6
Cooking Time: 4 Hours
Ingredients:
- 6 russet potatoes
- 2 tbsp. olive oil
- Salt, to taste
- 8 cooked bacon slices, crumbled
- ½ C. heavy whipping cream
- 4 oz. cream cheese, softened
- 4 tbsp. butter, softened
- 4 jalapeño peppers, seeded and chopped
- 1 tsp. seasoned salt
- 2 C. Monterrey Jack cheese, grated and divided

Directions:
1. Set the temperature of Traeger Grill to 225 degrees F and preheat with closed lid for 15 minutes.
2. With paper towels, pat dry the washed potatoes completely.
3. Coat the potatoes with olive oil sprinkle with some salt.
4. Arrange potatoes onto the grill and cook for about 3-3½ hours.
5. Remove the potatoes from grill and cut them in half lengthwise.
6. With a large spoon carefully, scoop out the potato flesh from skins, leaving a little potato layer.
7. In a large bowl, add potato flesh and mash it slightly.
8. Add bacon, cream, cream cheese, butter, jalapeno, seasoned salt and 1 C. of Monterrey Jack cheese and gently, stir to combine.
9. Stuff the potato skins with bacon mixture and top with remaining Monterrey Jack cheese.
10. Arrange the stuffed potatoes onto a baking sheet.
11. Place the baking sheet in grill and cook for about 30 minutes.
12. Serve hot.

Nutrition Info:
- Calories per serving: 539; Carbohydrates: 35.7g; Protein: 17.6g; Fat: 37g; Sugar: 2.8g; Sodium: 1355mg; Fiber: 5.5g

Cornish Game Hens

Servings: 6
Cooking Time: 1 Hour
Ingredients:
- 4 Cornish game hens, giblets removed
- 4 teaspoons chicken rub
- 4 sprigs of rosemary
- 4 tablespoons butter, unsalted, melted

Directions:
1. Switch on the Traeger grill, fill the grill hopper with mesquite flavored wood pellets, power the grill on by using the control panel, select 'smoke' on the temperature dial, or set the temperature to 375 degrees F and let it preheat for a minimum of 15 minutes.
2. Meanwhile, rinse the hens, pat dry with paper towels, tie the wings by using a butcher's strong, then rub evenly with melted butter, sprinkle with chicken rub and stuff cavity of each hen with a rosemary sprig.
3. When the grill has preheated, open the lid, place hens on the grill grate, shut the grill, and smoke for 1 hour until thoroughly cooked and internal temperature reaches 165 degrees F.
4. When done, transfer hens to a dish, let rest for 5 minutes and then serve.

Nutrition Info:
- InfoCalories: 173 Cal ;Fat: 7.4 g ;Carbs: 1 g ;Protein: 24.1 g ;Fiber: 0.2 g

Smoked Pork Ribs With Fresh Herbs

Servings: 6
Cooking Time: 3 Hours
Ingredients:
- 1/4 cup olive oil
- 1 Tbs garlic minced
- 1 Tbs crushed fennel seeds
- 1 tsp of fresh basil leaves finely chopped
- 1 tsp fresh parsley finely chopped
- 1 tsp fresh rosemary finely chopped
- 1 tsp fresh sage finely chopped

- Salt and ground black pepper to taste
- 3 pounds pork rib roast bone-in

Directions:
1. Combine spices and mix well
2. Coat chop with mixture
3. Start the pellet grill Set temperature to 225 °F and preheat, lid closed, for 10 to 15 minutes. Smoke the ribs for 3 hours. Place the ribs to you preferred container and serve while it is hot

Nutrition Info:
- Calories: 459.2 Cal Fat: 31.3 g   Carbohydrates: 0.6 g Protein: 41 g Fiber: 0.03 g

Cajun Rub

Servings: 3
Cooking Time: 5 Minutes

Ingredients:
- 1 teaspoon freshly ground black pepper
- 1 teaspoon onion powder
- 1 teaspoon coarse kosher salt
- 1 teaspoon garlic powder
- 1 teaspoon sweet paprika
- ½ teaspoon cayenne pepper
- ½ teaspoon red pepper flakes
- ½ teaspoon dried oregano leaves
- ½ teaspoon dried thyme
- ½ teaspoon smoked paprika

Directions:
1. In a small airtight container or zip-top bag, combine the black pepper, onion powder, salt, garlic powder, sweet paprika, cayenne, red pepper flakes, oregano, thyme, and smoked paprika.
2. Close the container and shake to mix. Unused rub will keep in an airtight container for months.

Smoked Cheese Dip

Servings: 8
Cooking Time: 1 Hour And 15 Minutes

Ingredients:
- Ice cubes
- 1 block cheddar cheese
- 8 tablespoons butter
- ½ cup carrots, chopped
- 1 onion, chopped
- 1 cup heavy cream
- 3/4 cup flour
- Hot sauce
- 1 teaspoon Worcestershire sauce

Directions:
1. Preheat your Traeger wood pellet grill to 180 degrees F for 15 minutes while the lid is closed.
2. Add ice cubes to a pan.
3. Place a cooling rack on top.
4. Put the cheese block on the rack.
5. Put this on top of the grill.
6. Smoke for 30 minutes.
7. Transfer the cheese to your freezer.
8. In a pan over medium heat, add the butter and let it melt.
9. Cook the onion and carrots for 15 minutes.
10. Stir in the rest of the ingredients.
11. Reduce heat and simmer for 15 minutes.
12. Take the cheese out of the freezer and shred.
13. Put the shredded cheese into the mixture.
14. Stir while cooking until cheese has melted.

Nutrition Info:
- Calories: 1230 Fats: 77 g Cholesterol: 145 mg Carbohydrates: 104 g Fiber: 8 g Sugar: 7g Protein: 40 g

Pizza Bianca

Servings: 2
Cooking Time: 3 Hours

Ingredients:
- 3cups all-purpose or bread flour, plus more as needed
- 2teaspoons instant yeast
- 2teaspoons kosher or coarse sea salt, plus more for sprinkling
- 2tablespoons good-quality olive oil, plus more for drizzling
- 1tablespoon or more chopped fresh rosemary

Directions:
1. Whisk the flour, yeast, and salt together in a large bowl. Add the oil and 1 cup water and mix with a heavy spoon. Continue to add water, 1 tablespoon at a time, until the dough forms a ball and is slightly sticky to the touch. In the unlikely event that the mixture gets too sticky, add flour 1 tablespoon at a time until you have the right consistency.
2. Lightly flour a work surface and turn out the dough onto it. Knead by hand for a minute until smooth, then form into a round ball. Put the dough in a bowl and cover with plastic wrap; let rise in a warm spot until it doubles in size, 1 to 2 hours. You can cut this rising time short if you're in a hurry, or you can let the dough rise more slowly, in the refrigerator, for up to 8 hours. You can freeze the dough at this point for up to a month: Wrap it tightly in plastic wrap or put in a zipper bag. Thaw in the refrigerator; bring to room temperature before shaping.
3. To shape, divide the dough into 2 or more pieces; roll each piece into a round ball. Put each ball on a lightly floured work surface, sprinkle lightly with flour, and cover

with plastic wrap or a towel. Let rest until slightly puffed, 25 to 30 minutes.

4. Start the coals or heat a gas grill for medium direct cooking. Make sure the grates are clean.

5. Roll or lightly press each ball into a flat, round disk, lightly flouring the work surface and the dough as necessary to keep it from sticking (use only as much flour as you need). To stretch the dough, push down at the center and outward to the edge, turning the round as you do. Continue pushing down and out and turning the dough until the round is the size you want; if you're making 2 pizzas, aim for rounds 10 to 12 inches in diameter. Sprinkle the tops evenly with the rosemary and a pinch or so coarse salt, then drizzle with olive oil.

6. Put the crusts on the grill directly over the fire. Close the lid and cook until the bottoms firm up and brown and the tops are cooked through, 5 to 10 minutes, depending on how hot the fire is; the top side of the dough will bubble up from the heat underneath but likely won't take on much color. Transfer to a cutting board and use a pizza cutter to slice into wedges or small pieces and serve.

Nutrition Info:
- Calories: 460 Fats: 17 g Cholesterol: 20 mg Carbohydrates: 56 g Fiber: 3 g Sugars: 7 g Proteins: 18 g

Traeger Smoked Italian Meatballs

Servings: 6
Cooking Time: 1 Hour 5 Minutes;
Ingredients:
- 2 lb beef, ground
- 2 slices white bread
- 1/2 cup whole milk
- 1 tbsp salt
- 1/2 tbsp onion powder
- 1/2 tbsp minced garlic
- 2 tbsp Italian seasoning
- 1/4 tbsp black pepper

Directions:
1. In a mixing bowl, mix all the ingredients until well combined using your hands. Turn on your Traeger and set it to smoke then line a baking sheet with parchment paper.
2. Roll golf size meatballs using your hands .and place them on the baking dish. Place the baking dish in the Traeger and smoke for 35 minutes.
3. Increase the Traeger heat to 3250F and cook for 30 more minutes or until the internal temperature reaches 1600F.
4. Serve when hot

Nutrition Info:
- InfoCalories 453, Total fat 27g, Saturated fat 10g, Total carbs 7g, Net carbs 7g Protein 0g, Sugars 2g, Fiber 0g, Sodium 550mg

Hickory Smoked Green Beans

Servings: 10
Cooking Time: 3 Hours
Ingredients:
- 6 cups fresh green beans, halved and ends cut off
- 2 cups chicken broth
- 1 tbsp pepper, ground
- 1/4 tbsp salt
- 2 tbsp apple cider vinegar
- 1/4 cup diced onion
- 6-8 bite-size bacon slices
- Optional: sliced almonds

Directions:
1. Add green beans to a colander then rinse thoroughly. Set aside.
2. Place chicken broth, pepper, salt, and apple cider in a pan, large. Add green beans.
3. Blanch over medium heat for about 3-4 minutes then remove from heat.
4. Transfer the mixture into an aluminum pan, disposable. Make sure all mixture goes into the pan, so do not drain them.
5. Place bacon slices over the beans and place the pan into the wood pellet smoker,
6. Smoke for about 3 hours uncovered.
7. Remove from the smoker and top with almonds slices.
8. Serve immediately.

Nutrition Info:
- Calories: 57 Total Fat: 3 g Saturated Fat: 1 g Total Carbs: 6 g Net Carbs: 4 g Protein: 4 g Sugars: 2 g Fiber: 2 g Sodium: 484 mg

Crusty Artisan Dough Bread

Servings: 6
Cooking Time: 2 Hours
Ingredients:
- 3 cups all-purpose flour
- 1/2 tsp Yeast
- 1-1/2 cups of warm water
- 1-1/2 tsp salt

Directions:
1. In a large bowl, combine all your ingredients and mix until it is sticky and has a shaggy texture. Cover with plastic wrap and allow to rest for 12 hours

2. After 12 hours, set the wood pellet smoker-grill to indirect cooking at 4250 F, using any pellet. Preheat the Dutch oven.
3. Transfer prepared mixture to a dry, floured surface and mold into a ball. Open the Dutch oven and place the dough in the middle—cover and bake for 30 minutes.
4. Remove the lid and bake for an additional 20 minutes.
5. Remove and allow to cool.

Nutrition Info:
- InfoPer Serving: Calories: 462kcal, Carbs: 41g, Fat: 18g, Protein: 5g

Smoked Pork Tenderloin With Mexican Pineapple Sauce

Servings: 6
Cooking Time: 3 Hours And 55 Minutes
Ingredients:
- Pineapple Sauce
- 1 can (11 oz) unsweetened crushed pineapple
- 1 can (11 oz) roasted tomato or tomatillo
- 1/2 cup port wine
- 1/4 cup orange juice
- 1/4 cup packed brown sugar
- 1/4 cup lime juice
- 2 tbsp Worcestershire sauce
- 1 tsp garlic powder
- 1/4 tsp cayenne pepper
- PORK
- 2 pork tenderloin (1 pound each)
- 1 tsp ground cumin
- 1/2 tsp pepper
- 1/4 tsp cayenne pepper
- 2 tbsp lime juice (freshly squeezed)

Directions:
1. Combine cumin, pepper, cayenne pepper and lime juice and rub over tenderloins.
2. Smoke grill for 4-5 minutes. Preheat, lid closed for 10-15 minutes
3. Smoke tenderloin for 2 ½ to 3 hours.
4. Rest for 5 minutes
5. For Sauce:
6. Combine ingredients and boil for 25 minutes
7. Remove from heat and cool.
8. Serve pork slices with pineapple sauce and lime wedges.

Nutrition Info:
- Calories: 277.85 Cal Fat: 3.49 g Carbohydrates: 24.31 g Protein: 32.42 g Fiber: 0.67 g

Grilled Fruit And Cream

Servings: 4
Cooking Time: 10 Minutes
Ingredients:
- 2apricots, halved
- 1nectarine, halved
- 2peaches, halved
- ¼ cup blueberries
- ½ cup raspberries
- 2tablespoons honey
- 1orange, peel
- 2cups cream
- ½ cup balsamic vinegar

Directions:
1. Preheat your smoker to 400 degrees F, lid closed
2. Grill peaches, nectarines, apricots for 4 minutes, each side
3. Place pan on the stove and turn on medium heat
4. Add 2 tablespoons honey, vinegar, orange peel
5. Simmer until medium-thick
6. Add honey and cream in a bowl and whip until it reaches a soft form
7. Place fruits on serving plate and sprinkle berries, drizzle balsamic reduction
8. Serve with cream and enjoy!

Nutrition Info:
- Calories: 230 Fats: 3g Carbs: 35g Fiber: 2g

Smoked Ribs

Servings: 8
Cooking Time: 6 Hours
Ingredients:
- 4 baby back ribs
- 1 cup pork rub
- 1 cup barbecue sauce

Directions:
1. Preheat your grill to 180 degrees F for 15 minutes while the lid is closed.
2. Sprinkle baby back ribs with pork rub.
3. Smoke the ribs for 5 hours.
4. Brush the ribs with barbecue sauce.
5. Wrap the ribs with foil.
6. Put the ribs back to the grill.
7. Increase temperature to 350 degrees F.
8. Cook for 45 minutes to 1 hour.
9. Let rest before slicing and serving.
10. Tips: Trim excess fat from the baby back ribs before cooking.

Grilled Peaches And Cream

Servings: 8
Cooking Time: 8 Minutes
Ingredients:
- 4halved and pitted peaches
- 1tbsp vegetable oil
- 2tbsp clover honey
- 1cup cream cheese, soft with honey and nuts

Directions:
1. Preheat your pellet grill to medium-high heat.
2. Coat the peaches lightly with oil and place on the grill pit side down.
3. Grill for about 5 minutes until nice grill marks on the surfaces.
4. Turn over the peaches then drizzle with honey.
5. Spread and cream cheese dollop where the pit was and grill for additional 2-3 minutes until the filling becomes warm.
6. Serve immediately.

Nutrition Info:
- Calories: 139 Total Fat: 10.2g Saturated Fat: 5g Total Carbs: 11.6g Net Carbs: 11.6g Protein: 1.1g Sugars: 12g Fiber: 0g Sodium: 135mg

Smoked Brats

Servings: 12 To 15
Cooking Time: 1 To 2 Hours
Ingredients:
- 4 (12-ounce) cans of beer
- 2 onions, sliced into rings
- 2 green bell peppers, sliced into rings
- 2 tablespoons unsalted butter, plus more for the rolls
- 2 tablespoons red pepper flakes
- 10 brats, uncooked
- 10 hoagie rolls, split
- Mustard, for serving

Directions:
1. On your kitchen stove top, in a large saucepan over high heat, bring the beer, onions, peppers, butter, and red pepper flakes to a boil.
2. Supply your smoker with wood pellets and follow the manufacturer's specific start-up procedure. Preheat, with the lid closed, to 225°F.
3. Place a disposable pan on one side of grill, and pour the warmed beer mixture into it, creating a "brat tub" (see Tip below).
4. Place the brats on the other side of the grill, directly on the grate, and close the lid and smoke for 1 hour, turning 2 or 3 times.
5. Add the brats to the pan with the onions and peppers, cover tightly with aluminum foil, and continue smoking with the lid closed for 30 minutes to 1 hour, or until a meat thermometer inserted in the brats reads 160°F.
6. Butter the cut sides of the hoagie rolls and toast cut-side down on the grill.
7. Using a slotted spoon, remove the brats, onions, and peppers from the cooking liquid and discard the liquid.
8. Serve the brats on the toasted buns, topped with the onions and peppers and mustard (ketchup optional).

Roasted Ham

Servings: 12
Cooking Time: 6 Hours
Ingredients:
- 2 quarts water
- 1/2 cup quick home meat cure
- 1/2 cup kosher salt
- 3/4 cup brown sugar
- 1 tablespoon pork rub
- 1 teaspoon whole cloves
- 10 lb. fresh ham
- 1 teaspoon whole cloves
- 1/4 cup pure maple syrup
- 2 cup apple juice

Directions:
1. In a large container, pour in the water and add the meat cure, salt, sugar, pork rub and whole cloves.
2. Mix well.
3. Soak the ham in the brine.
4. Cover and refrigerate for 1 day.
5. Rinse ham with water and dry with paper towels.
6. Score the ham with crosshatch pattern.
7. Insert remaining cloves into the ham.
8. Season ham with the pork rub.
9. Add ham to a roasting pan.
10. Smoke the ham in the Traeger wood pellet grill for 2 hours at 180 degrees F.
11. Make the glaze by mixing the maple syrup and apple juice.
12. Brush the ham with this mixture.
13. Increase heat to 300 degrees F.
14. Roast for 4 hours.
15. Tips: You can also inject the brine into the ham.

Savory Applesauce On The Grill

Servings: 2
Cooking Time: 45 Minutes
Ingredients:
- 1½ pounds whole apples
- Salt

Directions:
1. Start the coals or heat a gas grill for medium direct cooking. Make sure the grates are clean.
2. Put the apples on the grill directly over the fire. Close the lid and cook until the fruit feels soft when gently squeezed with tongs, 10 to 20 minutes total, depending on their size. Transfer to a cutting board and let sit until cool enough to touch.
3. Cut the flesh from around the core of each apple; discard the cores. Put the chunks in a blender or food processor and process until smooth, or put them in a bowl and purée with an immersion blender until as chunky or smooth as you like. Add a generous pinch of salt, then taste and adjust the seasoning. Serve or refrigerate in an airtight container for up to 3 days.

Nutrition Info:
- Calories: 15 Fats: 0 g Cholesterol: 0 mg Carbohydrates: 3 g Fiber: 0 g Sugars: 3 g Proteins: 0 g

Thanksgiving Turkey Brine

Servings: 1
Cooking Time: 5 Minutes
Ingredients:
- 2 gallons water
- 2 cups coarse kosher salt
- 2 cups packed light brown sugar

Directions:
1. In a clean 5-gallon bucket, stir together the water, salt, and brown sugar until the salt and sugar dissolve completely.

Smoked Sriracha Sauce

Servings: 2
Cooking Time: 1 Hour
Ingredients:
- 1 lb Fresno chiles, stems pulled off and seeds removed
- 1/2 cup rice vinegar
- 1/2 cup red wine vinegar
- 1 carrot, medium and cut into rounds, 1/4 inch
- 1-1/2 tbsp sugar, dark-brown
- 4 garlic cloves, peeled
- 1 tbsp olive oil
- 1 tbsp kosher salt
- 1/2 cup water

Directions:
1. Smoke chiles in a smoker for about 15 minutes.
2. Bring to boil both vinegars then add carrots, sugar, and garlic. Simmer for about 15 minutes while covered. Cool for 30 minutes.
3. Place the chiles, olive oil, vinegar-vegetable mixture, salt, and 1/4 cup water into a blender.
4. Blend for about 1-2 minutes on high. Add remaining water and blend again. You can add another 1/4 cup water if you want your sauce thinner.
5. Pour the sauce into jars and place in a refrigerator.
6. Serve.

Nutrition Info:
- InfoCalories 147, Total fat 5.23g, Saturated fat 0.7g, Total carbs 21g, Net carbs 18g, Protein 3g, Sugar 13g, Fiber 3g, Sodium: 671mg

Simple Roasted Butternut Squash

Servings: 8
Cooking Time: 25 Minutes
Ingredients:
- 1(2 pounds) butternut squash
- 2garlic cloves (minced)
- 2tablespoon extra olive virgin oil
- 1tsp paprika
- 1tsp oregano
- 1tsp thyme
- Salt and pepper to taste

Directions:
1. Start your grill on smoke mode and leave the grill open for 5 minutes, until fire Preheat the grill to 400°F.
2. Peel the butternut squash.
3. Cut the butternut squash into two (cut lengthwise).
4. Use a spoon to scoop out the seeds.
5. Cut the butternut squash into 1-inch chunks and wash the chunks with water.
6. In a big bowl, combine the butternut squash chunks and other ingredients.
7. Stir until the chunks are coated with the ingredients.
8. Spread the coated chunks on the sheet pan.
9. Place the sheet pan on the grill and bake for 25 minutes.
10. Remove the baked butternut squash from heat and let it sit to cool.
11. Serve.

Nutrition Info:
- Calories: 8 Total Fat: 3.7 g Saturated Fat: 0.5 g Cholesterol: 0 mg Sodium: 331 mg Total Carbohydrate 13.8 g Dietary Fiber 2.6 g Total Sugars: 2.5 g Protein: 1.2 g

Red Wine Beef Stew

Servings: 8
Cooking Time: 3 Hours 30 Minutes
Ingredients:
- 1-1/2 tsp kosher salt
- 4lb chuck roast, cut into 2-inch pieces
- 1 Tsp ground black pepper
- 1/4 cup tomato paste
- 1 Tsp olive oil
- 2 cups dry red wine
- 2 bay leaves
- 4 spring's fresh thyme
- 2 lb carrots, peeled and chopped
- 1lb red potatoes, cut into half
- 4 cups chicken broth
- 3 Tsp all-purpose flour

Directions:
1. Preheat wood pellet smoker-grill to 325ºF, with the lid closed for about 15 minutes
2. Place meat in a bowl and sprinkle in salt, pepper, and flour. Toss together until meat is adequately seasoned.
3. Heat oil in a cast-iron Dutch oven and cook the meat at Medium for about 8 minutes, until brown.
4. Remove meat and place on a plate. Add wine, broth, tomato paste, thyme, bay leaves, and 1/4 of carrots into the Dutch oven and bring to a boil. Transfer meat to Dutch oven and place on the grill grate for direct cooking. Cook meat for about 2 hours.
5. Remove cooked vegetables from Dutch oven and add remaining carrots and potatoes. Cook until meat is fork-tender, about 1 hour.
6. Serve.

Nutrition Info:
- InfoPer Serving: Calories: 402kcal, Carbs: 17.3g, Fat: 15.4g, Protein: 35.5g

Vegan Pesto

Servings: 4
Cooking Time: 10 Minutes
Ingredients:
- 1 cup cilantro leaves
- 1 cup basil leaves
- 1 cup parsley leaves
- ½ cup mint leaves
- ½ cup walnuts
- 1 tsp miso
- 1 tsp lemon juice
- ¼ cup olive oil

Directions:
1. In a blender place all ingredients and blend until smooth
2. Pour sauce in a bowl and serve

Cherry Smoked Strip Steak

Servings: 3
Cooking Time: 70 Minutes
Ingredients:
- Kosher or sea salt
- Olive oil
- Black pepper
- 1-1/2 pound of rib steak

Directions:
1. Preheat the grill for 15 minutes at 225°F. Use maple wood pellets.
2. Season the steak with salt and black pepper.
3. Place the seasoned steak directly on the grates and smoke for 2 hours or until internal temperature reads 160°F.
4. After smoking, rub olive oil on the steak then return it to the grates of the grill. Increase the temperature to 300°F and grill it for another 10 minutes.
5. Serve it hot.

Nutrition Info:
- InfoPer Serving: Calories: 289.5kcal, Protein: 35.9g, Fat: 40.5g, Carbs: 51g

Smoked Brisket Pie

Servings: 8
Cooking Time: 45 Minutes
Ingredients:
- 1 cup Onions, peeled and blanched (pearl)
- ½ cup Peas, frozen
- 1 Garlic clove, minced
- 1 Onion, chopped (yellow)
- 2 Carrots, chopped (peeled)
- 2 tbsp. of Butter
- 2 cups chopped Leftover Brisket
- 1 Egg
- 1 Sheet Pastry dough, frozen
- 2 cups of Beef Stock

Directions:
1. In a pot add the butter. Place it over medium - high heat. Once the butter is melted sauté the carrots for 10 minutes.
2. Add the onion. Cook 7 minutes and then add the garlic. Cook 30 seconds.
3. Add in the brisket, peas, and stock. Let it simmer until thick so that it coats the spoon. In case it doesn't thickens make a slurry from cornstarch and add it. Add black pepper and salt to season

4. Place mixture inside baking dish and cover with dough.
5. In a bowl whisk the egg and brush the pastry.
6. Preheat the grill to 350F with closed lid. Once heated place the baking dish on the grate and let it bake 45 minutes. Set aside.
7. Cool down for 10 minutes and serve. Enjoy!

Nutrition Info:
- Calories: 320 Cal Fat: 16 g   Carbohydrates: 22 g   Protein: 12 g Fiber: 0 g

Fall Season Apple Pie

Servings: 8
Cooking Time: 1 Hour
Ingredients:
- 8 C. apples, peeled, cored and sliced thinly
- ¾ C. sugar
- 1 tbsp. fresh lemon juice
- 1 tsp. ground cinnamon
- ¼ tsp. ground nutmeg
- 2 whole frozen pie crusts, thawed
- ¼ C. apple jelly
- 2 tbsp. apple juice
- 2 tbsp. heavy whipping cream

Directions:
1. Set the temperature of Traeger Grill to 375 degrees F and preheat with closed lid for 15 minutes.
2. In a bowl, add the apples, sugar, lemon juice, flour, cinnamon, and nutmeg and mix well.
3. Roll the pie crust dough into two (11-inch) circles.
4. Arrange 1 dough circle into a 9-inch pie plate.
5. Spread the apple jelly over dough evenly and top with apple mixture.
6. Dampen the edges of dough crust with apple juice.
7. Cover with the top crust, pressing the edges together to seal.
8. Trim the pastry, and flute the edges.
9. With a sparing knife, make several small slits in the top crust.
10. Brush the top of the pie with the cream.
11. Place the pie pan onto the grill and cook for about 50-60 minutes.
12. Remove from the grill and place the pie onto a wire rack to cool slightly.
13. Serve warm.

Nutrition Info:
- Calories per serving: 419; Carbohydrates: 79.5g; Protein: 2.2g; Fat: 12.3g; Sugar: 54.2g; Sodium: 214mg; Fiber: 6.1g

All-purpose Dry Rub

Servings: 2 And ½ Cups
Cooking Time:5 Minutes
Ingredients:
- ½ cup paprika, or 1/3 cup smoked paprika
- ¼ cup kosher salt
- ¼ cup freshly ground black pepper
- ¼ cup brown sugar
- ¼ cup chile powder
- 3 tablespoons ground cumin
- 2 tablespoons ground coriander
- 1 tablespoon cayenne pepper, or to taste

Directions:
1. Combine all ingredients in a bowl and mix well with a fork to break up the sugar and combine the spices. Mixture will keep in an airtight container, out of the light, for a few months.

Coffee-chile Rub

Servings: 1 Cup
Cooking Time:5 Minutes
Ingredients:
- ¼ cup finely ground dark-roast coffee
- ¼ cup ancho chile powder
- ¼ cup dark brown sugar, tightly packed
- 2 tablespoons smoked paprika
- 2 tablespoons kosher salt
- 1 tablespoon ground cumin

Directions:
1. In a small bowl, mix all the ingredients thoroughly, massaging the mixture with your fingers to break down the dark brown sugar into fine crystals.
2. Liberally sprinkle a thin layer of the rub onto the steak, then pat it in with your fingers so it adheres.

Pellet Grill Funeral Potatoes

Servings: 8
Cooking Time: 1 Hour
Ingredients:
- 1, 32 oz, package frozen hash browns
- 1/2 cup cheddar cheese, grated
- 1 can cream of chicken soup
- 1 cup sour cream
- 1 cup Mayonnaise
- 3 cups corn flakes, whole or crushed
- 1/4 cup melted butter

Directions:
1. Preheat your pellet grill to 350oF.

2. Spray a 13 x 9 baking pan, aluminum, using a cooking spray, non-stick.
3. Mix together hash browns, cheddar cheese, chicken soup cream, sour cream, and mayonnaise in a bowl, large.
4. Spoon the mixture into a baking pan gently.
5. Mix corn flakes and melted butter then sprinkle over the casserole.
6. Grill for about 1-1/2 hours until potatoes become tender. If the top browns too much, cover using a foil until potatoes are done.
7. Remove from the grill and serve hot.

Nutrition Info:
- Calories: 403 Total Fat: 37 g Saturated Fat: 12 g Total Carbs: 14 g Net Carbs: 14 g Protein: 4 g Sugars: 2 g Fiber: 0 g Sodium: 620 mg

Bruschetta

Servings: 4
Cooking Time: 25 Minutes

Ingredients:
- 8 1-inch slices baguette or Italian bread
- ¼ cup good-quality olive oil
- 1 or 2 cloves garlic, peeled

Directions:
1. Start the coals or heat a gas grill for medium-high direct cooking. Make sure the grates are clean.
2. Lightly brush both sides of the bread slices with the oil. Put them on the grill directly over the fire. Close the lid and toast, turning once, until the bread develops grill marks, 1 to 3 minutes per side. Transfer the slices to a platter. When the bread has cooled just enough that you can handle it, rub one or both sides of the bread with the garlic, and serve.

Nutrition Info:
- Calories: 45 Fats: 4 g Cholesterol: 70 mg Carbohydrates: 3 g
- Fiber 0 g Sugars: 2 g Proteins: 0 g

Banana Walnut Bread

Servings: 1
Cooking Time: 1 Hour 15 Minutes

Ingredients:
- 2-1/2 cup of all-purpose flour
- 1 cup of sugar
- 2 eggs
- 1 cup ripe banana, mashed
- 1/4 cup whole milk
- 1/4 cup walnut, finely chopped
- 1 tsp salt
- 3 Tbsp of Vegetable oil
- 3 tsp baking powder

Directions:
1. Set the wood pellet smoker-grill for indirect cooking at 3500 F.
2. Combine all the ingredients in a large bowl. Using a mixer (electric or manual), mix the ingredients. Grease and flour the loaf pan. Pour the mixture into the loaf pan.
3. Transfer loaf pan to the grill and cover with steel construction. Bake for 60-75 minutes. Remove and allow to cool.

Nutrition Info:
- InfoPer Serving: Calories: 548kcal, Carbs: 69g, Fat: 36g, Protein: 14g

Grilled Bacon Dog

Servings: 4 To 6
Cooking Time: 25 Minutes

Ingredients:
- 16 Hot Dogs
- 16 Slices Bacon, sliced
- 2 Onion, sliced
- 16 hot dog buns
- As Needed The Ultimate BBQ Sauce
- As Needed Cheese

Directions:
1. When ready to cook, set the Traeger to 375°F and preheat, lid closed for 15 minutes.
2. Wrap bacon strips around the hot dogs, and grill directly on the grill grate for 10 minutes each side. Grill onions at the same time as the hot dogs, and cook for 10 -15 minutes.
3. Open hot dog buns and spread BBQ sauce, the grilled hot dogs, cheese sauce and grilled onions. Top with vegetables. Serve, enjoy!

Fennel And Almonds Sauce

Servings: 4
Cooking Time: 10 Minutes

Ingredients:
- 1 cup fennel bulb
- 1 cup olive oil
- 1 cup almonds
- 1 cup fennel fronds

Directions:
1. In a blender place all ingredients and blend until smooth
2. Pour sauce in a bowl and serve

Grilled Pizza

Servings: 4
Cooking Time: 10 Minutes
Ingredients:
- 2tablespoons all-purpose flour, plus more as needed
- 6-8 ounces of pizza dough
- 1tablespoon canola oil, divided
- 1/2 cup Alfredo sauce
- 1cup mozzarella cheese, shredded
- 1/2 cup ricotta cheese, pieces
- 14pepperoni slices
- 1/2 teaspoon of dried oregano for serving, optional

Directions:
1. Place the grill grate inside the unit and close the hood.
2. Set temperatures to Max and let it preheat for 8 minutes.
3. Meanwhile, spread flour on a clean flat surface, roll the dough onto surface, and use a rolling pin
4. Roll the dough and then cut in rod shape that it fits inside the grill grate.
5. Brush the dough evenly with canola oil and flip to coat the dough form another side as well.
6. Poke the dough with the fork.
7. Place it on the grill grate and close the hood.
8. Cook for 4 minutes and then flip to cook from another side by opening the hood.
9. Cook for 4 more minutes.
10. Now open the unit and spread sauce, cheeses, and pepperoni on top.
11. Close the hood and let it cook for 3 minutes.
12. Once it's done, serve with a sprinkle of oregano.

Nutrition Info:
- Calories: 465 Total Fat: 31.6g Saturated Fat: 10.3g Cholesterol: 39mg Sodium: 1335mg Total Carbohydrate: 30.1g Dietary Fiber 1.6g Total Sugars: 0.2g Protein:15g

Smoked Teriyaki Tuna

Servings: 4
Cooking Time: 2 Hours
Ingredients:
- Tuna steaks, 1 oz.
- 2 c. marinade, teriyaki
- Alder wood chips soaked in water

Directions:
1. Slice tuna into thick slices of 2 inch. Place your tuna slices and marinade then set in your fridge for about 3 hours
2. After 3 hours, remove the tuna from the marinade and pat dry. Let the tuna air dry in your fridge for 2-4 hours. Preheat your smoker to 180 degrees Fahrenheit
3. Place the Tuna on a Teflon-coated fiberglass and place them directly on your grill grates. Smoke the Tuna for about an hour until the internal temperature reaches 145 degrees Fahrenheit.
4. Remove the tuna from your grill and let them rest for 10 minutes. Serve!

Nutrition Info:
- Calories: 249 Cal Fat: 3 g Carbohydrates: 33 g Protein: 21 g Fiber: 0 g

Classic Apple Pie

Servings: 8
Cooking Time: 2 Hours
Ingredients:
- 2 Tbsp all-purpose flour
- 2 pie dough rounds
- 6 cups of apple, peeled and sliced
- 1 Tbsp lemon juice
- 3/4 cup of sugar
- 1/4 tsp powdered nutmeg
- 1/2 tsp powdered cinnamon
- 1/2 tsp salt

Directions:
1. Set the wood pellet smoker-grill to indirect cooking at 4250 F
2. In a large bowl, combine all your ingredients (except for the pie dough) and mix well. Gently press one of the pie dough unto a 10-inch pie dough plate. Make sure it is firm and covers the sides.
3. Pour in your apple mixture. Cover the filling with the second pie dough, gently clip the two doughs together. Make a crosshatch slit on the top with a knife—transfer dough plate to the cooking grid.
4. Bake for 45-60 minutes or until the crust browns. Allow to cool for 1 hour before serving.

Nutrition Info:
- InfoPer Serving: Calories: 542kcal, Carbs: 41g, Fat: 20g, Protein: 10g

Bradley Maple Cure Smoked Salmon

Servings: 6
Cooking Time: 1 Hour And 30 Minutes
Ingredients:
- 1 large sized salmon fillet
- 1 quart of water
- ½ a cup of pickling and canning salt
- ½ a cup of maple syrup
- ¼ cup of dark rum
- ¼ cup of lemon juice

- 10 whole cloves
- 10 whole allspice berries
- 1 bay leaf

Directions:

1. Take a medium sized bowl and add the brine ingredients. Mix them well. Place the salmon fillet in a cover with brine. Cover it up and let it refrigerate for about 2 hours. Remove the Salmon and pat dry then air dry for 1 hour. Preheat your smoker to a temperature of 180 degrees Fahrenheit and add Bradley Maple-Flavored briquettes. Smoke the salmon for about 1 and a ½ hour.

Nutrition Info:

- Calories: 223 Cal Fat: 7 g Carbohydrates: 15 g Protein: 21 g Fiber: 0 g

Baked Breakfast Casserole

Servings: 8
Cooking Time: 1 Hour
Ingredients:

- 6 bread slices, cut into cubes
- 6 eggs
- 3/4 teaspoon ground mustard
- 1 cup milk
- Salt and pepper to taste
- 1 onion, chopped
- 1 bell pepper, chopped
- 6 ounces chorizo
- 6 ounces ground turkey
- 1 cup baby spinach
- 4 slices bacon, cooked crispy and chopped into bits
- 1 cup Swiss cheese, grated
- 2 cups cheddar cheese, grated

Directions:

1. Set the Traeger wood pellet grill to 350 degrees F.
2. Preheat for 15 minutes while the lid is closed.
3. Spray your baking pan with oil.
4. Arrange the bread cubes in the baking pan.
5. Beat the eggs in a bowl.
6. Stir in the mustard, milk, salt and pepper.
7. Spray your pan with oil.
8. Place the pan over medium heat.
9. Cook the onion, bell pepper, ground turkey and chorizo.
10. Stir in the spinach.
11. Cook for 1 minute.
12. Place the meat mixture on top of the bread.
13. Pour egg mixture on top.
14. Sprinkle cheeses on top.
15. Repeat layers.
16. Cover the baking pan with foil.
17. Bake in the wood pellet grill for 40 minutes.
18. Remove cover and bake for another 10 minutes.
19. Tips: You can also cook ground turkey and chorizo in advance to less preparation time.

Dill Seafood Rub

Servings: 5
Cooking Time: 5 Minutes
Ingredients:

- 2 tablespoons coarse kosher salt
- 2 tablespoons dried dill weed
- 1 tablespoon garlic powder
- 1½ teaspoons lemon pepper

Directions:

1. In a small airtight container or zip-top bag, combine the salt, dill, garlic powder, and lemon pepper.
2. Close the container and shake to mix. Unused rub will keep in an airtight container for months.

Smoked Up Salmon And Dungeness Crab Chowder

Servings: 6
Cooking Time: 45 Minutes
Ingredients:

- 4 gallons of water
- 3 fresh Dungeness crabs
- 1 cup of rock salt
- 3 cups of Cold-Hot Smoked Salmon
- 3 cups of ocean clam juice
- 5 diced celery stalks
- 1 yellow diced onion
- 2 peeled and diced large sized russet potatoes
- 14 ounces of sweet corn
- 12 ounce of clam chowder dry soup mix
- 4 bacon slices crumbled and cooked

Directions:

1. Bring 4 gallons of water and rock salt to a boil. Add the Dungeness crab and boil for 20 minutes
2. Remove the crabs, let it cool and clean the crabs and pick out crab meat. Place it over high heat.
3. Add clam juice, 5 cups of water, diced potatoes, diced celery, and onion. Bring the mix to a boil as well. Add corn to the liquid and boil.
4. Whisk in the clam chowder and keep mixing everything. Simmer on low for about 15 minutes and add the crumbled bacon. Add bacon, garnish with ½ cup flaked smoked salmon and ½ cup Dungeness crabmeat. Serve!

Nutrition Info:

- Calories: 174 Cal Fat: 5 g Carbohydrates: 12 g   Protein: 8 g Fiber: 0 g

Grilled Lime Chicken

Servings: 6
Cooking Time: 45 Minutes
Ingredients:
- 2 teaspoon sugar
- 1 teaspoon chili powder
- 1 1/2 teaspoons granulated garlic
- 1 1/2 teaspoons ground cumin
- Salt and pepper to taste
- 12 chicken thighs, skin removed
- 1 1/2 tablespoons olive oil
- 1 1/2 tablespoons butter
- 4 tablespoons pineapple juice
- 4 tablespoons honey
- 1 1/2 tablespoons lime juice
- 1/4 teaspoon red pepper flakes
- 1 1/2 tablespoons hot sauce

Directions:
1. Set the Traeger grill to 375 degrees F.
2. Preheat it for 10 minutes.
3. In a bowl, mix the sugar, chili powder, garlic, cumin, salt and pepper.
4. Coat the chicken with the olive oil and sprinkle with the dry rub.
5. Grill the chicken for 7 minutes per side.
6. In a pan over medium heat, simmer the rest of the ingredients for 10 minutes.
7. Remove from heat and transfer to a bowl.
8. Brush the mixture on both sides of the chicken.
9. Cook for another 7 minutes per side.
10. Tips: Add more hot sauce to the glaze if you want your chicken spicier.

Rosemary-smoked Lamb Chops

Servings: 4
Cooking Time: 2 Hours, 5 Minutes
Ingredients:
- 4½ pounds bone-in lamb chops
- 2 tablespoons olive oil
- Salt
- Freshly ground black pepper
- 1 bunch fresh rosemary

Directions:
1. Supply your smoker with wood pellets and follow the manufacturer's specific start-up procedure. Preheat the grill, with the lid closed, to 180°F.
2. Rub the lamb chops all over with olive oil and season on both sides with salt and pepper.
3. Spread the rosemary directly on the grill grate, creating a surface area large enough for all the chops to rest on. Place the chops on the rosemary and smoke until they reach an internal temperature of 135°F.
4. Increase the grill's temperature to 450°F, remove the rosemary, and continue to cook the chops until their internal temperature reaches 145°F.
5. Remove the chops from the grill and let them rest for 5 minutes before serving.

Bourbon Braised Beef Short Ribs

Servings:6
Cooking Time: 3 Hours 15 Minutes
Ingredients:
- 2 Tbsp Worcestershire sauce
- 3 Tbsp soy sauce
- 2 Tbsp bourbon
- 1/2 cup Dijon mustard
- 1 cup beef stock
- 12 beef short ribs

Directions:
1. Preheat wood pellet smoker-grill to 250ºF, with the lid closed for about 15 minutes
2. Mix the Worcestershire sauce, mustard, and molasses.
3. Brush sauce on each side of the rib.
4. Prepare the mop sauce by mixing the soy sauce, beef stock, and bourbon in a food-safe plastic spray bottle.
5. Arrange the ribs directly on the grill and braise for 2 hours, until an internal temperature of 165ºF is reached. Spray the mop sauce over the rib occasionally for tender perfection.
6. Remove rib from the grill and place on an aluminum foil. Pour remaining mop sauce over the ribs and wrap the foil over the ribs.
7. Transfer foil enclosed rib for direct cooking to the grill grate. Braise the ribs until the Instant read thermometer reads a temperature of 195ºF, about one hour.
8. Remove foil enclosed rib from grill and place on a platter to rest for 15 minutes
9. Take out ribs from foil and serve.

Nutrition Info:
- InfoPer Serving: Calories: 591kcal, Carbs: 78g, Fat: 13g, Protein: 8g

Potluck Favorite Baked Beans

Servings: 10
Cooking Time: 3 Hours 5 Minutes
Ingredients:
- 1 tbsp. butter
- ½ of red bell pepper, seeded and chopped
- ½ of medium onion, chopped
- 2 jalapeño peppers, chopped
- 2 (28-oz.) cans baked beans, rinsed and drained
- 8 oz. pineapple chunks, drained
- 1 C. BBQ sauce
- 1 C. brown sugar
- 1 tbsp. ground mustard

Directions:
1. Set the temperature of Traeger Grill to 220-250 degrees F and preheat with closed lid for 15 minutes.
2. In a non-stick skillet, melt butter over medium heat and sauté the bell peppers, onion and jalapeño peppers for about 4-5 minutes.
3. Remove from heat and transfer the pepper mixture into a bowl.
4. Add remaining ingredients and stir to combine.
5. Transfer the mixture into a Dutch oven.
6. Place the Dutch oven onto the grill and cook for about 2½-3 hours.
7. Remove from grill and serve hot.

Nutrition Info:
- Calories per serving: 364; Carbohydrates: 61.4g; Protein: 9.4g; Fat: 9.8g; Sugar: 23.5g; Sodium: 1036mg; Fiber: 9.7g

Smoked Sausage & Potatoes

Servings: 4 To 6
Cooking Time: 50 Minutes
Ingredients:
- 2 Pound Hot Sausage Links
- 2 Pound Potatoes, fingerling
- 1 Tablespoon fresh thyme
- 4 Tablespoon butter

Directions:
1. When ready to cook, set the Traeger to 375°F and preheat, lid closed for 15 minutes.
2. Put your sausage links on the grill to get some color. This should take about 3 minutes on each side.
3. While sausage is cooking, cut the potatoes into bite size pieces all about the same size so they cook evenly. Chop the thyme and butter, then combine all the ingredients into a Traeger cast iron skillet.
4. Pull your sausage off the grill, slice into bite size pieces and add to your cast iron.
5. Turn grill down to 275°F and put the cast iron in the grill for 45 minutes to an hour or until the potatoes are fully cooked.
6. After 45 minutes, use a butter knife to test your potatoes by cutting into one to see if its done. To speed up cook time you can cover cast iron will a lid or foil. Serve. Enjoy!

Butter-braised Springs Onions With Lots Of Chives

Servings: 3
Cooking Time: 25minutes
Ingredients:
- 1lb spring onions, trimmed
- Kosher salt
- 1/4 tsp chives, chopped
- 4 Tbsp unsalted butter

Directions:
1. In a large skillet, add onions, 1/2 cup water, two tablespoons butter and sprinkle in the salt. Cover skillet and bring to a boil. Reduce heat and simmer onion until almost tender, about 15 minutes. Remove cover, stir continuously and leave onions to cook for another 5 minutes, until fork-tender.
2. Take out onions and place them on a plate. Heat the liquid in skillet until it reduces to about two teaspoons, then add the remaining butter. Transfer onions to the skillet and stir it in with the sauce. Garnish with chives.

Nutrition Info:
- InfoPer Serving: Calories: 129kcal, Carbs: 4.0g, Fat: 12g, Protein: 2.0g

Barbecue Pork Belly

Servings: 6
Cooking Time: 3 Hours
Ingredients:
- 3 lb. pork belly
- Salt and pepper to taste
- Barbecue dry rub

Directions:
1. Preheat your Traeger wood pellet grill to 275 degrees F for 15 minutes while the lid is closed.
2. Sprinkle all sides of pork belly with salt, pepper and dry rub.
3. Cook for 3 hours.
4. Let rest for 10 minutes before slicing and serving.
5. Tips: You can also coat with barbecue sauce before serving.

Lemon And Thyme Roasted With Bistro Chicken

Servings: 4
Cooking Time: 25 Hours
Ingredients:
- 1 4pounds chicken
- 3 Tbsp of unsalted butter, melted
- 1 lemon
- 1 Tbsp of thyme, fresh and chopped.
- Salt and ground black pepper, to taste

Directions:
1. Season chicken with salt and pepper as desired. Make sure to rub seasoning all over, including the inner cavities. Refrigerate seasoned chicken, uncovered, for 24 hours.
2. Preheat the grill for direct cooking at 420°F (High). Use mesquite wood pellets for a distinctive, strong woody taste.
3. Put the lemon zest, chopped thyme, and butter in a bowl, then mix. Rub the mixture all over the chicken, and put half lemon in the chicken.
4. Place the chicken in a roasting pan and roast for about 35 minutes. Turn it to the other side and roast for 15 minutes or until internal temperature reads 160°F.
5. Cool for 10 minutes before slicing and serving.

Nutrition Info:
- InfoPer Serving: Calories: 388.9kcal, Protein: 41.8g, Carbs: 73.4g, Fat: 52g.

Roasted Almonds

Servings: 6
Cooking Time: 1 Hour And 30 Minutes
Ingredients:
- 1 egg white
- Salt to taste
- 1 tablespoon ground cinnamon
- 1 cup granulated sugar
- 1 lb. almonds

Directions:
1. Beat the egg white in a bowl until frothy.
2. Stir in salt, cinnamon and sugar.
3. Coat the almonds with this mixture.
4. Spread almonds on a baking pan.
5. Set your Traeger wood pellet grill to 225 degrees F.
6. Preheat for 15 minutes while the lid is closed.
7. Roast the almonds for 90 minutes, stirring every 10 minutes.
8. Tips: Store in an airtight container with lid for up to 1 week.

Grapefruit Juice Marinade

Servings: 3
Cooking Time: 1hours 10 Minutes
Ingredients:
- 1/2 reduced-sodium soy sauce
- cups grapefruit juice, unsweetened
- 1-1/2 lb. Chicken, bone and skin removed
- 1/4 brown sugar

Directions:
1. Thoroughly mix all your ingredients in a large bowl.
2. Add the chicken and allow it to marinate for 2-3 hours before grilling.

Nutrition Info:
- InfoPer Serving: Calories: 489kcal, Carbs: 21.3g Fat: 12g, Protein: 24g

RECIPES INDEX

A

All-purpose Dry Rub 97
Apple-smoked Bacon 17
Applewood-smoked Whole Turkey 33
Aromatic Herbed Rack Of Lamb 30
Authentic Holiday Turkey Breast 45

B

Baby Back Ribs 25
Bacon-swiss Cheesesteak Meatloaf 15
Bacon-wrapped Chicken Tenders 33
Baked Breakfast Casserole 100
Baked Cheesy Corn Pudding 68
Banana Walnut Bread 98
Barbecue Chicken Wings 50
Barbecue Pork Belly 102
Barbecued Shrimp 58
Barbecued Tenderloin 20
Barbeque Shrimp 57
Bbq Oysters 55
Bbq Party Pork Ribs 12
Bbq Sauce Smothered Chicken Breasts 46
Bbq Sweet Pepper Meatloaf 15
Beef Shoulder Clod 22
Beer Can Chicken 38
Blackened Salmon 57
Blackened Steak 27
Blt Pasta Salad 74
Bourbon Braised Beef Short Ribs 101
Bradley Maple Cure Smoked Salmon 99
Braised Lamb Shank 14
Braised Pork Carnitas 86
Broccoli-cauliflower Salad 83
Bruschetta 98
Buffalo Chicken Flatbread 39
Bunny Dogs With Sweet And Spicy Jalapeño Relish 74
Butter-braised Springs Onions With Lots Of Chives 102
Buttered Crab Legs 63
Buttered Thanksgiving Turkey 45
Buttermilk Pork Loin Roast 26

C

Cajun Catfish 57
Cajun Chicken 40
Cajun Double-smoked Ham 21
Cajun Rub 91
Cajun Seasoned Shrimp 54
Cajun Smoked Catfish 62
Cajun-blackened Shrimp 50
Caldereta Stew 69
Charleston Crab Cakes With Remoulade 61
Cheeseburger Hand Pies 28
Cheesy Lamb Burgers 12
Cherry Smoked Strip Steak 96
Chicken Cordon Bleu 36
Chicken Tortilla Soup 77
Chicken Wings 34
Chilean Sea Bass 63
Chili Rib Eye Steaks 25
Chinese Bbq Pork 17
Chinese Inspired Duck Legs 43
Christmas Dinner Goose 40
Cider Salmon 59
Citrus Salmon 53
Citrus-smoked Trout 54
Classic Apple Pie 99
Coconut Bacon 80
Cod With Lemon Herb Butter 53
Coffee-chile Rub 97
Corn Chowder 81
Cornish Game Hens 90
Crispy Maple Bacon Brussels Sprouts 82
Crusty Artisan Dough Bread 92

D

Deliciously Spicy Rack Of Lamb 16

Dijon-smoked Halibut 50

Dill Seafood Rub 100

E

Easy Smoked Vegetables 79

Enticing Mahi-mahi 67

F

Fall Season Apple Pie 97

Feisty Roasted Cauliflower 86

Fennel And Almonds Sauce 98

Flavorsome Pork Loin 23

French Onion Burgers 20

G

Game Day Chicken Drumsticks 38

Garlic And Herb Smoke Potato 80

Garlic And Rosemary Potato Wedges 83

Ginger And Chili Grilled Shrimp 89

Glazed Chicken Thighs 42

Grapefruit Juice Marinade 103

Grilled Artichokes 70

Grilled Asparagus With Wild Mushrooms 81

Grilled Bacon Dog 98

Grilled Blackened Salmon 53

Grilled Butter Basted Porterhouse Steak 28

Grilled Butter Basted Rib-eye 18

Grilled Clam With Lemon-cayenne Butter 88

Grilled Corn On The Cob With Parmesan And Garlic 83

Grilled Corn With Honey & Butter 69

Grilled Filet Mignon 23

Grilled Fruit And Cream 93

Grilled Hanger Steak 30

Grilled Herbed Tuna 59

Grilled King Crab Legs 63

Grilled Lamb Chops With Rosemary 22

Grilled Lime Chicken 101

Grilled Lingcod 56

Grilled Lobster Tail 66

Grilled Peaches And Cream 94

Grilled Pineapple With Chocolate Sauce 87

Grilled Pizza 99

Grilled Rainbow Trout 56

Grilled Salmon 57

Grilled Shrimp 67

Grilled Shrimp Kabobs 65

Grilled Shrimp Scampi 51

Grilled Sugar Snap Peas 76

Grilled Sweet Potato Planks 79

Grilled Teriyaki Salmon 67

Grilled Tilapia 55

Grilled Tuna Burger With Ginger Mayonnaise 87

Grilled Venison Kabob 31

Grilled Zucchini 71

Grilled Zucchini Squash 78

H

Halibut 64

Halibut In Parchment 54

Halibut With Garlic Pesto 58

Hellfire Chicken Wings 39

Herb Roasted Turkey 42

Hickory Smoked Chicken 48

Hickory Smoked Green Beans 92

Honey Garlic Chicken Wings 34

Hot And Sweet Spatchcocked Chicken 31

Hot-smoked Salmon 53

J

Jamaican Jerk Chicken Quarters 32

Jerk Shrimp 52

Juicy Smoked Salmon 62

K

Kalbi Beef Ribs 24

Korean Style Bbq Prime Ribs 26

L

Leg Of A Lamb 19
Lemon And Thyme Roasted With Bistro Chicken 103
Lemon Chicken Breast 36
Lively Flavored Shrimp 62
Lobster Tails 65

M

Maple And Bacon Chicken 40
Mexican Street Corn With Chipotle Butter 76
Midweek Dinner Pork Tenderloin 16

N

Naked St. Louis Ribs 24
No-fuss Tuna Burgers 66

O

Octopus With Lemon And Oregano 53
Oysters In The Shell 51

P

Paprika Chicken 47
Pellet Grill Funeral Potatoes 97
Peppercorn Tuna Steaks 59
Perfect Roast Prime Rib 26
Perfectly Smoked Turkey Legs 37
Pizza Bianca 91
Potluck Favorite Baked Beans 102
Potluck Salad With Smoked Cornbread 71

R

Ramen Soup 77
Red Wine Beef Stew 96
Roasted Almonds 103
Roasted Chicken With Pimenton Potatoes 40
Roasted Ham 94
Roasted Hasselback Potatoes 82
Roasted Okra 80
Roasted Parmesan Cheese Broccoli 85
Roasted Peach Salsa 72
Roasted Pork With Blackberry Sauce 29
Roasted Root Vegetables 69
Roasted Sheet Pan Vegetables 73
Roasted Vegetable Medley 75
Roasted Whole Chicken 42
Rosemary Chicken Glazed With Balsamic With Bacon Pearl Onions 88
Rosemary Orange Chicken 42
Rosemary-smoked Lamb Chops 101
Rub-injected Pork Shoulder 23
Rustic Maple Smoked Chicken Wings 31

S

Salt-crusted Baked Potatoes 79
Santa Maria Tri-tip 30
Savory Applesauce On The Grill 95
Savory-sweet Turkey Legs 35
Scampi Spaghetti Squash 84
Seared Tuna Steaks 64
Serrano Chicken Wings 38
Simple Roasted Butternut Squash 95
Simple Traeger Grilled Lamb Chops 14
Simple Wood Pellet Smoked Pork Ribs 21
Simply Delicious Tri Tip Roast 15
Skinny Smoked Chicken Breasts 46
Smo-fried Chicken 34
Smoked Airline Chicken 41
Smoked And Fried Chicken Wings 47
Smoked Baked Beans 73
Smoked Balsamic Potatoes And Carrots 77
Smoked Brats 94
Smoked Brisket Pie 96
Smoked Cheese Dip 91
Smoked Chicken Drumsticks 47
Smoked Chicken With Apricot Bbq Glaze 49
Smoked Deviled Eggs 75
Smoked Eggs 79
Smoked Fried Chicken 45
Smoked Ham 14
Smoked Healthy Cabbage 74
Smoked Hummus 73
Smoked Lamb Chops 21
Smoked Mashed Red Potatoes 79

Smoked Midnight Brisket 22

Smoked Mushrooms 75

Smoked New York Steaks 27

Smoked Pickles 70

Smoked Pork Ribs With Fresh Herbs 90

Smoked Pork Tenderloin With Mexican Pineapple Sauce 93

Smoked Pumpkin Soup 68

Smoked Ribs 93

Smoked Roast Beef 28

Smoked Sausage & Potatoes 102

Smoked Scallops 63

Smoked Shrimp 56

Smoked Soy Sauce 87

Smoked Spicy Candied Bacon 17

Smoked Sriracha Sauce 95

Smoked Stuffed Mushrooms 82

Smoked Teriyaki Tuna 99

Smoked Tomato And Mozzarella Dip 70

Smoked Tuna 88

Smoked Turkey Breast 46

Smoked Up Salmon And Dungeness Crab Chowder 100

Smoked Whole Chicken 33

Smokey Roasted Cauliflower 81

Smoking Burgers 89

South-east-asian Chicken Drumsticks 32

Southern Slaw 86

Special Occasion's Dinner Cornish Hen 39

Spicy Pork Chops 13

Spicy Shrimp 64

Spicy Shrimps Skewers 51

Split Pea Soup With Mushrooms 76

Sriracha Salmon 59

St. Louis Bbq Ribs 27

St. Patrick Day's Corned Beef 26

Succulent Lamb Chops 89

Super-tasty Trout 52

Sweet And Spicy Cinnamon Rub 88

Sweet Jalapeño Cornbread 84

Sweet Sriracha Bbq Chicken 44

T

Teriyaki Pineapple Pork Tenderloin Sliders 24

Teriyaki Smoked Shrimp 61

Texas Shoulder Clod 19

Thai Beef Salad 18

Thai Beef Skewers 13

Thanksgiving Dinner Turkey 48

Thanksgiving Turkey Brine 95

Traditional Tomahawk Steak 29

Traeger Asian Miso Chicken Wings 49

Traeger Bacon 21

Traeger Beef Jerky 17

Traeger Beef Short Rib Lollipop 14

Traeger Chicken Breast 49

Traeger Fries With Chipotle Ketchup 83

Traeger Grilled Buffalo Chicken Legs 49

Traeger Grilled Lingcod 51

Traeger Kalbi Beef Short Ribs 25

Traeger Lobster Tail 60

Traeger Rockfish 55

Traeger Salmon With Togarashi 66

Traeger Smoked Cornish Hens 41

Traeger Smoked Italian Meatballs 92

Traeger Smoked Mushrooms 73

Traeger Smoked Shrimp 65

Traeger Stuffed Peppers 20

Trager Smoked Spatchcock Turkey 35

Turkey Legs 44

Turkey Meatballs 36

Twice Grilled Potatoes 90

Twice-smoked Potatoes 72

V

Vegan Pesto 96

Vegan Smoked Carrot Dogs 72

Vegetable Skewers 85

Versatile Beef Tenderloin 13

W

White Bbq Sauce 87
Whole Roasted Cauliflower With Garlic Parmesan Butter 78
Whole Smoked Chicken 35
Wild Turkey Egg Rolls 32
Wine Braised Lamb Shank 16
Wine Infused Salmon 60
Wood Pellet Cold Smoked Cheese 68
Wood Pellet Grilled Aussie Leg Of Lamb Roast 12
Wood Pellet Grilled Buffalo Chicken 48
Wood Pellet Grilled Chicken Kabobs 43
Wood Pellet Grilled Lamb With Brown Sugar Glaze 19
Wood Pellet Grilled Mexican Street Corn 78
Wood Pellet Grilled Scallops 61
Wood Pellet Grilled Vegetables 78
Wood Pellet Grilled Zucchini Squash Spears 71
Wood Pellet Rockfish 52
Wood Pellet Sheet Pan Chicken Fajitas 46
Wood Pellet Smoked Asparagus 85
Wood Pellet Smoked Buffalo Shrimp 58
Wood Pellet Smoked Cornish Hens 44
Wood Pellet Smoked Spatchcock Turkey 33
Wood Pellet Smoked Spatchcock Turkey 37
Wood Pellet Teriyaki Smoked Shrimp 58
Wood-fired Chicken Breasts 48
Wood-fired Halibut 60

Manufactured by Amazon.ca
Acheson, AB